MISADVENTURES OF A CIVIL WAR SUBMARINE

ED RACHAL FOUNDATION NAUTICAL ARCHAEOLOGY SERIES

Misadventures of a Civil War Submarine

Iron, Guns, and Pearls

James P. Delgado

TEXAS A&M UNIVERSITY PRESS
College Station

Library of Congress Cataloging-in-Publication Data

Delgado, James P.
Misadventures of a Civil War submarine : iron, guns, and pearls /
James P. Delgado.—1st ed.
p. cm.—(Ed Rachal Foundation nautical archaeology series)
Includes bibliographical references and index.
ISBN 978-1-60344-472-9 (cloth : alk. paper)—
ISBN 1-60344-472-6 (cloth : alk. paper)—
ISBN 978-1-60344-381-4 (e-book)—
ISBN 1-60344-381-9 (e-book)
1. Kroehl, Julius, 1820–1867. 2. Sub Marine Explorer—History.
3. Pacific Pearl Company—History. 4. Engineers—United States—Biography.
5. German-Americans—United States—Biography. 6. Submersibles—History.
7. Shipwrecks—Panama—Pearl Islands—History—19th century. 8. Pearl industry
and trade—United States—History—19th century. 9. Pearl industry and trade—
Panama—Pearl Islands—History—19th century. 10. United States—History—
Civil War, 1861–1865—Naval operations—Submarine.
I. Title. II. Series: Ed Rachal Foundation nautical archaeology series.
VM140.K69D45   2012
623.82'05—dc23
2011049843

This explorer will be able to
traverse the bed of the ocean without difficulty,
and . . . the men working it . . . will be as free to labor there
as in the streets of the city.

—*Brooklyn Daily Eagle*, November 12, 1865

*To all who labor in the depths,
especially those who never return.
To John M. McKee, who has done more
than most to bring Julius Kroehl back to life, and
to John W. McKay, who has done more
than most to bring* Sub Marine Explorer
back to life.

Contents

Acknowledgments

The genesis of this book was the chance discovery in 2001 of Julius Kroehl's incredible, and then forgotten, craft, *Sub Marine Explorer*, on the edge of the beach at Isla San Telmo in Panama's Archipiélago de las Perlas. Little did I realize then, on vacation and standing on a beach unequipped and unprepared for documenting what turned out to be one of the world's earliest successful deep diving submarines, that I would return, again and again, to document this submarine and research its history. Ten years after that first morning on the narrow beach of San Telmo, the submarine has been reconstructed on paper, and the story of Julius Kroehl, at least all that we have been able to find thus far, is told, and this book is complete.

None of that would have happened without the assistance and kindness of a variety of friends and strangers in libraries and archives, colleagues who joined the work on the submarine in the field, supporters who funded the fieldwork, and experts who reviewed the various incarnations of this tale and suggested corrections and changes.

The thanks begin with Richard Fagan, who first reported the presence of a mysterious submarine on the beach while on an earlier Zegrahm Expeditions "Rainforests and Reefs" cruise, and my other friends at Zegrahm, including Mike Messick, who loaned me the Zodiac craft and agreed to my checking out the submarine, and Jeff Gneiser and all the passengers who helped on the initial surveys of *Explorer* on two cruises. Thanks also go to Sandi Gerstung and Pete Bancroft, both of whom provided initial photos, and to my wonderful assistant (and wife) on the survey, Ann Goodhart, and fellow lecturer, oceanographer, and scientist Joe Valencic.

The initial quest for an identity for the submarine saw the assistance of Wendy Coble, Bob Mealings, Eugene B. Canfield, who correctly placed it in the Civil War era, and finally, Richard Wills, who provided the names of Julius Kroehl and *Sub Marine Explorer*. Thanks to Richard's scan of Baird's 1902 drawings and description of the craft, I was able to see, using our initial surveys, that the measurements matched up, and that we could "pin the name on the wreck" at last.

The opportunity to conduct a more thorough examination of the submarine came thanks to my friend John B. Davis at Eco-Nova Productions Ltd., when he agreed to produce an episode of the National Geographic International Television series *The Sea Hunters* that included *Sub Marine Explorer*. I want to thank the "Sea Hunters" team of Susan MacDonald, Lisa Bower, Mike Fletcher, Warren Fletcher, Marc Pike, and John Rosborough for their hard work on Isla San Telmo and for making the first film about the wreck. That episode ultimately reached hundreds of millions of viewers around the world.

My colleagues at the Council of American Maritime Museums, especially president Jerry Ostermiller, treasurer Paul Fontenoy, and the rest of the CAMM board, answered the call to support the documentation of *Sub Marine Explorer* by lidar (light detection and ranging) and by the Historic American Engineering Record.

Dr. Robert Neyland of the Naval History and Heritage Command provided an invitation to Doug DeVine and Carlos G. Velazquez of Pacific Survey and Epic Scan, Ltd., who conducted the lidar documentation of the submarine and graciously helped sponsor the documentation in 2004. Todd Croteau of the National Park Service's Historic American Engineering Record began the laborious process of documenting the submarine, and was a constant and helpful companion on countless dives, half-drowning inside the craft as we measured and drew. His initial plans of *Explorer* formed the basis of the final drawings of the submarine by another good friend, John W. McKay, whose insights into nineteenth-century technology and engineering also made a positive difference. The 2004 field team also included and was greatly assisted by Mark K. Ragan and Jacinto Almendra.

Another friend who provided support, information, and the best small research vessel I have worked on, the M/V *Cheers*, is Captain Jim Dertien. A "CZ (Canal Zone) brat" with an extensive local knowledge, Jim is the man to go to if you want to get to the Pearl Islands and explore them. The crew of *Cheers*, indefatigable Captain Arnulfo Abrego and chief mate, deckhand, and cook Zayda Zobrowski formed an essential part of the team in the 2006 and 2008 seasons. They navigated the waters, operated the small craft, offered exceptional Panameño cuisine, and nursed a clumsy archaeologist with three snapped ribs and internal injuries as he daily squeezed in and out of a wetsuit and a certain rusty iron craft in 2008.

The 2006 field season at the submarine was funded by the National Oceanic and Atmospheric Administration's Office (NOAA) of Ocean Exploration & Research. I'd like to thank Craig McLean, Jeremy Weirich, Frank Cantelas, Nicholas Alvarado, and Kate Elliot of NOAA. The 2006 team included Michael "Mack" McCarthy (Western Australian Maritime Museum), Larry E. Murphy (National Park Service), Dr. Donald L. Johnson (University of Nebraska–Lincoln), Lt. Cdr. Joshua S. Price, USN (Office of the Supervisor of Salvage), Bert Ho (National Oceanic and Atmospheric Administration), Jacinto Almendra (Instituto Nacional de Cultura de Panamá), Todd Croteau (National Park Service), Jim Dertien, Arnulfo Abrego, and Zayda Zobrowski.

That season made great and significant strides in understanding the submarine. Dr. McCarthy provided invaluable archaeological and cultural observations, thanks to his extensive research on pearl diving, and his background in shallow and intertidal metal shipwrecks was also a great boon. His work on the iron steamship *Xantho* proved not only to be a guide but also an inspiration. Mack and Jacinto also made a survey of the beach area and found the likely site of the Pacific Pearl Company's 1869 camp on the island. The archaeological and corrosion science expertise of Larry Murphy was also invaluable. Bert Ho and Todd Croteau worked hard to document and measure the submarine, Bert conducted a detailed hydrographic survey, and Josh Price dived, assessed, and helped to make the corrosion survey happen—he was the essential team member, always there, ready to help with each and every job. Jacinto Almendra was a font of knowledge about local history, culture, and iron conservation. I also want to acknowledge and thank the crew from *Der Spiegel* television and magazine, in particular Karl Vandenhole, Torsten Mehlretter, and Sven Robold. None of this would have been possible were it not for the assistance of Kathy Smith and Betty Marshall, who arranged travel, assisted in global connections, and facilitated communications.

The 2008 field season at the submarine was funded by the Waitt Institute for Discovery of San Diego. I'd like to thank Ted Waitt for his generous support, Dr. Dominique Rissolo, executive director of the Waitt Institute of Discovery for arranging it and working as a partner on the permit and logistics, Mike Dessner and Capt. Dave Passamore and the crew of the R/V *Plan B* for logistical support, Joe LaPorte for being an exceptional boat driver and diver, and once again, Jim Dertien, Arnulfo Abrego and Zayda Zobrowski. The 2008 team included Frederick "Fritz" Hanselmann of Indiana University, John W. McKay and Clyde P. Smith of the Institute of Nautical Archaeology, and

Steve Bilicki, Mike Purcell, Dr. Erich Horgan, and Greg J. Packard of Woods Hole Oceanographic Institution. John, Clyde, and Fritz assessed and helped to document the submarine's features and damage in the final season of work, and conducted a metal detector survey of the beach. Steve Bilicki and Joe LaPorte conducted a magnetometer survey of the cove where *Explorer* lies and discovered a large iron beam that may have been its mooring. Mike Purcell and Greg Packard conducted an extensive autonomous underwater vehicle (AUV) survey of the waters off San Telmo, charting the pearl beds and the submerged maritime landscape where *Explorer* worked in 1869. Erich Horgan conducted a detailed biological survey of the submarine and assessed the pearl beds. Additional footage and images of *Explorer* were expertly captured by Lance Milbank.

The privilege of working in Panama on the submarine came thanks to the Instituto Nacional de Cultura de Panamá, which issued archaeological research permits in 2004, 2006, and 2008. I want to particularly thank Dr. Tomas Mendizabal for all his assistance and guidance, and I thank Andrea Hamel for introducing me to Tomas. I want to acknowledge the support of the three past directors of the Instituto Nacional who granted our permits, Carlos Fitzgerald Bernal, Domingo Varela, and Linette Montenegro. The support of Ambassador Luis E. Arreaga, then the deputy chief of mission in Panama, is also very much appreciated, as is the US Embassy's reception for our team and the introduction of leading cultural authorities in Panama in 2006. I also wish to acknowledge and thank ANCON (La Asociación Nacional para la Conservación de la Naturaleza), Isla San Telmo, and the submarine's stewards and guardians along the *cabildo* and the people of La Esmeralda, who graciously extended their hospitality with each visit we made to their village. Our final reports were greatly assisted by Melissa Delgado Steinhoff of San Jose, who volunteered to undertake their translation, which made a great difference. *Gracias y felicidades*, Meli!

Additional documentation of the submarine was provided between our expeditions in 2005 by Roger D. Cooper, Technical Director, Navtech Systems Ltd., Sulby, North Welford, Northamptonshire, UK, for which I am grateful. The analysis of the metal and corrosion of *Sub Marine Explorer* was made possible through the hard work and scientific expertise of Dr. Donald L. Johnson and Dr. Brent M. Wilson of the Department of Mechanical Engineering, University of Nebraska–Lincoln, and Dr. James D. Carr of the Department of Chemistry, University of Nebraska–Lincoln, with contributions from Larry E.

Murphy and Paul Mardikian, and with support from the Omaha Section of the National Association of Corrosion Engineers, who provided undergraduate scholarship funding for student laboratory assistance at the University of Nebraska–Lincoln.

The initial, considerable historical research and followup work by Mark K. Ragan, the leading Civil War submarine historian, made a substantial contribution. Mark has remained a true friend of mine and of the project, and his observations in the field in 2004 were also invaluable. A great deal of additional research was done by my good friend Robert Schwemmer of the Maritime Heritage Program of the Office of National Marine Sanctuaries, National Oceanic and Atmospheric Administration. Without Mark and Bob's help, much of this story would not have been known. Richard K. Wills also provided some of his research, including the previously mentioned Baird article of 1902 that proved to be the "smoking gun" in establishing the sub's identity. I am also indebted to the research and assistance of the late Henry "Hank" Silka, who identified Ariel Patterson as the partner who worked with Kroehl to build *Explorer*. The world lost an exceptional historian when Hank passed away unexpectedly during this project. Another good friend, fellow archaeologist Rhonda K. Robichaud, did extensive research for me in San Francisco at the San Francisco History Room, the Society of California Pioneers, and the California Historical Society, adding much to my understanding of William H. Tiffany and Mark Brumagim. I also thank John Ulrich of Harvard University's Student Services, who transcribed the various entries for Kroehl's partners Peter V. Husted, John Chadwick, William Henry Tiffany, Mark Brumagim, and George Wrightson in the R. G. Dun Records of Harvard's Baker Library. Tomas Mendizabal, in addition to all his other support, researched Kroehl and the submarine in Panama's historic newspapers and archives. James A. Goold provided the means for accessing Kroehl's will. Lisa Stansbury conducted additional research for me at the National Archives in the Coast Survey records. Captain Albert "Skip" Theberge and John Cloud of the NOAA Central Library in Silver Spring, Maryland, provided helpful insights into Ferdinand Gerdes, Alexander Bache, the role of Germans in the Coast Survey, photography and survey in the Coast Survey, and a high-resolution copy of Julius Kroehl's survey of the obstructions in front of the forts at the mouth of the Mississippi.

The participation and support of Bruce Kroehl and his family provided insights into the Kroehl family, especially when Bruce, an avid genealogist, shared what he had found. In late 2007 I made the online acquaintance of

John M. McKee of Oklahoma City. John, a member of the Masonic Order and a historian and genealogist, had become fascinated with Julius Kroehl and had commenced work on a biography. John also authored, and has continued to substantially edit and add to, the online Wikipedia entries on Julius Kroehl, the Pacific Pearl Company, and *Sub Marine Explorer*; in this he has done more than anyone else to ensure Julius Kroehl's twenty-first-century fame. When contacted, John became an avid correspondent and collaborator, and I greatly appreciate his collegial sharing of research and insights. My good friend Dr. Stephen Lunsford made a trip to San Diego to examine documents pertaining to Van Buren Ryerson and his diving bell. I am indebted to Ralf Mulhern for sending me a photocopy of Ryerson's original patent document. My colleague Dr. Robert Chandler of Wells Fargo Bank's History Department, as he has in the decades we have been friends, sent me helpful references and was especially a help with Mark Brumagim's history.

I am indebted to the following institutions, archives, and libraries for access to their collections and for the assistance of their staff: Baker Library, Harvard University; California Historical Society, North Baker Library, San Francisco; Henry E. Huntington Library and Archives, San Marino, California; New York Historical Society Library, New York City; United States National Archives, Washington, DC; Library of Congress, Washington, DC; Society of California Pioneers Library, San Francisco; San Francisco Room of the San Francisco Public Library; United States Naval History and Heritage Command Library, Washington, DC; New York Historical Society, New York City; New York Public Library, New York City; Sharlot Hall Museum and Archives, Prescott, Arizona; Yale University Library; W. B. and M. H. Chung Library of the Vancouver Maritime Museum, Vancouver, British Columbia; British Columbia Provincial Archives, Victoria, British Columbia; and Evans Library, Texas A&M University, College Station, Texas. I'd also be remiss if I did not acknowledge the incredible work and resources available on the Internet now, thanks to JSTOR and especially to Google Books, which gave me hitherto unparalleled access to an incredible array of nineteenth-century publications.

My friend W. Peter House, MD, provided invaluable insights from a diving physician's viewpoint on the submarine's operation, decompression sickness, and comparative symptoms of decompression sickness and "fever."

The final reconstruction of *Sub Marine Explorer*, thanks to the extensive fieldwork of the various team members in 2004, 2006, and 2008, and especially the hard work and initial drawings by Todd Croteau, was assembled in close partnership with my friend John W. McKay of Fort Langley, British Columbia, who is often credited as an "architectural draftsman." That title that does not convey a sense of his exceptional knowledge, engineering, and technical abilities, and his innate understanding of machines and ships, let alone his obsessive drive to research, revise, and get it right. I am deeply indebted to John for his hard work and commitment to the project and for the exceptional plans and drawings of the submarine. Julius Kroehl would have been very impressed, too. The maps for the book were drawn by another friend and colleague, Jack Scott of Chicago.

I also wish to acknowledge and thank the boards of the Vancouver Maritime Museum and the Institute of Nautical Archaeology for their support of this project, which spanned nearly a decade, and the gracious granting of time to spend in the field working on *Sub Marine Explorer*. The staffs at both institutions have also been a great help, and I particularly want to thank Betty Marshall, Guy Mathias, and Kennith Chan at the Vancouver Maritime Museum.

I am grateful for the review of the various versions of the manuscript and suggestions made by Dr. David L. Conlin, Dr. Mack McCarthy, John M. McKee, Paula Martin, Vickie D. Jensen, and my assistant Kathy Smith, who tackled the initial edit of the final manuscript and helped stickhandle it through to final publication. I also acknowledge the helpful and comprehensive edits of Lona Dearmont. Despite all this help, however, any errors are mine. I am also grateful to my publishers at Texas A&M University Press, the premier publishers of nautical archaeology scholarship in the world. I particularly wish to thank Charles Backus, Mary Lenn Dixon, and the editorial staff at Texas A&M University Press. My wife, Ann Goodhart, is as always my muse, inspiration, and the one who covers the bases when I am away diving, researching, and writing. This time she was there to help make the "discovery" and capture data. As always, thank you, darling.

Preface

Captain Nemo's Submarine
on Robinson Crusoe's Island

THE ISLAND sits on the edge of the Bay of Panama, its western shore facing the open Pacific. Known as Isla San Telmo, it is the last outpost of dry land—or the first—that a sailor sights when sailing from or to the fabled port of Panama. The name is strangely appropriate, for St. Elmo (also known as Saint Erasmus of Formiae), a forth-century martyr and the namesake of the island, is the patron saint of mariners. As to why or when the island gained its name, no one knows, but it appears on Spanish charts of the sixteenth century. Its forested shores nurtured the native peoples who inhabited the islands until the Spaniards came, and perhaps its streams and forests succored thirsty or starving sailors who blessed it with the name of their saint.

San Telmo is one of the smallest of several islands that comprise the Archipiélago de las Perlas, a cluster of volcanic-spawned tips of drowned mountains. They sit in what once was a coastal valley, now a bay, at the edge of a drowned river. That ancient waterway once flowed west, dropping to the sea out of the mountain chain that forms the Central American isthmus. The river is now a deep submarine canyon, its depths and currents combining with the shallows of the bay and the depths of the ocean to form nutrient-rich waters teeming with marine life. The molluscs and fish of the archipelago have nurtured life on the islands for thousands of years. One of the shellfish, the black tip oyster, also yielded the pearls that gave these islands their European name.

European greed for those pearls depopulated the islands, and no descendants of those first people remain in the archipelago. The people who live here now are black descendants of slaves brought to fish the waters, and even their numbers have declined as the pearl fishery died out in the years surrounding World War II. Scattered settlements of subsistence fishermen and their families remain, harvesting red snapper, tuna, grouper, amberjack, wahoo, sailfish, and other species. Some of the men still free dive for pearl oysters, engaging in an age-old lottery with the sea to hopefully wrestle a fabulous pearl from its grasp, a pearl that will transport the fisherman and his family from their current circumstances, perhaps even to the mainland and the big city of Panama itself.

What separates the dreams of the modern inhabitants from their ancestors' is an outboard motor on the stern of their dugout bongos, or canoes, and the molded rubber fins, masks, and snorkels of the modern diver. The outside world also intrudes in the form of satellite television, visiting yachts of blue water cruisers, sportfishing charters from Panama City, and the occasional small cruise ship carrying a few dozen ecotourists. There are also the whispered tales of fast boats and darkened, unmarked planes from nearby Colombia that use the uninhabited islands' isolation as drug drops.

These intrusions, however, do little to disrupt the ebb and flow of life here. The basic rhythm in the Archipiélago de las Perlas has remained substantially unchanged from the seventeenth to the twenty-first centuries. The sea continues to provide sustenance. The people harvest the eggs of the iguana and air-dry them for food, and they husk rice in wooden mortars unchanged in their basic form from those of their West African ancestors. Clothes dry on the breeze, and a visiting boat still brings the entire village to the beach to see just who has come to call. And then there are the old stories, passed down the generations. Among them is the tale of the submarine of death that lies off the beach of Isla San Telmo.

The submarine has lain off that beach for a long time, longer than the memory of their oldest fishermen. Streaked with rust, pocked with holes, its dark, empty iron shell rises out of the sea with each falling tide. For as long as people have fished these waters, they knew of the mysterious hulk, but if it had a name or an identity, it had long since been forgotten. What was known was its reputation as a craft of death, perhaps even the source of a poison many believed had spread throughout the islands, killing off the oyster beds and depriving the fishermen of their pearls. One story about the rusting iron craft seemingly confirmed its sinister purpose. "Everyone who enters it dies," was the legend, and perhaps for that reason, very little scavenging of the hulk had occurred.

In 1948, at the request of the government of Panama, the US government sent a scientist to Panama to try and learn why the oysters had died. Amazingly, though the scientist visited Isla San Telmo, his report did not mention the submarine, but perhaps it was when the tide was high and the submarine was hidden from view. From a passing boat, it is small and easily lost among the rocks that line the shore, its rusted hull covered with guano from seabirds at low tide. But other outsiders learned of the submarine, including other Americans from the Panama Canal Zone. In the late 1950s, a passing boat, *Observer*, anchored off San Telmo. The boat owner's sister took her two nephews out for an excursion in a skiff and found the submarine rising before them at low tide.[1] They were soon followed by others. In 1969 a group of Sea Scouts from the Canal Zone took a cruise to the islands. Stopping at San Telmo, they spotted the stranded hulk, and soon there were eager and excited children and adults scrambling over its rusty sides, peering into its water-filled dark interior and wondering what it was and how it came to rest on this isolated shore.

Memories of the last war, a conflict in which some of their fathers had served, perhaps sparked the thought that this submarine was a relic of World War II. Perhaps it was a Japanese "suicide sub," one of the two-man "midget" type that has gained notoriety for participating in the December 7, 1941, attack on Pearl Harbor. Other midget submarines, which rode piggyback on the decks of the Japanese navy's larger I-class submarines, had carried out an attack against the British fleet off Madagascar in the Indian Ocean and a daring penetration of Sydney Harbor in Australia to attack shipping there in 1942. Maybe this was another midget, launched and lost on a secret mission to attack the Panama Canal and wreak havoc. To help answer the question, a return trip to San Telmo brought the Japanese ambassador to Panama. It was not one of his country's wartime craft, he said. Perhaps it was the boiler of a lost ship.

Rumors die hard, and so do tales of secret wartime missions. Visitors to the islands heard the amazing tale, but the submarine remained an elusive target for divers, as one German group complained. Their inquiries met with varying results: "Some had heard of it, but when we asked, it always lay somewhere else," wrote the German divers in a Web blog. When they found it at last, they described their discovery as doubtless a Japanese *piratengeschicten* lost in 1942 when the Japanese intended to "destroy the strategically important Panama Canal."[2] Obviously, one of the submarines, rendezvousing with others "inconspicuously between the many islands in the archipelago," had stranded in the shallows or had been abandoned by its crew due to a technical defect, saving themselves on Isla San Telmo.

For the most part, the story remained a tale circulated among German-speaking divers and sailors who had read the blog, as well as passing mariners, some of whom searched in vain, as the submarine's position was never precisely noted and the tide hid and exposed it daily. Unless you knew exactly where to look—knew that it was in the surf zone or just beneath the surface—you could pass within 50 feet and never spot it.

And so, over the course of five decades, the mystery submarine of Isla San Telmo remained one of the great sea stories of the Central American coast. For whatever reason, it never reached a wide audience, one of so many mysteries of the sea that remain a local tale shared with those passing through, and like so many such tales, one that was usually discounted, if not disbelieved, except by the very few who actually spotted it, like the German divers. After the war, in fact, Japanese naval officers confessed that Japan had developed gigantic aircraft-carrying subs, the I-400 class of the Imperial Japanese Navy. The I-400 submarine squadron had trained to attack the Panama Canal, launching their planes from sea after surfacing in a daring repeat of the Pearl Harbor attack. The ending months of the war and the collapsing Japanese sea frontier had doomed the plan.

One would think that the fantastic tale of a stranded Japanese submarine lost on a top-secret attack on the Panama Canal would have inspired an expedition to find the sub and unlock the truth. Historians of the Pacific War have speculated that there may be untold Japanese submarine warfare tales. Burl Burlingame, author of an exhaustively researched and compelling account of Japan's opening moves against the United States by the "midget" submarine corps, writes that "because unsuccessful submarine sorties tend to disappear without a trace, many details of Japanese naval operations of World War II may never be known." Open-ended questions like that tend to excite the interest of professional and amateur sleuths.

Japan launched five "midgets" at Pearl Harbor, and the fates of only three were known, leading to a variety of theories. Then, in June 1960, US Navy divers on a training exercise off Oahu discovered a lost midget from the Pearl Harbor attack lying in 76 feet of water, where it had lain undiscovered since December 1941. When it was raised in July 1960, the craft was empty, with no trace of its crew, exciting tales of how the crew may have swum to shore and melted into the island's local Japanese American population. Memories of this discovery may very well have played into the misidentification of the mystery submarine of Isla San Telmo.

However, either no one believed the story or no one cared. Ongoing hunts for the first Japanese midget lost at Pearl Harbor, sunk just before the attack in the deep waters off the harbor entrance, and one of two midgets lost in the attack on Sydney, Australia, occupied a great deal of time and attention throughout the 1990s and early years of the twenty-first century. Despite the "discovery" of the San Telmo submarine, however, no official investigation—as far as is known—was ever launched.

In a twist that has particular bearing on the submarine at Isla San Telmo, interest in submarines older than the midgets of World War II surfaced in the 1980s. In July 1980 adventure novelist and shipwreck hunter Clive Cussler began to devote his attention and funding to a decades-long search of the waters of Charleston Harbor for the ill-fated Confederate Civil War submarine *H. L. Hunley*, which had been lost in a successful attack against the Union warship *Housatonic* on February 17, 1864. *Hunley*'s fate had fired Cussler's (and many others') imagination. *Hunley* had cast an irresistible spell over him, so much so that he spent two field seasons in 1980 and 1981 hunting for it.

After a 13-year hiatus and many successful hunts for other famous lost ships under his belt, Cussler returned to Charleston to give it another try. A discouraging season in 1994 sent Cussler home, but he kept his field crew, archaeologists Wes Hall and Ralph Wilbanks, on his payroll to keep hunting. On May 3, 1995, with archaeologist Harry Pecorelli, the crew found the lost sub buried in sediment. It had taken four seasons of work, stretching out over 15 years, and $130,000 of Clive Cussler's own money, to discover *Hunley*. The discovery sparked a multiyear project to excavate, raise, and begin the costly process of preserving and restoring *H. L. Hunley* as a sacred relic of Civil War undersea combat and the heroic sacrifice of its crew. By the time the project ends, millions will have been spent, and appropriately so, on *H. L. Hunley*.

The *Hunley* project coincided with the British discovery of the 1879 submarine *Resurgam*, the world's first mechanically powered submersible. In 1995 *Resurgam* was found off the coast of Wales after a multiyear survey effort that commenced in 1975. The discovery came only after a fisherman snagged *Resurgam* in his nets. The submarine remains on the seabed, awaiting a *Hunley*-type project such as the one mounted by the Royal Navy in 1981 when it found and raised its first submarine, *Holland I*, a 1901 craft lost in 1913 and now a signature exhibit at the Royal Navy Submarine Museum in Gosport.

The interest in old submarines in the 1990s and the early 2000s also included projects to document preserved historic submarines or to better understand relics such as a presumed Confederate submarine in New Orleans, or New York's *Intelligent Whale*, an 1866-built craft considered by some to be a deadly post–Civil War failure. It was actually not a failure but was unfairly relegated to that category—but that is another story. Another search, for the US Navy's first sub, an 1861-built slender craft christened as USS *Alligator*, began in the new century as a cooperative venture of the US Navy and the National Oceanic and Atmospheric Administration.

In what would be one of the greatest ironies in the archaeology of the submarine, the mystery of Isla San Telmo was about to be solved. The lost submarine of the archipelago, ignored and largely unknown to the outside world, would turn out to be a Civil War craft at least equal in significance to *Resurgam*, *Intelligent Whale*, or USS *Alligator*, and in its own way, a unique counterpoint to *H. L. Hunley*. The resolution of the mystery required only that an archaeologist finally reach Isla San Telmo, albeit on vacation, without a clue as to what he was about to see. In an escalating scale of ironies, the archaeologist was one who had earlier searched for and documented Japanese midget subs of World War II and had worked with Clive Cussler, but not on *H. L. Hunley*. In many ways, the hapless archaeologist was the right person who at last reached the right place at the right time. I should know, because I was that archaeologist.

In 2000, one of America's leading ecological and cultural touring companies, Zegrahm Expeditions of Seattle, Washington, decided to launch a series of trips, by small cruise ship, that would essentially "circumnavigate" Central America. Initially sailing from Cancun and later Belize City, the 16-day long trips were billed as "Rainforests to Reefs." On the voyage, passengers would experience little-visited islands, cays, bird sanctuaries, coral reefs, Mayan ruins, and the Panama Canal. They would also sail through the Archipiélago de las Perlas and stop at Isla San Telmo. San Telmo was touted as a great stop for birders. A nature preserve since 1996, and protected by ANCON, San Telmo is a migratory haven for red-footed boobies and pelicans.

In early 2000 the first Zegrahm Rainforests cruise reached Isla San Telmo on the chartered Royal Caribbean sailing cruise ship *Wind Star*. Historian/

lecturer Dr. Richard Fagan, a Stanford University retired professor, stepped ashore to investigate tales of the mystery sub of San Telmo. His beachside hike led to the submarine, and despite less than ideal tides and a heavy sea surge, Dr. Fagan made a careful sketch of it, noting it was heavily built, sophisticated, and had enough room forward "for an explosive charge quite large enough to disable one of the Panama canal locks." The latter explanation came via Panamanian guides who "knew" the story of the submarine. In April 2000 Dr. Fagan sent in a two-page letter with sketches of the mysterious submarine to Zegrahm's head office. His letter was for the next year's lecturing "historian"— me—who hopefully as a maritime archaeologist might be able to shed more light on the subject.

The story seemed incredible, to say the least, and Fagan's sketch only vaguely resembled the typical Japanese midget submarine of World War II. As it turned out, Dr. Fagan had accurately depicted the sub, and he had correctly identified some key features such as its ballast system—but that is ahead of the story. In April 2000, when the fax crossed my desk, it seemed an incongruous but plausible story, and even if the mystery sub did not appear to be the standard World War II Japanese midget, it might still be Japanese. A few years earlier I had documented the only surviving prototype for the Japanese midgets, and at approximately half the size of the 80-foot-long wartime models, it did resemble Fagan's drawing. Who knew exactly what lay off San Telmo? I filed away the drawing and, in time, forgot about it.

In February 2001 my wife, Ann Goodhart, and I boarded *Wind Star* in Cancun for "Rainforests to Reefs," with me lecturing on board as a visiting archaeologist/historian in exchange for our passage. This happy arrangement with Zegrahm has resulted in incredible vacations around the world, opportunities to meet and interact with an incredible range of remarkable people, and some amazing sights. We cruised down the coast of Mexico to Belize, Honduras, Nicaragua, Costa Rica, and Panama, stopping off for a daylong excursion by battered ex-Soviet air transports to Honduras's classical Maya site at Copan. We reached Panama on February 19, stopping at the isolated coastal port of Bocas del Toro before lining up the following morning for a daylight transit of the Panama Canal. That evening we anchored near the Bridge of the Americas, off Balboa, and waited for the falling tide to carry us under the bridge and into the Bay of Panama.

The following morning's light found us in the Archipiélago de las Perlas en route to Isla San Telmo. The day's plan was to land in inflatable Zodiac boats and then hike the beach with birder Greg Homel and guides from ANCON, the island's stewards. At this stage, we had spent days of what, for birders, must have been sheer heaven, visiting colonies of coastal birds galore. My sailor's perspective on the flying creatures of the sea had been honed by the pungent odors of guano and the resultant fear of a direct hit from the skies. Less than enthusiastic about the day's offering, I nonetheless had resigned myself to my fate when Zegrahm Expedition leader Mike Messick, in response to my query about the mystery sub, offered me a Zodiac to land on the beach where it was said to lie to "scout it out."

Soon I was zooming across the water, around the corner and out of sight of *Wind Star* to land on a narrow beach. There was no submarine in sight, but my driver, before landing me, told me to wait for the tide to fall. Resting beneath a nearby tree at the edge of the beach, out of the sun and safe from the numerous boobies and pelicans hovering above, I patiently waited. After an hour, the dropping tide slowly revealed first a small conning tower, and then the unmistakably rounded hull of a submarine, streaked with rust as the waves continue to wash over it. I had not come equipped for a snorkel, believing the craft to be up on the beach. The lack of a wetsuit was no obstacle, however. Out of sight of the ship, clad only in boxer shorts, I swam out and clambered aboard, ignoring the scrapes and cuts of rusted iron as I excitedly explored what proved to be a strange and unique craft.

In form it resembled a modern submarine's football-shaped hull, only it was small, no more than 36 feet long and 10 feet in diameter at its greatest breadth. Holes rusted through it revealed hand-forged spokes—bars of iron that had apparently braced the submarine. They looked far older, and I had the vague feeling I was looking at something at least 100 years old. But how could such an old craft have survived? Perhaps this was an early twentieth-century submarine, a prototype from naval testing, probably related to the United States' long presence at the Panama Canal and not Japanese at all. Having studied the Pearl Harbor Japanese midget submarines in detail, one thing that I knew for sure was that San Telmo's submarine was not one of them. My vacationing encounter with the submarine was a mystery that tugged at my archaeologist's soul and would not let go. I needed to solve the mystery now that I had seen the submarine. Encountering this odd vessel on the shores of an island inhabited only by seabirds felt like finding Captain Nemo's abandoned craft on the shores of Robinson Crusoe's island.

When Zegrahm offered another Rainforests tour in 2002, I agreed, offering this time to lead some of the passengers in a hands-on archaeological experience to help map the submarine. On March 20, 2002, *Wind Star* again anchored off Isla San Telmo, and my group of "explorers" and I scrambled over and around the rusty craft, taking measurements and photographs while I sketched a plan of the submarine on sheets of waterproof Mylar. Thanks to that morning on the beach, I now had a set of photographs of the exterior of the sub and the exposed chamber full of reinforcing rods, as well as measurements.

The interior, however, remained a mystery, because there were no underwater flashlights or scuba gear. The water roared into the sub and forced air and sea foam out of the conning tower—surely not a good sign for a snorkeling diver who might be caught on a projecting piece of metal or jammed into a narrow space that constantly flooded with each wave. Naturalist friend Joe Valencic, another of the lecturers on the cruise, had also warned of Panamanian sea snakes, whose venom is similar to a cobra's. A few of the snakes were sunning on a nearby rock, and the thought of encountering one inside a darkened submarine was not my idea of fun, even though there are no reports of anyone having been bitten by one.

At high tide, as I snorkeled around the submarine, I had come face-to-face with a small moray eel tucked in a hole in the sub, and as he eyed me with his mouth of curving fangs, I had kept a respectful distance, again glad I was in open water and not in the interior of the sub. Discretion is the better part of valor—we stayed out of the sub and confined our work to the exterior until the last Zodiac from *Wind Star* came and plucked the last man—a certain reluctant archaeologist—off the beach. This would be the last year Zegrahm stopped at Isla San Telmo, and I was not sure how I would get back.

I sent photos of the mystery sub out to colleagues all over the world. Inquiries at the US Naval Historical Center came up blank—the only subs the United States had lost in or around the Panama Canal had been much larger. Perhaps the craft was foreign, they suggested. An e-mail from another colleague, Gene Canfield, suggested that instead of an early twentieth-century craft, the San Telmo submarine was older. It looked similar to the Civil War–era *Intelligent Whale*, an unfairly characterized "grand failure" that the US Navy had paid for and ultimately rejected. *Intelligent Whale* had been displayed for years at the Washington Navy Yard's museum, where I had seen her, looking like a swollen football with a flat bottom. A renovation of the navy yard's museum facilities had relegated *Intelligent Whale* to the National Guard and Militia Museum in Sea Girt, New Jersey.

With Canfield's suggestion in mind, in early 2003 I e-mailed the photos from San Telmo to submarine researcher Richard Wills. Then a graduate student in the nautical archaeology program at Texas A&M University, Rich had researched nineteenth-century American subs and authored a master's thesis on the Civil War–era sub in New Orleans. I didn't hear from Rich for a while, which was not unexpected. He works as an archaeologist for JPAC (Joint POW/MIA Accounting Command)—the CSI-styled lab where America's lost soldiers, sailors, fliers and marines are identified when human remains are found far afield on foreign soil. When I had last seen Rich, he was part of a team preparing to excavate the graves of US Marines killed during a daring raid on the Pacific island of Butaritari (Makin) in August 1942.

When I heard back from Rich, he agreed with Canfield. The San Telmo submarine was, in his opinion, an old craft. He suggested that it might be a submarine mentioned in a 1902 article on Civil War "submarine torpedo boats." That craft, manufactured by Julius H. Kroehl of the Pacific Pearl Company, "was built in New York in 1864, and carried to the Pearl islands, near the Bay of Panama, where it was successfully used." Reading Rich's e-mail, I sat straight up. It seemed too simple. I immediately e-mailed back and asked if the article had any illustrations. Rich answered back that it did, including a plan and dimensions of Kroehl's submarine. His scan of the plan was soon on my screen, and there was no mistaking it. The mystery was solved. The Zegrahm "sub explorers" of 2002 had in fact helped to map Kroehl's *Sub Marine Explorer*, one of many ironies surrounding the saga of the tiny craft. Thus began a multiyear quest to unlock all the submarine's secrets and rescue its story, and then to rescue its rusted mass from Isla San Telmo.

The truth behind this forgotten submarine is stranger than fiction. The *Sub Marine Explorer* and its inventor, Julius Kroehl, were forgotten footnotes to history. It is one of the world's oldest submarines, a vehicle for undersea combat and exploration and a product of the Industrial Revolution—forged in the passionate fires of both the Civil War and the foundry. It was the brainchild of an engineer and inventor as forgotten as his incredible machine. It was seen as a means of winning the war and of wresting wealth from the depths. Instead, it may have killed its crew, and it ended up discarded and forgotten in an isolated corner of the world. The submarine, in its operations in Panama, dived too deep, as we will see, and stayed too long, exposing its crew to decompression sickness and probable death.

While this is the saga of an incredible craft, it is first and foremost a human story. Julius H. Kroehl is a German American engineer who, had he not died an early death in Panama, might well have continued on to become one of the "fathers of the modern submarine." As it is, Kroehl's contributions to the development of the submarine were forgotten by most, and at best, relegated to a footnote in the history of submersible craft.

Kroehl was one of a number of mid nineteenth-century engineers and inventors whose interest and enthusiasm were captured by the new industrial age. Kroehl's career, devoted to iron, underwater explosives, and submersible craft, paralleled those of a number of his contemporaries, some of whom gained fame. Many others, like Kroehl, remained in obscurity. It was an age of incredible technological achievement; the nineteenth century witnessed the "triumph" (to use the word of the time) of the steam engine, the railroad, ocean steamships, iron and steel construction, the telegraph, photography, rifled guns, aerial balloons, and, of course, the submarine.

That the submarine ended up in Panama is no accident of history. American entrepreneurs and capitalists with ambitions to dominate and profit from the control and extraction of the mineral and natural resources of the West, particularly in Latin America, paid for Kroehl's submarine and sent it to Panama as yet another Yankee technological innovation that would not only conquer an area considered a "frontier" but also get the job done easier, faster, and more profitably—or so it was believed—than the "natives" of the region. Had those entrepreneurs sought the advice of the natives, however, something they would not do because of racism and their belief in their technological superiority, they would have found that the pearls they sought to harvest with the submarine were largely gone, and those that were left lay in deeper waters in lesser quantity and quality. Their much-vaunted technological advantage, while initially good, ultimately was for naught.

The tale of Kroehl and his invention is one of tragedy as well as technological triumph. Julius Kroehl was not the first nor would he be the last inventor to inadvertently kill through his invention. Sometimes the inventor pays the price, but oftentimes it is others who suffer. It is a tale as old as Prometheus and fire, Icarus who flew too close to the sun, or the fabled Dr. Frankenstein of Mary Shelley's classic. While Kroehl did not die at the hands of his submarine, it is possible that the crew who followed him did. In that lies the probable origin of the Pearl Islands' legend of "everyone who enters it dies." But the submarine also represented the adaptation of technology in an industrial process to harvest mechanically resources at a scale beyond ordinary human capacity. The overuse of technology in such a fashion ultimately leads to the complete destruction of natural resources.

There are many nuances to the tale of *Explorer*, and its complexities are a metaphor for its age—an age of iron, gunpowder, and pearls. It is a relevant tale for the twenty-first century as well, with lessons about the consequences of unbridled capitalism, audacious speculation, and the overexploitation of resources. Here follows the tale.

MISADVENTURES OF A CIVIL WAR SUBMARINE

1

Kleindeutschland

The Age of Gold and the Age of Bronze
have given place to the Age of Iron. . . . Iron is a great power
in the present age. It is revolutionizing the world . . .
the uses of the metal are endless, and its
supply almost inexhaustible.

—*Merchants' Magazine and Commercial Review,* 1854

KLAIPEDA, the hometown of Julius Kroehl, is a small city of just over 187,000 people. It is a busy place, with ships loading and discharging cargoes 24 hours a day, year-round, in this ice-free eastern Baltic harbor. It is Lithuania's only port. Until the end of World War II, Klaipeda was the German settlement of Memel. Memel once lay in the Kingdom of Prussia, occupied lands wrested from Poland and Lithuania following centuries of war and colonization. *Ostpreußen,* or East Prussia, where Memel is situated, came under Hohenzollern sovereignty in 1772 as a province of the kingdom, and largely remained under German control until the end of World War II.

One of the oldest German enclaves in East Prussia was Memelland, a territory on the banks of the Memel River near the Baltic Sea. Memel prospered as a strategically located port on the Baltic, although it was not in the Hanseatic League or on a major trade route.[1] Memel joined the province of East Prussia in 1773 and entered a period of economic growth as the northernmost German city in Europe, 91 miles north of the port of Königsberg. The key to Memel's success was its role in the British timber trade.

Britain's large forests began to vanish in the eighteenth century in the face of increased city and town construction and an expanding fleet of merchant and naval vessels. To fulfill its needs, Britain turned to two ready sources—the Baltic and North America. Because of its relative proximity, the Baltic dominated the trade through the early-nineteenth century.[2] By the time the British began to dominate the timber trade, Memel, only 1,100 nautical miles from England's eastern shores, had assumed a leading role as a timber trade port.[3] High duties in Riga, the region's greatest port, induced British merchants to bypass Riga in favor of Memel. As part of a strategy to control as much of the trade as they could, British merchants established branch offices in Memel, created strong partnerships with native Memellander merchants, in time even intermarrying, and built steam-powered sawmills in Memel to boost its output.

The flow of timber was immense no matter how it was measured—in 1762, when British timber ships started calling in greater numbers, 133 vessels arrived at Memel. By 1788, 784 timber ships loaded at Memel, which remained the average for the remainder of the eighteenth century until disrupted by the Napoleonic Wars. In 1804, 831 ships arrived at Memel.[4] The ships that called for timber arrived with a wide variety of British manufactures and "colonial wares"—woolens, sugar, coffee, tea, and tobacco, which along with corn, hemp, and flax filled the warehouses of Memel's merchants. The town was described in 1854: "The quays and streets relay a lively scene and a motley throng in the trading season,—German and Russian merchants, English, French and Dutch captains and sailors,—Lithuanian boatmen, foresters and farmers,—Jew dealers and pedlars, and occasionally some country people."[5] Historian Robert Greenhalgh Albion, writing on the timber trade, describes Memel and other Baltic timber ports as dreary seaports crowded with warehouses filled with "timber and corn . . . whose inhabitants lived almost entirely in a world of contracts, discounts and demurrages."[6]

One of Memel's merchants was Jacob Kröhl (also spelled Kroehl or Krehl), born in Memel in 1751 and married in 1776 to Anna Susanna Rosenbergerin. The family's origins may be Scottish Jacobite, or Scots introduced to the area through the lumber trade and Scotland's maritime ties to the Baltic. They may have been the descendants of John Crail, who emigrated from Scotland around 1660. Crail was living in Königsberg in 1676 under the name Johann Krehl. A petition for citizenship noted that although he was a foreigner, he had settled in Prussia as a boy and had carried on his business for nearly 16 years. He had a son who, as of 1682, was considered a citizen.[7]

The destruction and loss of many of Prussia's and specifically Memel's early records through war leaves gaps that can only be speculatively filled in. It is possible that Jacob and Anna, whose first child was a daughter, another Anna Susanna, later also had a son, who in turn passed on his father's name to Jacob when he was born sometime around 1795. Jacob married Johanna Philippine Dorothea, and they had two sons. The first was Heinrich, born on May 9, 1818, and the second was Julius Hermann Kröhl, whose exact birth date is unknown. When Julius died in early September 1867, his age was listed as 47, meaning his birthday had passed, suggesting that Johanna Kröhl delivered Julius between May and July 1820.

Nothing is known of the family's early life, but several clues besides Memel's role in the timber trade suggest that as a merchant Jacob had ties to Britain. A cousin, Wilhelm Kröhl, arrived in England and assumed British citizenship in the 1830s. Furthermore, by 1848, Johanna Kröhl had remarried, and her second husband was British-born merchant John Heanes.[8]

In 1826 Jacob Kröhl relocated to Berlin and lived there until at least 1833, possibly until 1837. There are many possible explanations for the Kroehl family's departure from Memel. Jacob's business may have not done well, or he may have sought a better life for himself and his family in the resurgent economy of an industrializing Prussia. Memel's fortunes had declined during the Napoleonic Wars, as Napoleon and his allies controlled the Baltic ports, and Memel timber prices skyrocketed due to their scarcity in England.[9] Memel mast imports dropped from nearly 1,000 to 500 in 1807, and then to a mere 42 masts in 1808–9, picking up to 204—20% of the pre-war shipments—in 1809–14.[10] It follows that British exports to the Baltic, and the profits Memel merchants could make from them, also declined. After the war, a combination of high British duties on timber and a shift in policy to bring more timber from Canada meant that Memel never fully recovered, nor would all of its merchants. Perhaps one of them was Jacob Kröhl.

Whether Jacob's family joined him in Berlin is unknown. He may have left Johanna and the children behind in Memel because of a divorce, also leaving her free to marry John Heanes. Not much is known of Heanes; it is possible that he was a merchant in Memel, and there met Johanna. The date of Heane's marriage to Johanna was sometime between 1826 and 1848. Both John and Johanna Heanes are buried next to Heinrich Kroehl in the family plot in Brooklyn, New York.

FLEEING PRUSSIA

Julius Kroehl most likely came to the United States not only to seek opportunity but also to flee difficulties at home. He arrived in New York at a time of

European unrest, especially in what is now Germany, then a confederation of 39 states and kingdoms of various sizes. Prussia and the Austrian Empire, the two largest powers, dominated the confederation. The rising power of Prussia both excited support in other states in the German Confederation for a united Germany, but it also inspired resistance in others, especially Austria, which remained apart from a Prussian-led customs union, the *Zollverein,* established in 1834 under Prussian leadership, which had gradually incorporated most of the other states. Despite the seeming unity of the *Zollverein,* Prussia's domination of the German Confederation was not universally accepted.[11]

Despite mistrust of Prussia, many of the other German states shared, in addition to the German language, a common history of association in the Holy Roman Empire. They had experienced the Napoleonic Wars under French occupation, which had ended with a Prussian-led revolution against Napoleon in 1813–14. The German states also shared, to varying degrees, famine, economic hardship, civil unrest, and growing nationalism in the "hungry 1840s," a decade also marked by the same struggles in other European states, including famine-ravaged Ireland, the Italian states, and Hungary.[12]

Internal dissension in Prussia, beginning in the 1830s, focused on the 1817 decision by Prussian ruler Friedrich Wilhelm III to merge the country's Lutheran and Calvinist churches into a single new entity. By the 1830s opposition to the new church by the "Old Lutherans" had spread throughout Prussia, engendering secret underground services, arrests and imprisonment, and the immigration of thousands of Lutherans to Australia and the United States.[13] A surge in religious revivalism also led to challenges from Prussia's Catholics, who pushed against a Prussian law that children of "mixed religion" marriages be educated in the faith of the father—a sticking point that the Pope and the Prussian archbishop ignored. This led to the arrest of the archbishop, which led to demonstrations and Catholic clashes with troops sent to keep order through 1837–38.[14]

The death of the king in 1840 brought a new ruler, Friedrich Wilhelm IV, to the throne. The new king's initial actions were more liberal than in his predecessor's reign, freeing prisoners, relaxing religious strictures, and talking of representative politics as opposed to a strict monarchy. The post-Napoleonic era in Prussia had been marked by the growth of the bureaucracy and the military, and a resultant struggle between a desire for tolerance and freedom matched by a need for obedience to the law and public order, a conflict underscored by an anonymous Prussian poem of the late 1830s:

For us who live in Prussia's land
The King is always lord;
We live by law and the bonds of order,
Not like some bickering horde.[15]

The Industrial Revolution, population growth, crop failures, food shortages, an oversupply of labor, a resultant lowering of wages, poor working conditions, a fear that the ruling class was seeking to "pauperize" the working classes, agitation for religious freedom, and distrust of an increasingly authoritarian Prussian state, now combined with a desire for political change into a series of clashes, "hunger riots," and deep-rooted internal dissension.

The social conditions of Germany were bleak in the decade Julius Kroehl passed from adolescence into young adulthood, and in Prussia, they were such that the kingdom was in a state of "social emergency" from 1844 to 1847. In 1848 the tensions erupted in Germany, Prussia, and throughout Europe in a wave of popular uprisings that sought to overthrow absolutism and introduce representative governments. In Germany, a growing sense of nationalism also featured into the movement as the "radicals" called for a united Germany.

Revolutionary democratic, nationalistic, popular liberal and socialist fervor inspired revolutions in Switzerland, the Italian States, the Austro-Hungarian Empire, France, Poland, and Wallachia. An outright movement for independence ended in military defeat of the revolutionaries. Barricades in Berlin were swept aside by the military, and ultimately the Prussian aristocracy, led by a ruthless new chancellor, Otto von Bismarck, worked with the king to institute a new constitutional monarchy that retained significant royal control. Under Bismarck, Prussia would manipulate, provoke, and finally wage war with Austria and then France to merge the German states into a new, united German Reich with a decidedly Prussian flavor. However, a large number of Germans had fled their homeland for Great Britain, the United States, and South America. Among them were the Kroehls.

What is known is that Heinrich, his name anglicized to Henry Kroehl, "attended the German government schools, removed to Berlin, where he served as a junior clerk in a banking house until his twentieth year," and then immigrated to the United States, arriving in New York in 1838.[16] There he settled, eventually entering the family business by becoming a merchant. He was followed by his brother, Julius, who arrived from Liverpool on the immigrant packet *Fairfield* on July 29, 1844. The passenger manifest listed him as a 24-year-old "engineer."[17] Julius had previously been a member of the Prussian artillery, according to Civil War records stating that he had "served in the artillery abroad."[18] He arrived in a city and a nation seemingly in need of his talents, and a New York then in the midst of rapid social and technological change. Julius Kroehl threw himself into his new life with zeal, seeking to tap into the technological revolution to make his own version of the American dream come true.

KLEINDEUTSCHLAND

When the Kroehls arrived, New York was a city in flux, expanding rapidly to become America's principal seaport and city. Its population skyrocketed from 123,706 in 1820 to 813,669 in 1860, with most of the new residents immigrants.[19] Author Washington Irving, writing to his sister in 1847, described a city changed from their youth, "pulled to pieces, burnt down and rebuilt. . . . I can hardly realize that within my term of life, this great crowded metropolis . . . [once] a quiet little City . . . is . . . now one of the most rucketing cities in the world."[20] It reminded him "of one of the great European cities Frankfort [*sic*] for instance in the time of an annual fair."[21]

The analogy to Frankfurt was apt, for thanks to a flood of immigrants, the city hosted the largest German population outside Europe. In 1840 there were more than 24,000 Germans in New York, and by 1860 the German population had grown to more than 200,000 owing to the unrest in the German states. Germans were the second largest immigrant group in New York after the Irish.[22] The Germans represented a quarter of New York's population and America's first large immigrant community that spoke a foreign language.[23] German immigration to the United States dated to the seventeenth century, and at the time of the American Revolution, German was the second most spoken language in the new nation.

The Germans of New York settled on Commercial Street in the 1820s. By the 1840s they had expanded into a larger, primarily German neighborhood in the 10th and 17th Wards, east of the Bowery and north of Division Street. Known variously as "Dutch Town," or *Kleindeutschland* ("Little Germany"), it was the German American center of the United States.[24] It was into this neighborhood that the Kroehls settled. Henry, the first arrival, worked as a clerk, and in September 1847, he married Cornelia R. Turfler. Their first child was born two years later, in 1849, and in 1851 Henry established a bristle and brush importing business with fellow immigrant Otto Dill in Little Germany. The partners remained together as a firm until Dill died in 1861.

Julius's residence and activities immediately after his 1844 arrival are not known, but he apparently lived in New York, probably in proximity to Henry.[25] He was a resident of New York when he became a naturalized citizen of the United States on October 26, 1849.[26] In 1850 he joined the newly formed *Sozialistische Turnverein,* a clear indication of his political sensitivities and perhaps a clue as to why he had left Prussia. The Turnverein (gymnastic club) movement was founded in Prussia by Friedrich Ludwig Jahn in 1811 to foster the rebirth of Germany, then under French occupation, through promoting physical health and mental acuity under the banner of "A Sound Mind and a Sound Body." The Turner movement, as it was called, blossomed in the 1840s during the period of unrest leading to the revolutionary movements of 1848, and in Germany, a number of the most ardent liberals and socialists in the revolution were Turners. In the aftermath of the defeat of the revolutionary movement, many Turners fled to the United States.[27]

The Turnverein movement spread nationwide, thanks to the new arrivals. Its "liberal-radical-reformer" nature led many of the clubs to associate with the German freethinker movement. Freethinkers were part of a "spectrum that started with something approximating Unitarianism/Universalism, extended through rationalism, deism, and secularism, and included an extremist undercurrent of crusading atheism."[28] Given his later marriage in a religious ceremony, Julius Kroehl most likely was at the beginning of that spectrum religiously, although politically he was more radical.

As a member of the Sozialistische Turnverein, Kroehl would have vowed to "give all available support to the essence of the Turners with both word and action," and "apart from physical gymnastics against the pressure of mind and material goods to strong encourage true freedom, prosperity and education for all classes."[29] Abolition played an important role in the club, too, as "the republican principles of the Turners carried many of them into the struggle against slavery, and eventually into the Republican party."[30] During the Civil War, the membership of the club strongly supported the Union, many joining to fight. Among them would be Julius Kroehl.

Julius embraced the emerging technology of photography as a source of income and as an outlet for his creative talents. The 1837 invention of photography by Louis Daguerre of Paris reached the United States in 1839 and quickly spread throughout the country. By 1850 New York was a hub of photographic daguerreotype activity, with 77 galleries employing 184 people. Three years later, in 1853, nearly a thousand New Yorkers were employed in daguerreotype galleries, with more than a third of them on Broadway.[31]

In 1851, as Henry entered into business with Otto Dill, Julius appears to have been the partner in the daguerreotype firm "Messrs. Kroehl & Vetter" of No. 499 Broad Street. That year, they entered "colored photographs" (hand-tinted daguerreotypes) in the Fair of the American Institute.[32] They also entered "phototypes," or photogravure reproductions of photographs, and won a silver medal for their submission.[33] "They are beautiful pictures, and resemble correct oil painted miniatures than sun drawn likenesses. They are really a credit to our city and to the talented artists who produced them."[34] It is possible, since *vetter* means "cousin" in German, that Kroehl had entered into a working partnership with a relative, perhaps his cousin Otto Sackersdorff, who like Julius was noted to have photographic interests later in life. No other record of the firm has been found, but later in his life, during the Civil War, Julius Kroehl carried "photographic apparatus," and when he died in Panama, photographic chemicals were among his personal effects.

The partnership does not appear to have lasted long and is not listed in the New York directories at the time—nor, for that matter, are Kroehl or Vetter. Julius first appears in the New York City directories on his own in 1855, listed as an engineer at 4 Broadway at the tip of Manhattan near Battery Park in close proximity to the waterfront.[35] However, he was in the city, as shown not only by his Turnverein membership and the Kroehl and Vetter partnership but also by his involvement in the 1853–54 construction of a new iron and glass landmark in New York, the fabled Crystal Palace, and then in a series of articles detailing the patent he received for a device to form flanges in wrought iron beams.[36] Ever inventive, it seems that Julius Kroehl had set aside his photographic interests to pursue another avenue for advancement. Like other industrious, engineering-minded men of his time, Julius Kroehl embraced the new "age of iron."

THE AGE OF IRON

The world was in the throes of a new iron age in the first half of the nineteenth century. The Prussians were among the first to take to the new uses for iron, casting a series of bridges beginning with a copy of the Iron Bridge for the Duke of Anhalt-Dessau in 1791, a full-sized span across the Striegauer Wasser near Laasen completed in 1796, and another in Berlin in 1797.[37] The French followed suit, not only with Napoleon adopting it for military purposes, but also with the nation building civic projects ranging from bridges and fireproof iron roof frames for a series of buildings including the Louvre (in 1779), to the world's first cast iron and glass dome for the Halle au Blé in Paris, completed between 1809 and 1813.[38]

Julius Kroehl's later affinity for iron working should not surprise us, given the strong Prussian interest in it. In addition to the tools of war, the Prussians turned to iron for memorialization. In particular, royal architect Karl Freidrich Schinkel (1781–1841) carried out his king's command for iron memorials to Prussia's struggles against Napoleon by erecting Gothic monuments such as the 64-foot-high Kreuzberg Memorial, rising still from a high Berlin hill with its 12 eight-foot-high cast iron statues, topped by a massive cast iron cross. Also, it was Schinkel in 1813 who designed and cast Prussia's highest military decoration, the *Eisernes Kreuz,* or Iron Cross.

Iron working in America dated to colonial times. By the mid-eighteenth century, most of the colonies hosted ironworks that drew their ore from nearby mines or bogs and refined and smelted iron, using charcoal culled from America's vast forests, to make a variety of household goods and farm implements and machinery.[39] New York's first ironworks, the Ancram Iron Works, was built around 1743. It later manufactured cannonballs for the Continental Army and an iron chain used to block the Hudson River during the Revolutionary War.

In New York State, the beginning of the nineteenth century brought the early stages of development in the Champlain iron district, which grew into the "most important iron district in the state, containing rolling mills, blast furnaces, and forges."[40] Pennsylvania and Ohio became the most prominent iron-producing states, with New York in third place by midcentury, but what New York lacked in massive iron-producing facilities it made up for in manufacturing finished products, especially large industrial castings and forgings. The development of rolling mills in the early-nineteenth century had moved iron working to an industrial level as mills began rolling angle iron and bars in 1817.[41] By 1830 American mills had produced 113,000 tons of rolled and hammered iron. Three decades later, more than 500,000 tons of rolled iron, the product of 256 ironworks in 20 states, helped to make America an emerging industrial power.[42]

New York at midcentury was an ideal place for Julius Kroehl. It was the industrial center of the United States. The shores of Manhattan were lined with ironworks "that hunkered down along the East River and Hudson River waterfronts, attended like economic royalty by flotillas of barges full of New Jersey pig iron and Pennsylvania coal . . . each acres in extent and employing hundreds of workers. . . . [They] were creatures of the boom in railroads and steamships, producing entire trestles, thirty-ton marine engines, and the enormous bed-plates on which a ship's machinery rested."[43]

After his foray into professional photography, Julius Kroehl turned his attention to iron. In 1853, following the success of the Great Exhibition of 1851 in London and its magnificent iron and glass Crystal Palace, New York prepared to host its own world's fair, called the "Exhibition of the Industry of All Nations." The exhibition would also be an opportunity for America and New York to demonstrate their industrial prowess, so the organizers opened a design competition to select a Crystal Palace that would outclass London's. The winning design came from a collaborative effort of two foreign-born architects, Georg Carstensen, a Dane, and Charles Gildemeister, a German immigrant.

Carstensen and Gildemeister hired a small team of eight architectural assistants, most of them also foreign born. Julius H. Kroehl was listed as the first assistant, a position of considerable responsibility, including his assignment to the project's building department as the assistant engineer. Kroehl would have worked on all aspects of the palace's design, from calculations to preparation of the drawings, and then the translation of drawings into castings and finally a standing building. Work on the site began in early 1853, and by March, much of the framework was in place, as shown in an image of the site depicted in the March 19, 1853, edition of the *Illustrated News*. Twenty-eight ironworks and foundries, most in New York, provided the masses of cast and wrought iron required for the palace. Like the London version, New York's Crystal Palace would be glass and cast iron, but different in shape, and larger. The building, shaped like a Greek cross, featured a central part surmounted by a 100-foot-diameter dome that towered 125 feet into the air. The 54-foot-wide naves, rising 67 feet to the ridge of the roof, housed the exhibition spaces and offices.

The dome, a critical part of the structure, was assigned to Julius Kroehl.[44] The dome's final assembly, as described by the architects, documents the complexity of the job:

> The lantern was completed on the ground, and raised between two poles, about 10 feet higher than the required height of the dome. Four derricks were then placed on the bed-plate of the dome, by

which the ribs, brought to the spot, on account of their length, in three different pieces each, were, after having been riveted together on the ground, hoisted to their placers, bolted and keyed to the bed-plate, and bolted to their shoes in the upper ring, supporting the lantern. . . . The contractors for raising the building deserve great credit for their skill in raising the dome, which was accomplished in 4½ working days; much is also due to the contractors for the iron works, the assistant engineer . . . and last but not least, to the efficient body of mechanics who, in sunshine and storm, applied themselves steadily to their labors.[45]

This was not the only praise Kroehl received from the architects. After the completion of the Crystal Palace in early 1854, Carstensen and Gildemeister noted their thanks to their staff, "among whom we have particular pleasure in mentioning Messrs. Kroehl, O. Dietz, A. Bauer, J. Kay and A. Monte Lilla." For the next few years, newspaper accounts referred to Kroehl as the "engineer of the Crystal Palace."

In March 1854, following the Crystal Palace project, Kroehl's experience in ironworking was reflected in his filing of a patent claim for "an improvement in machinery for bending flanges in wrought iron beams." The description of the patent claim also noted how the beams and their flanges could be shaped into a "taper or elliptic, or other curved form" with Kroehl's improved machinery.[46] The US government granted and published Kroehl's patent in January 1855.[47]

During this time Julius showed that he was indeed a practicing nineteenth-century liberal, as would be expected given his membership in the Turnverein. In the fall of 1853 he attended meetings to commend Commander Duncan Nathaniel Ingraham, who had aided Martin Kozsta, a fugitive patriot who had been arrested after the abortive 1849 rebellion against the Austro-Hungarian Empire. Because Kozsta had lived in the United States for awhile and declared his intention to become an American citizen, US officials protested his arrest, but to no avail. Ingraham, the commanding officer of the corvette USS *St. Louis,* trained his ship's guns on the Austrian ship on which Kozsta was imprisoned, forcing his release.[58] Besides Commander Ingraham receiving the praise of immigrants who had fled oppression in their native lands, Kroehl brought another case to public attention, that of Henry von Oensche (or Rensche), who had been arrested by Prussian officials over his activities as a writer.[48]

Kroehl's patent was part of his push to continue to work in the newly developed field of prefabricated building construction utilizing cast iron architectural elements like those employed in the Crystal Palace. Cast iron building elements were the brainchild of New Yorker James Bogardus, who "developed and patented a method for mass producing prefabricated building elements such as columns, panels, and arches, which were cast from molds in any architectural style. In 1849, he designed a complete cast iron façade for a Broadway drugstore, and in 1850 he patented an all cast iron building."[49] The rise of prefabricated iron "broke the logjam in commercial construction, and his structures—inexpensive to make, easy to erect and maintain, supposedly fireproof—were soon in great demand. Foundries were created or converted to supply them."[50]

In 1856 Kroehl successfully outbid James Bogardus and won a contract from the City of New York to erect a cast iron fire watchtower in Mount Morris Park (which lies between West 120th and West 124 Streets along the alignment of 5th Avenue in East Harlem, Manhattan). Following a disastrous fire in 1832, New York erected a series of wooden watchtowers, hired watchmen, and constructed reservoirs and an aqueduct to protect the city. The early wooden towers were susceptible to fire, but Bogardus's invention of architectural cast iron resolved the problem. In 1851 Bogardus erected the first cast iron tower at 9th Avenue and West 33rd Street, which was followed by a second tower in 1853 on Spring Street, which cuts across town in the East Village, close to Julius Kroehl's neighborhood in Little Germany.

Kroehl may have seen the Spring Street tower under construction and been inspired to compete for the next. In September 1855, when the city announced the competition for the third tower, Kroehl submitted a bid for $2,300. Bogardus submitted a $5,750 bid, which the city noted as received on January 14, 1856.[51] On April 14 the mayor approved the award of a contract to Kroehl, who began work on his tower, which stood atop a rocky summit in the park.[52] Kroehl used the natural elevation of the rock to cut his costs by essentially building half the tower Bogardus had envisioned.

However, while Kroehl had won the contract with less cost, he did not win it through major innovation. When completed in early 1857, the three-story, 47-foot-high octagonal tower featured cast iron Doric columns and iron girders suspending the large alarm bell, with the lookout atop the tower reached by a spiral staircase. Its design was, according to architectural historians, "dependent upon and representative" of Bogardus's earlier towers.[53] Bogardus also thought so, and launched a patent infringement lawsuit against the City of New York in April 1857 and asked for payment of a $289 royalty plus tens of thousands of dollars in damages. The city agreed to the fee but fought the damages and won; in April 1858 the court awarded Bogardus the $289 but not his court costs.[54] The suit and settlement evidently did not cloud Kroehl's reputation, as he was, at the time of the settlement, working on another civic project, one that saw Kroehl's adaptive abilities put to work not in iron but in gunpowder and underwater blasting. Julius Kroehl's new career beneath the water, however, would in time bring him back full circle to building with iron.

ᴗ2ᴗ

Americans Discover the World Below

Though the natural constitution of man
entirely unfits him for remaining in water with safety
for more than two minutes at a time, the desire of obtaining
valuable articles lying at the bottom of the sea has led him
to devise numerous expedients.

—*The New American Cyclopaedia,* 1859

E DUCATED nineteenth-century Americans knew that the world beneath the rivers, lakes, and oceans was a strange, terrible, and yet
marvelous place, filled with creatures fantastic and treasures waiting to be extracted through the technological triumph of human, and ideally,
American genius. The history of European diving bells was also known, one
encyclopedia reminding its readers, "the principle is seen in pressing any vessel like a tumbler mouth downward into the water. The air within the vessel
prevents the water from rising and filling it."[1] In this simple fashion, diving
bells, cast and shaped like their namesake church bells, had been employed in
marine salvage for centuries. In the late-seventeenth century, Edmund Halley
"improved" the simple bell by sinking two weighted, tightly sealed barrels
with air trapped within, alongside the bell, to replenish air inside a reinforced
wooden diver's bell; "the air contaminated by breathing was let off by a stop-
cock in the roof, and pieces of glass set in here admitted the light."[2]

Halley's invention was the first true forerunner of the "modern" diving
bell.[3] The next breakthrough was the use of a forced-air pump by British engineer John Smeaton, who in 1788 built a cast iron box he called a "diving chest."
It featured a pump mounted atop the chest, a reservoir for extra air, and a non-
return valve to retain air inside the chest if the pump failed. Small at 4½ feet

by 4½ feet high and long, and 3 feet wide, Smeaton's "chest" held two divers.[4] Using Smeaton's system, other inventors created versions of the bell in Britain, Europe, and the United States.

One of the earliest American diving bells known to have survived is a cast iron chest that has been sitting in Delaware City's Battery Park since 1941. Manufactured in Philadelphia, the bell was used in repairs on the Chesapeake and Delaware Canal from 1829 until the latter nineteenth century and the introduction of dive equipment.[5] The use of any diving bell limited a diver to the immediate area of his bell; bolder divers would hold their breath and dive down to fasten lines or recover items, but their mobility was limited by the length of their safety line and their lung capacity.

An early nineteenth-century invention, the diving helmet and "diver's dress" was the next change, introduced in 1827. John Deane of England and his brother Charles, with German-born instrument maker and inventor Augustus Siebe, created an underwater helmet. It was open to the sea at its bottom, so that if a diver fell over, the helmet would flood, killing the hapless diver. Siebe worked to perfect the helmet, and in 1840 developed a two-piece design with a breastplate that attached to the suit, and a separate helmet that screwed on to the neck ring of the breastplate like the lid of a jar. Siebe also added a spring-loaded air exhaust valve. The "Siebe helmet" or "hard hat" dive rig would remain essentially unchanged for over a century.[6] With tenders on a barge above pumping air continuously into the helmet and suit to pressurize it against the depths, a diver was free to walk a distance on the bottom, weighted with lead overshoes and a belt.

The Deanes used their helmets as early as 1832. They then used them in 1836 to salvage cannon from the sixteenth-century wreck of the ship *Mary Rose* off Portsmouth, and in 1839–44 to salvage the eighteenth-century wreck of the warship *Royal George,* which lay in 65 feet of water off Portsmouth.[7] A team of Royal Engineers, led by Colonel Charles William Pasley (1780–1861), pioneered the extensive use of the new diving system, as well as underwater explosives in the arduous but successful *Royal George* salvage. The project made Colonel Pasley and "submarine armour"[8] famous, and the talk of both sides of the Atlantic.[9]

American inventors were not idle during the period. Charles Condert of Brooklyn developed a sealed diving suit with a tank made of looped copper tubing that wrapped around the body. Filled with air using a pump made from a gun barrel, Condert's device functioned well enough for a few test dives in the East River. In August 1832, however, Condert drowned on a 20-foot-deep test dive when his breathing tube broke and his suit flooded.[10] While Condert's invention failed him, that of another American, Leonard Norcross of Maine, was more successful. He developed a gum-elastic-covered diving suit in 1834, the key feature of which was a relief valve at the top of the suit's helmet.[11] The invention crossed the Atlantic in 1837, when Augustus Siebe incorporated modified Norcross valves into his helmets in England. The next successful invention by an American came the following year, in 1838.

THE TWO "CAPTAIN TAYLORS" AND THEIR "SUB-MARINE ARMOR"

At the same time the Deane brothers and Colonel Pasley and his army divers were at work off Portsmouth, an enterprising American inventor and pioneer diver captured the attention of New Yorkers with his own version of "submarine armor." The *Knickerbocker,* New York's "monthly magazine," reported in its "gossip with readers and correspondents" section that the editors had a great attraction to the subject of submarine exploration, and recounted a September 1838 "performance of '*A Man in Sub-marine Armor*' off the Battery" in which the "diver" looked "very much like a robustious beer-barrel on skids": "He had an inverted head-piece, or hat, like a topsy-turvy iron pail, with a small glass-door on hinges in front. This was attached to an India-rubber jacket, terminating near the middle of the body in a strong copper hoop, which was screwed to another and corresponding hoop, fastened to . . . 'trowserloons,' which terminated in bronze or brass 'leggins' and impervious boots. He had a long cord in his 'mailed right hand,' and there was a small engine-hose coiled up on the deck, which he alluded to as 'that air-pipe.'"[12] The exploits of the "diver" in question, Captain William H. Taylor, marked the beginning of New York—and the nation's—heightened awareness and fascination with "submarine" technology. In an age of rapid industrial growth, a surge in patented inventions, the birth of publications like the *Scientific American,* and a burgeoning sense of America's manifest destiny, the underwater world was another frontier, real and metaphorical, for Americans to conquer.

William H. Taylor was the scion of an old North Carolina family with roots that dated to before the American Revolution.[13] Taylor first attracted attention in 1837 with the publication of a brochure, "New and Alluring Sources of Enterprise in the Treasures of the Sea, and the Means of Gathering Them," describing himself as "most particularly familiar with the Venezuelan coast, where both pearls and rich wrecks abound."[14]

Captain Taylor's missive suggests that he knew the South American coast, a route long traveled by Spanish treasure ships and worked for centuries by native and enslaved black pearl divers. Fearing the attack of sharks, in 1837 Taylor designed and built his armored diving suit to harvest the deeper areas of the fished-out pearl beds off Isla Margareta and to seek lost treasure. To publicize his invention and to seek investors, Taylor launched a series of public demonstrations beginning in August 1837.[15] These continued on to the demonstration admiringly described by the editors of the *Knickerbocker.*

On December 23, 1837, Taylor applied for a US patent for his suit, which he described as "Taylor's Submarine Armor."[16] The armor clothed "the diver in a dress which will protect him from the pressure of the water and from danger from fishes, etc., and at the same time give him the free use of his limbs and enable him to be supplied with air for breathing."[17] Taylor's application was successful, and on June 20, 1838, he was issued Letters Patent No. 578. Among his partners was George W. Taylor, no relation. This native of New Jersey, and a purveyor of India rubber, had an interest in the undersea world and his namesake's invention.[18]

In early 1838 William Taylor commenced the salvage of a wreck off Rockaway Beach and chartered the "Sub Marine Armor Company" of New York to raise $200,000 to expand the business. In September, Taylor conducted a series of demonstrations at the annual Mechanics' Fair, including the one witnessed by the editors of the *Knickerbocker,* and won a gold medal for "the originality and real merit of your inventions and submarine experiments."[19] The editors of the *Knickerbocker* were also impressed, conversing with Taylor as he sat on his diving barge, sipping champagne through his open helmet and telling them of his dives on the wreck at Rockaway, the *Bristol,* where he had recovered "a large amount in iron, steel and gold."[20] Obviously an avid student of Colonel Pasley's work, he concluded his demonstration by igniting two charges beneath the river, throwing up a mass of "mire and dirt" and water some 15 feet into the air:

> This sub-marine armor is a most wonderful invention, and we
> are glad to learn, that a 'Sub-Marine Armor Company'" has been
> established, and that nearly all its stock has already been taken. Its
> gains cannot fail to be intense. Our coasts and rivers teem with

wrecks, as do similar waters elsewhere; and when it is considered, that with this armor one can descend to the bed of the ocean, and work for hours among the treasures of the deep, it needs no seer to predict, that CAPTAIN TAYLOR, the ingenious inventor, and the Company who have brought his labors to account, will be well rewarded for their united genius and enterprise.[21]

Joined by George W. Taylor and other partners, William Taylor headed south after the demonstrations to spend the winter of 1838–39 salvaging wrecks. Within several weeks of his arrival in South Florida, however, Taylor died under mysterious, "if not sinister," circumstances.[22] He was apparently never mentioned again, the only reference to his death a listing of his widow's name in the New York City directory of 1840.[23]

In February 1839 the partners, with George Taylor advertising himself as "Captain Taylor" and also falsely claiming to be from North Carolina, arrived in Charleston and demonstrated the armor and underwater explosives, literally replacing the late, unmentioned inventor.[24] From Charleston they returned to New York. There, they held "submarine" demonstrations in early April before large crowds and awed bystanders during which "the convulsed waters lifted up her burden, and held it for a moment as in a bowl, until with tremendous force it burst into innumerable fragments, shooting high into the air, and falling with impetuous plunge within a wide circumference."[25]

Captain Taylor's demonstrations captured the attention of the government, especially the US Navy, but success eluded him. Diving operations, experiments in blasting, and marine salvage in Long Island Sound and in the Great Lakes occupied Taylor's attention from 1840 through 1845. Taylor's interest in underwater demolition and his invention of India rubber pontoons to help float stranded vessels off sandbars resulted in a brief stint as a civilian contractor for the navy during the Mexican War of 1846–48, including a foray up the Tabasco River in June 1847 and an opportunity to blast free a group of piles driven into the riverbed to obstruct the advance of the American fleet. The piles, once blasted loose, were pulled free by USS *Spitfire*, then under the temporary command of Lt. David D. Porter, USN.[26] This work provided an income for Taylor, his wife, and a daughter, but he was either far from comfortable or restless. In 1850 a government contract to examine the wreck of the US steam frigate *Missouri*, sunk at Gibraltar, sent him out at age 43 to conduct an arduous set of dives. Taylor became ill there, and after failing to recover his health in Madeira and Havana, returned to the United States where "his lungs became more oppressed, and he kept on declining" until he died.[27]

At the time of the second Captain Taylor's death, a number of inventors were hard at work perfecting devices to descend and work beneath the sea, and divers were busy working on a variety of projects ranging from underwater construction to demolition and salvage. They included James A. Whipple, son of a Boston brass finisher and machine shop owner. Fascinated by a demonstration of Taylor's "submarine armor," Whipple designed a helmet for his own use with an escape valve in the helmet, which did away with the need for two hoses. According to a published description, "the method used by Taylor, the only man then engaged in the business in this country, was to have two air pipes, one to carry the air down, the other to bring it up. The dispensing of the one hose . . . was a great relief to the operator below, as well as the tender above."[28]

From 1846 to 1858, Whipple worked at the "business of raising sunken property and submarine engineering upon foundations and piers." He was, he said, "a practical diver," with "the best apparatus in the United States, consisting of Steam Engine, Bell, Submarine Armors, Patent Pumps, Wrenches, Power Capstans, Chains, &c."[29] Whipple's projects included continuing Taylor's work on the sunken *Missouri,* the salvage of the Spanish warship *San Pedro de Alcantara* off the coast of Colombia, salvaging iron plates from the steamer *Pioneer* in the Hudson River, naval dry-dock work in Pensacola, water-pipe laying in New York, and salvage work in the Bay of Fundy and the Gulf of St. Lawrence before retiring from diving in 1859.[30]

Whipple was one of America's better known divers, as was a Great Lakes–based diver and salvor, John Green. Green was involved in a number of notable salvages, including the steamers *Erie* and *Atlantic,* and his exploits thrilled the public at a time when submarine adventures were as exciting as early space flight was in the late-twentieth century. The "otherworldliness" of underwater exploits and the risks taken by Green and other divers offered vicarious thrills, as noted in an 1853 account of Green's dives to the wreck of *Erie:* "By means of the submarine armor . . . the diver is enabled to remain uder water, from three to four hours without inconvenience, and in one instance, Mr. GREEN remained over five hours on the *Erie.* Air is supplied to the diver through a flexible tube force-pump. . . . In descending, if lowered quickly, a painful sensation and dizziness is experienced by the diver during the first 30 feet; if lowered slowly, however, the lungs gradually become accustomed to the pressure of the air, and little inconvenience is occasioned."[31] The effect on the public was remarkable; indeed, "the novelty and impact of graphical representations of the underwater world" was powerful in the early to mid-nineteenth century, with interest aroused in the worlds of science, art and commerce, with diving technology, and human endeavor to apply it, in a very Victorian sense, offering a new sense of life and learning.[32]

The worlds of technology and commerce were in the forefront of the 1850s development of diving apparatus. By then, rather than limit themselves to a man working in isolation in "submarine armor" or a diving suit, new inventors sought to perfect the diving bell or other forms of submersible craft that could carry more than one man. In the account of William Taylor's 1838 diving demonstrations, the *Knickerbocker*'s editors had opined that "such was sub-marine exploration, before the era of daguerreotypes, and land and ocean telegraphs. It is a different matter now.[33]

The Nautilus Sub-Marine Company

The "different matter" referred to the trials of the "Nautilus Sub-Marine Company's Diving Bell" in Glen Cove, New York. The Nautilus bell was one of a series of three sophisticated bells invented between 1849 and 1858. On April 3, 1849, J. Avery Richards and John W. Wolcott of Boston patented a "deep-sea diving bell."[34] Made of two hemispherical pieces of cast iron bolted together, the craft was entered by a hatch on the top, and with its sealed bottom, was actually a primitive bathysphere with glass-sealed portholes and a leather stuffed gland through which the "working rod" passed, with its "outer end . . . in the form of a hook, pike, scoop or forceps or other shape as experience shall show to be the most convenient."[35]

Apparently experience did not show Richards and Wolcott's bell to be convenient. Another team of inventors, however, was busy developing the next step in the evolution of the diving bell. Edgar W. Foreman of New Rochelle joined with Major Henry B. Sears of New York to create the first diving bell to use compressed air and water ballast chambers. Sears was a former artillery officer and a veteran of the Mexican War—the rank of "major" may have been a self-promotion to lend weight to his endeavors, as service records indicate that his Mexican War rank was at its highest a brevet 1st lieutenant.[36] The two started work in April 1852, building what Sears later called a "model successfully constructed to exemplify the principle" of the bell. When Foreman drowned on July 9, 1852, Sears continued, with Foreman's father's approval, on the project.[37]

As the previously noted circumstances of the two "Captain Taylors" demonstrates, there are problems inherent in partnerships in invention because of human nature and the need for individual reward. In the mid-nineteenth century, brilliant and clever people around the industrialized world were working to perfect new technologies and create inventions utilizing iron, steam, and electricity, and were competing to make scientific breakthroughs or "conquer" some geographical obstacle. It was an age of great egos, hubris, and risk-taking. Problems arose in the scramble to achieve funding, or when fame and fortune came with achievement, especially when there were conflicting claims, allegations of not giving credit where credit was due, or when misrepresentation or even fraud were suggested.

In 1854 Sears responded to an anonymous critic who had chastised media reports of his role in the development of the Nautilus bell. He wrote that he had asked Foreman's father to patent the bell in his dead son's name even though they had co-invented the bell and the bell at the time of Foreman's death was not yet of practicable use: "For two years and a half I have improved, added new features, conquered obstacles which seemed insurmountable, and produced a finished whole. I have received able assistance from my Engineers. They have all received their due need of credit. The model, with principle as first developed, is now at my office, where all can judge whether I may be considered the inventor of the finished machine. I have never failed to mention, with deep feeling, the assistance rendered to me in the first instance by the deceased Mr. F., or to admit that his mind, practically trained, was perhaps superior to my own."[38] Sears's remarks came after a public demonstration of the bell alongside the bark *Emily Banning* in Brooklyn. A *New York Times* reporter was among those who made a series of dives in the bell, describing the experience to his editors: "A body of air was first let in, the density being increased or diminished at will . . . from reservoirs of condensed air. A sensation of pressure is first felt on the drum of the ear by the ingress of air, but only temporarily. Our reporter was submerged about ten minutes, and at the bottom, a distance of thirty feet under the surface."[39]

Reporters, editors, government officials, politicians, and engineers acclaimed the Nautilus bell. In a subsequent test for the government, Jesse Gay, chief engineer of the US Navy, wrote his superiors that "it can be brought from the surface to the bottom of the water with considerable rapidity, or it can be moved up and down quite slowly." The compressed air tank of the bell allowed the operator to expel water from the ballast tanks, and provided sufficient lift to raise a four-ton block of stone off the bottom. The tanks also replenished air inside the bell with "no unpleasant sensation, such as are produced in the common diving-bell, by the action of the pump. When necessary to admit air, it is done so evenly."[40]

Sears, with his principal backer, Samuel Hallett, promoted the Nautilus bell as ideal for a variety of uses. It was capable of subsurface construction, functioning as an underwater crane. It could be used to remove large rocks, or as a moveable cofferdam, or to recover riches from the seabed. The *New York Times* account of the first public trial of the bell noted, "The *Emily Banning,* from which the experiments were made, will sail this week with four of the Nautilus machines for the Pacific to engage in the pearl fisheries."[41] The plan to sail to Baja California's pearl fishery, then the subject of American entrepreneurial interest, did not take place until 1856. In February of that year, the *New York Daily Tribune* reported that "the bark *Emily Banning* arrived at Acapulco on the 24th December for supplies. She is engaged in pearl fishing and wrecking, and has been successful, as she had on board $20,000 worth of old silver and pearls. Until Dec. 12 she was engaged in surveying the pearl grounds from Panama to Acapulco . . . having arrived at the Bay of Panama in the latter part of October. The machinery used on board the *Emily Banning* is the 'Nautilus' machine, owned by the Nautilus Submarine Company . . . the expedition belonging to the Wilmington Pearl-Fishing Company."[42] The expedition may not have been a complete success, since no other record of dives using the bell in Baja has surfaced.[43] Sears and Hallett found other avenues to exploit the bell's capabilities.

In April 1856 the *New York Times* reported that the schooner *Searsville,* under the command of "Captain Sears," had returned from Trinidad "loaded principally with old iron guns and an anchor, from the remains of Spanish men-of-war that were burnt in the Gulf of Paria, near the Port of Spain, in 1797." Diving in 36 feet of water, the expedition recovered 90 iron cannon, two bronze six-pounder guns, all shipped to New York to be scrapped in the city's iron foundries.[44]

Ever eager to promote the bell, Sears and Hallett traveled to England in 1857, where Sears read a paper at the Society of Arts and held dockside demonstrations at Victoria Dock. Advocating the Nautilus bell as a "new mode of operations," Sears gave a long and thorough briefing on the craft. At the surface, it displaced more water than it weighed, and floated. To dive, the operator closed the "man hole" and flooded the ballast chamber that surrounded the working chamber. By regulating the influx of water and the exhaust of air from the ballast tanks, the operator controlled the descent of the bell. The bell, connected to the surface by a "flexible" hose, was linked to a pressurized air tank on a dock or the deck of a support vessel.

The operator opened a valve in the bell to pressurize the interior to match the ambient sea pressure outside. Once the gauges inside and outside the bell marked "equal points, showing the equilibrium of forces," the operator lifted the covers on the bottom of the bell, allowing access to the seedbed. Cables with pulleys attached to the outside of the bell allowed the crew to stand on the bottom and move it by pushing. Cables, passing outside the bell through stuffing boxes, and connected to small windlasses, provided the means to lift or shift large stones or other weight.[45]

Sears and Hallett formed the "Nautilus Submarine Company" to capitalize their efforts, and as late as 1859, they and the craft were mentioned in a variety of magazines and dictionaries as exemplars of American ingenuity and pride. And yet the craft and company drop from the pages roughly around the time Hallett was engaged in a protracted lawsuit with financier and Rhode Island textile mogul Rowland G. Hazard,[46] and as others took what Sears had started and modified it further—notably a New York inventor named Van Buren Ryerson, who would in time design the *Sub Marine Explorer.* Hallett shifted his promotional and entrepreneurial drive to promoting the transcontinental railroad in Kansas, where he settled in the 1860s.[47] Although it passed out of public mention, the Nautilus diving bell had played a significant role in advancing diving technology in America and in maintaining the keen interest of the public begun by pioneer divers like the Captains Taylor and James Whipple. It was not alone, as other types of craft were also being developed, both abroad and in the United States, that presaged the development of a new type of vessel, the submarine.

EARLY SUBMARINES

Concurrent to the development of the diving bell, which operated suspended and linked to the surface, the true "submarine" was an automobile craft that operated independent of surface control. The concept of such a craft dates to the sixteenth century, when William Bourne drew upon Archimedes' principle of buoyancy to propose a "Shipe or Boate that may goe under the water unto the bottom, and so to come up againe at your pleasure."[48] Bourne's craft was never built. In 1622 Dutch inventor Cornelis van Drebbel built a submarine craft with a bow-mounted "battering ram."[49]

A variety of submarine craft were proposed and tested by inventors over the next century, but most historians agree that the first "successful" submarine was not invented until 1775–76, when David Bushnell of Connecticut built a one-person craft named the *American Turtle.* Described in 1775 as having "the nearest resemblance to the two upper shells of a tortoise joined together," *Turtle* "doth not exceed 7½ feet from the stem to the upper part of the rudder; the height not exceeding 6 feet." "The person who navigates it enters at the top. It has a brass top or cover, which receives the person's head as he sits on a seat."[50] Ballasted with lead and propelled and steered by hand-cranked rudders and "oars," *Turtle* was said to carry explosive charges that would be set underneath British ships to sink them. In September 1776, under the control of Sergeant Ezra Lee of the Continental Army, *Turtle* reportedly set out to sink HMS *Eagle,* then moored off New York. The mission failed, and after two other attempts to destroy a ship, *Turtle* was sunk with the ship carrying it on the Hudson River a few days after its initial foray.[51]

Some historians, notably British submarine scholar Richard Compton-Hall, doubt that *Turtle* was built, or if constructed, was used, but others, citing contemporary correspondence and the reminiscences of George Washington, are convinced that the craft did sortie on a mission. The story of the intrepid Yankee sergeant who trusted to an experimental craft and tried against the odds to be the first submariner to sink an enemy vessel entered American folklore. Whether or not *Turtle*'s mission occurred as legend has it, the story of Bushnell's submarine became part of a national dialogue on American ingenuity and bravery in adopting submarine technology to warfare.[52]

The next American inventor to turn his talents toward a submarine was Robert Fulton (1765–1815), better known for building *Clermont,* the first commercially viable steamboat in the United States, in 1807. Prior to this, Fulton spent nearly a decade in Europe, alternately trying to sell his concept of a "submarine boat" to France and the United Kingdom. The craft he proposed was a boat that sailed with a collapsible rig into position and then submerged. In 1799 the French agreed to build the craft, and in May 1800 Fulton's *Nautilus* was launched into the Seine from the yard of Perrier Frères in Paris. After an initial trial, Fulton took *Nautilus* to Brest for more tests, which reportedly involved taking the boat down to depths of 25–30 feet. However, the craft proved difficult to handle, and the French admiralty canceled Fulton's contract. He scrapped *Nautilus* in 1801 and ventured to England in 1804, where he developed "submarine bombs," or floating mines, and tested them for the British admiralty. Fulton adopted the word "torpedo" to describe his floating bombs, naming them for the Atlantic ray (*Torpedo nobiliana*), which emits strong electric shocks of up to 200 volts.[53]

While Fulton's "torpedoes" worked—he sank a target ship, the brig *Dorothea,* on October 15, 1805—the admiralty demurred, one admiral citing the "baseness and cowardice of this species of warfare." Fulton returned to New York in December 1806 and turned his hand to new endeavors, such as steamboats, while retaining an interest in submarines and torpedoes through the War of 1812.[54] Fulton's work was widely distributed and translated, and submarine historian Norman Friedman suggests that Fulton's work, especially combining the concepts of the submarine and the torpedo, inspired other inventors through the period of the US Civil War and beyond.[55]

Inventors proposing submarine craft in the first decades of the nineteenth century varied from a French naval captain Jacques-Phillipe Mérigon de Montgéry, who designed but did not build an all-iron craft in 1823, to the enthusiastic inventor Brutus de Villeroi, who introduced his first submarine at Noirmoutiers, near Nantes, France, in August 1832.[56] That 10-foot-long, 3-foot-wide craft was again demonstrated in 1835, but repeated efforts by the inventor to sell his designs were for naught. Villeroi ultimately made his way to the United States in 1856, where he designed and built a submarine for maritime salvage, and with the outbreak of Civil War, he successfully sold his idea, through an audacious demonstration to the public and a subsequent naval evaluation, to the US government. The craft he built and christened *Alligator* was the first submarine commissioned by the United States Navy.[57]

As development of diving bells and "submarine armor" picked up in the late 1830s and 1840s, the concept of autonomous submarine craft continued slowly, with fatal results for two inventors. One was in Spain, an inventor named Cervo, who died in 1831 when his spherical craft failed to return from a dive, and the other was in France in 1834, a Dr. Jean-Baptiste Petit of Amiens, who asphyxiated when his small submarine failed to surface from the Somme.[58] In 1842 a French scientist, Dr. Prosper Antoine Payerne (1806–86), experimenting with air replenishment in enclosed spaces, worked with Colonel Pasley and watched the use of "submarine armor" during the salvage of the sunken British

warship *Royal George.* To test his equipment for air purification, and with a
mind to branch out into submersible development, Payerne decided to build
a better means of working underwater. The result was first a diving bell built
in 1844 and then a submarine he termed a *bateau-cloche* (diving boat) made
of riveted iron, which he completed in 1846. It was later described as being
about 35 feet in length with a 10-foot diameter: "Inside it was divided into two
parts by a convex bulkhead, the fore-part constituting the air reservoir and the
after portion the room in which the propeller was turned by a hand-crank.
The vessel steered by vertical and horizontal rudders, and the divers emerged
into the water by means of an 'air-lock' or small chamber in which the air was
compressed till its pressure was sufficient to stop the inrush of water when the
outer hatch was opened."[59] "The only means of moving this craft when submerged was by the men inside 'punting' it with poles," but Payerne soon built
another craft, *Belledonne,* in 1846. It was "propelled mechanically by a screw
propeller."[60] Payerne's work on *Belledonne* at Cherbourg inaugurated a period
of intense work and international fame for Payerne, including his plans, announced in 1852, for a submarine tunnel connecting England and France. That
year he also built a second submarine, *Belledonne II,* a larger, steam-powered
craft (which he termed a "Pyrhydrostat") more than 60 feet in length. Financial setbacks, however, doomed Payerne's plans for expansion of his business,
and by 1863 he was bankrupt, returning to his original career in medicine.[61]
However, Payerne's work had significant consequences; *Belledonne* was a work-
able and efficient craft and its design was copied and brought to America.
There it would have a prominent (and until now unacknowledged) influence
on the development of subsequent American submersible craft.

As Payerne was working, a German inventor, Wilhelm Bauer (1822–75),
designed and built a small three-person submersible for the Prussian military
during the 1848–51 war between Denmark and the German states. To try and
break a naval blockade, Bauer proposed and received a limited amount of funds
to build first a model and then a full-scale craft. Named *Brandtaucher* ("marine
diver") by Bauer, the 26-foot-long, 35-ton riveted submarine was designed to
carry a 500-pound "torpedo" against enemy vessels. A single propeller, driven by
a hand-cranked flywheel, and a small rudder at the stern maneuvered *Brandtaucher.* Constrained by limited finances, Bauer dispensed with internal ballast
and air tanks, instead installing pumps to bring water into the open bilge to
dive and to pump it out to the surface. Also to save money, the hull was made

thinner, prompting Bauer to warn his backers that the submarine could not dive deeper than 30 feet.

Built at Kiel by the firm of Schweffel und Howald, *Brandtaucher* was completed in early 1851. The first trial dive, on February 1, was disastrous. As the water poured into the sub, Bauer could not keep it level, and the stern dropped. Loose cast-iron ballast tumbled aft, and *Brandtaucher* sank deeper than 30 feet. The hull flexed and deformed with the pressure, rivets cracked, and the flywheel came out of its mounts and broke. Finally, *Brandtaucher* hit the bottom of Kiel harbor, coming to rest in the mud in 52 feet of water. As the water poured in, Bauer either convinced or cowed his two companions to wait until the pressure inside the boat equalized, and then they opened the hatch and floated to the surface.[62] Wilhelm Bauer would later take his designs and build an improved submarine for the Russian Navy, and today is considered the father of the *unterseeboot* in Germany. But in 1851 his was but another seemingly failed idea for a self-propelled submarine.

In the United States, a former shoemaker turned engineer, Lodner D. Phillips, designed and built a submarine in Michigan City for marine salvage in the Great Lakes in 1850. Described as cigar-shaped and 40 feet in length with a 14-foot diameter, Phillips's submarine also employed ballast tanks and compressed air to regulate buoyancy and to keep the crew alive. It was called, appropriately enough, *Marine Cigar.*[63] Popular history insists that the craft sank due to its flaws and that Phillips was killed by his invention, but like so much early submarine history, the story is not true. *Marine Cigar* is said to have sunk on an unmanned test over the wreck of the steamer *Atlantic* in Lake Erie in 1853, and yet Phillips noted in a letter to the US Navy in 1864 that the submarine had operated until 1855. As for Phillips's "demise," in 1856 he patented a one-atmosphere diving suit, and during the Civil War, he offered his designs to the navy. These facts point to the success of *Marine Cigar* a decade earlier. However, until recent research proved otherwise, Phillips and his incredible craft were also relegated to the category of failure.[64]

Rumors of failure notwithstanding, the concept of submarines continued to fire the imagination of inventors, would-be undersea explorers, treasure seekers, and salvagers, and the general public. That enthusiasm was evident in late 1851 and through 1852, when both the *New York Times* and the *Scientific American* reported on an egg-shaped submarine then being tested at the Brooklyn Navy Yard. It had been built locally, at "Messrs. Pease & Murphy's engineering works, this city, for the Submarine Exploring Company."[65] Thirty feet long and 10 feet in diameter, it weighed ten tons, was hand-cranked with a single propeller, and featured a "manhole" through which a diver could lower his arms into the water to attach lines to objects. It was connected to the surface by an air hose, with a hollow copper float, and it had external cast-iron ballast supports, hinged and capable of being dropped to let loose ballast stacked on them. It had pumps inside the craft to help trim the craft with water and to send compressed air from cylinders into the working chamber.

An air purification system, which sprayed water through caustic lye, "which abstracts the carbon and returns pure oxygen," meant that three to seven men could work inside the craft for up to seven hours, at pressures up to 2½ atmospheres, "without fatigue."[66] The *Scientific American* named the inventor, a M. Alexandré, who was actually Lambert Alexandré, a salvage diver from France and one-time associate of Dr. Payerne. An account in the *Scientific American* noted the craft was invented in France and was employed in "the harbor of Cherbourg . . . [where] one of these machines, 40 feet long, is employed daily to remove some submarine rocks which obstruct the entrance to one of the basins."[67] Whether Alexandré was acting on his own or for Payerne is not known, but the claim that he was the inventor and owner suggests the former and that Alexandré was in America violating Payerne's patent.

The *Scientific American*'s correspondent in 1851 termed it a "very excellent and ingenious invention" and claimed not only that it would be "very useful about our harbor" but also "with such a vessel as this, no enemy's fleet could be safe on our coast."[68] The *New York Times,* in a March 1852 account of a dive, termed the craft "the most perfect submarine boat we have ever seen" after a detailed description of both it and the test dive it had taken.[69] "M. Alexandré" named his craft *Submarine Explorer,* and as such, he not only tested it in Brooklyn but also demonstrated it during the annual fair of the American Institute off New York's Battery. This American copy of Payerne's *Belledonne* had several features that would later be emulated in Sears's *Nautilus,* Merriam's *Intelligent Whale,* Villeroi's *Alligator,* and Kroehl's *Sub Marine Explorer:* "Inside it was divided into two parts by a convex bulkhead, the fore-part constituting the air reservoir and the after portion the room in which the propeller was turned by a hand-crank. The vessel steered by vertical and horizontal rudders, and the divers emerged into the water by means of an 'air-lock' or small chamber in which the air was compressed till its pressure was sufficient to stop the inrush of water when the outer hatch was opened."[70] Julius Kroehl was probably among the members of the American Institute present at the New York demonstration, and within a few years his interests would shift to a new type of work—submarine blasting. That field, pioneered and spurred on by international and national developments in submarines, diving bells, "submarine armor," and "torpedoes," would take firm root in New York in the decade before the Civil War. It would also frame a rivalry between Kroehl and another submarine entrepreneur, Benjamin Maillefert.

3

Rivals beneath the River

When the authorities become thoroughly awakened
to the importance of removing dangerous rocks from the paths
of commerce, many on which our vessels are often
wrecked will be removed.

—*New York Times,* August 11, 1853

THE use of submarine armor and diving bells came to the forefront in clearing obstructions to navigation on the oceanic and river routes to the great port of New York. For nearly two centuries, ships had risked hitting shoals and rocks in the river. And they had to navigate the narrow straits that connected New York's crowded waterfront port with Long Island Sound and the open Atlantic. One of the worst was Hell Gate, where the Harlem River flows into the East River. and where the East River connects to Long Island Sound. Filled with rocks that choked it, the aptly named Hell Gate gained its name not only because of these obstacles but also because of the strong currents and tidal rips that ebbed and flowed through the rocks. Washington Irving spread the fame and notoriety of Hell Gate in the early-nineteenth century:

> About six miles from the renowned city of the Manhattoes [*sic*], and in that Sound, or arm of the sea, which passes between the main land and Nassau or Long Island, there is a narrow strait, where the current is violently compressed between shouldering

promontories and horribly irritated and perplexed by rocks and shoals. Being at the best of times a very violent, hasty current, it takes these impediments in mighty dudgeon; boiling in whirlpools; brawling and fretting in ripples and breakers; and, in short, indulging in all kinds of wrong-headed paroxysms. At such times, woe to any unlucky vessel that ventures within its clutches.[1]

In time, as New York sailor, sociologist, and historian William Kornblum relates, the sailors who threaded the passage gave names to the obstacles. These ranged from terms of respect to gallows humor—"Pot Rock, Greater and Little Mill Rocks, Hen and Chickens, Frying Pan, Negro Head, Bald Headed Billy, Bread and Cheese, the Hog's Back, Flood Rock Island, and others."[2]

In response to a petition from New York merchants and shippers, the US Navy sent three officers, lieutenants Charles F. Davis, David Dixon Porter, and Isaac Woodhull, to survey Hell Gate in 1849. They reported that one in 50 sailing vessels that passed through were damaged, "forced by the violence of the currents on the rocks and shoals," and that steamships were also at risk. They recommended clearing the channel for mercantile reasons, and because the port was also of strategic importance. In response, New York underwriters, the harbor commissioners, and the chamber of commerce petitioned Congress for money to clear Hell Gate and other harbor obstructions, including Diamond Reef, Prince's Reef, and other rocks off the Battery at the eastern tip of Manhattan. The petition did not attract the attention of Congress, but it did get the attention of engineer Benjamin Maillefert, who offered "to contract for the removal of the rocks . . . by means of blasting under water, without drilling, using the surface water for a fulcrum, and igniting the powder by means of a wire attached to a galvanic battery."[3]

Maillefert's proposal attracted considerable attention, coming as it did in a time when New Yorkers were still in awe of the submarine exploits of the Captains Taylor, James Whipple, and other divers. Many doubtless remembered Captain Taylor's explosive displays off the Battery. As well, the readers of most of the town's mercantile, engineering, and scientific magazines were aware of the electric blasting undertaken by Colonel Pasley in England. Now, the new technologies of submarine apparatus and underwater explosives would be put to use to resculpt nature and remake New York harbor for commercial benefit.

BENJAMIN MAILLEFERT

In 1849 Benjamin S. H. Maillefert was 35 years old, a recent immigrant to the United States, and a veteran "submarine engineer." Born in Barcelona in November 1813 to a French father and Spanish mother who subsequently migrated to England after the peninsular wars, Maillefert emigrated from there to Nassau in the Bahamas in 1846. "Being of an active turn, he had previously passed a life of considerable adventure, a decided spice of romance being mixed up in his career."[4] In 1847 Maillefert's life took a new direction when he was hired to blow up the sunken ship *Sybella* of Boston, which had wrecked on the rocks off Nassau. Maillefert's experience suggested to him a new theory, that if he placed his charges directly on top of the wreck, the pressure of the water would exert force against the blast and shatter the hulk.

After successfully blasting *Sybella* for salvage, Maillefert blasted 900 tons of coral off Rockfish Shoal at the entrance of Nassau Harbor in a four-month job. When the project was done, he sailed for New York, "determined to repair to the United States . . . with the idea of making his second great effort at the famous Hell Gate."[5] Maillefert's proposal was to blast the rocks without diving or drilling; he proposed lowering charges and detonating them with an electric charge. The proposal was first "treated as the wildest and most absurd," but Maillefert patiently and persistently pursued the plan, and finally, after nearly two years, a group of New York businessmen led by Henry Grinnell financed the project and Maillefert went to work. "His mode of operation is to sink a tin canister of powder down upon the top of the rock and there ignite it through a wire by means of a galvanic battery."[6] Beginning work in August 1851, Maillefert began blasting Pot Rock, "the principle obstruction," detonating 301 charges, "being a total of 27,981 pounds of powder, at an expense of about $6,000 to blast 19 feet of rock off the top of the 235 by 75 foot boulder" by December.[7]

Resuming operations in February 1851, Maillefert continued blasting, firing off 284 more charges ranging from 125 to 78 pounds of powder.[8] Maillefert's activities attracted a great deal of attention, starting as they had with a great deal of public skepticism. There was also excitement, because Maillefert and his assistants worked in full view of many, in the midst of the river in the heart of an urban setting, and in a notorious spot. There was a sense of the dramatic in the blasting:

A large float is anchored in the channel about eight feet from the rock. Precisely at high water, there being but three or four minutes' cessation of the current, the large tin canister is carried from the float and sunk upon the top of the rock. The boat returns to the float, bringing up the end of the wire attached to the canister, Mons. Maillefert attaches the wire to his battery and completes the circuit. Instantly a report is heard, and the mass of waters over the rock rise into the air. There seems to be a solid body of water, perhaps twenty feet in diameter, rising to a height of fifteen or twenty feet, and then towering up in broken fragments and jets twenty or thirty feet higher.[9]

A fatal accident on March 26, 1852, underscored the danger and drama of the work. One of the charges went off in the boat as it was being placed, killing two of Maillefert's assistants and wounding three others, including Maillefert, who was badly burned, "the powder having penetrated his face and hands."[10] While setting and firing four charges, one after the other, the crew had damaged one charge, which floated to the surface. Hauling it alongside their boat, they set it aside and prepared a new charge.

Somehow, instead of handing Maillefert the wire for the new charge, they mistakenly handed him the one for the damaged charge, which was still alongside their boat. The explosion of 125 pounds of powder destroyed one boat, mangling and killing two of the men in it, and threw Maillefert's boat 150 feet, injuring him and his brother-in-law, who was in the boat with him. Maillefert's boat was a patented iron "Francis Metallic Lifeboat," which shielded its occupants from much of the blast. Bystanders on shore launched boats and rescued the injured men as they floated in the river.[11]

Maillefert's recovery took several months as his burns healed and his eyesight, damaged by the powder blown into his eyes, gradually returned. In June 1852 he returned to work, blasting Pot Rock down to 20½ feet, and then heading out to other rocks, including Diamond Reef, between Governor's Island and the Battery, where Maillefert shaved off 2 feet.[12] He then moved on to Long Island Sound, blasting a rock near the entrance to the harbor at New Haven, Connecticut. Maillefert's gamble in tackling Hell Gate paid off; in August 1853, the *New York Times* noted the judgment of the community: "The results obtained at 'Hell's Gate,' and other places of less note, have given the public full confidence in his method of blasting."[13]

Maillefert patented his "improvement in blasting rocks under water" on March 2, 1852, even as he was busy blasting Hell Gate.[14] With his patent, and with other jobs, including an examination of the sunken steamer *Atlantic* in Lake Erie and a trip to Louisiana's Red River in the winter of 1853–54 to blast the rapids blocking passage upriver to Natchitoches, Maillefert was the man of the hour, the American authority on underwater blasting, salvage, and harbor clearance.

Maillefert, it would seem, was therefore the logical choice for New York's next major harbor clearance project, a city-funded blasting of Diamond Reef. In a move that shocked both Maillefert and his backers, however, the contract went to a lower bidder who employed Maillefert's own techniques— Julius Kroehl, an engineer previously limited to iron casting and no stranger to controversy, then being embroiled in the Mount Morris Park fire watchtower controversy.

HUSTED & KROEHL AND DIAMOND REEF

While Kroehl was engaged in the construction of the fire watchtower, he was working with Peter V. Husted as "Husted and Kroehl, Submarine Engineers," at 4 Broad Street in downtown New York.[15] Born in Greenwich, Connecticut, the 38-year-old Husted had previously listed himself in the city directories of 1850–51 as a tailor and in 1851–52 as a clerk.[16] Active in politics, Husted was an inspector of elections for the 11th Ward in the City elections of November 1851, and in September 1852, he was elected as the 11th Ward's delegate to the Whig Party's primary meetings in Syracuse, New York, where the Northern Whigs overturned the reelection hopes of President Millard Fillmore by nominating Mexican War hero General Winfield Scott.[17] He was also an inventor on the side, later patenting spirally threaded wire and barbed nails.[18] Husted's politics also extended to a relationship with city hall; in 1852 the city paid Husted $700 for drawing and engraving a likeness of Henry Clay, US senator from Kentucky and founder of the Whig Party, and another $1,650 for a bust of the statesman for a civic memorial service for Clay, who died in June 1852.[19] Husted was compensated handsomely for his artistic endeavors, as the payments exceeded his annual salary as a clerk.

Husted's clerking job was in the Naval Office, where the principal customs officer of the Port of New York oversaw and documented all vessel entries and departures, cargoes and tonnages.[20] He worked under naval officers Philip

Hone (1849–51) and David A. Bokee (1851–53).[22] In an interview with a commercial reporting agency in June 1855, Husted explained that he left the Naval Office after Bokee's replacement and "then engaged in the sub-marine blasting" business.[23] The clerk's positions were patronage jobs—Hone was a Whig who received his post thanks to his connections, and when he died in May 1851, President Millard Fillmore appointed Bokee, a former Whig congressman from Brooklyn, to the post.[24] When Bokee left office, and a new, non-Whig officer came in, all of Bokee's clerks left with him.

How Husted and Kroehl met is unknown. Given Husted's position with the Naval Office, they may have met there as Kroehl investigated the possibilities of submarine blasting. They may have met as fellow Whigs. Husted lived at 129 Columbia Street, close to the East River in the Lower East Side. Kroehl resided in Kleindeutschland, and so he was a close enough neighbor, even if their association came from mutual interest in politics, technology, or business, not proximity. They may have also been fellow Masons. Kroehl had experience in iron and engineering, and perhaps blasting, but not funding, which he gained from Husted, with Husted earning a lucrative percentage.

In 1855, at the time of their partnership, Husted was privately described as an "active and enterprising" man.[25] The partnership was one in which Kroehl pursued the business and Husted provided the funding but was inactive, as was the case with a saloon and hotel business he bankrolled at the same time. In April 1860 he was described in notes for a commercial report as "the principal man & furnished the principal part of the capital. He operates consid'y [sic] in corporative [sic] contracts & it is said is sure to make money in all his operations, believed to own consid means amt. not known."[26]

The new partners joined forces sometime in latter 1854, and in January 1855 submitted a petition to blast Hell Gate.[27] That petition was not answered, but they began work in early 1855 with two jobs, one in New York Harbor at Diamond Reef, an obstruction in the East River off 33rd Street, and the other at Merlin Rock at the entrance to St. John's Harbor in Newfoundland. The job in Newfoundland came courtesy of a fellow Whig, Peter Cooper, a director and principal financier of the New York, Newfoundland and London Telegraph Company, organized in March 1854 to lay the first transatlantic telegraph cable.[28] The rock, which lay inside the entrance to the harbor, required blasting to a depth of 27 feet to allow the cable company's vessels easier passage in and out of the narrow entrance to St. John's. Kroehl may have been busy, as Husted apparently made the trip to Newfoundland in April 1855 to superintend the job, which was successfully completed in short order.[29] Journalist and author Bayard Taylor, visiting St. John's, commented on the project, which he reported near completion in August 1855, and enthusiastically described Husted's blasting:

> As we were passing Chain Rock Battery, on the afternoon of our departure, we noticed the boats of Mr. Huested [*sic*] anchored over the Merlin rock, lying in the channel, the removal of which had completed during our visit. Mr. Huested hailed us, saying he would give us a parting salute. Nearly all the passengers were gathered on the hurricane-deck at the time, looking their last on the receding harbor. There was a movement on Mr. Huested's boat; a handling of wires; a touch—and then followed a dumb, heavy explosion which shook our steamer—then not fifty yards from the spot. In a second a circle of water forty or fifty feet in diameter over the rock was violently agitated; a narrower circle was hurled into the air to the height of thirty feet; and from the centre a sheaf of silvery jets sprang seventy or eighty feet above the surface of the sea. The enormous masses of water curved outward as they ascended, and stood for an instant as colossal plumes waving against the sun, which shone through their tops and blinded our eyes with the diamond lustre. It was the Great Geyser of the sea—a momentary but sublime picture which no volcanic well of the Icelandic valleys can surpass. As it fell, the shower of airy spray drifted down upon us, drenching ourselves and the decks, but creating a sudden rainbow over the paddle-boxes, an arch of promise which spanned our course for an instant, and melted into air with the sound of our parting cheers.[30]

There were no cheers in New York, however, on the Diamond Reef job. When, in January 1855, New York's Common Council had passed a resolution to direct the city's street commissioner to advertise for bids to remove Diamond Reef, 13 bidders replied, among them Maillefert and Husted & Kroehl. The bidding was complex. Some bid by the square yard, while others bid on the whole job.[31] The lowest bidder was one Cornelius Smith, and Maillefert, apparently the only bidder with experience, was the highest bidder. He bid nearly double what Husted & Kroehl did. Confusion over how to rate the bids ended with a decision to allow Husted & Kroehl to change their bid from by the yard to the whole project, which now made them the lowest bidder at $35,000, beating out Smith's $40,000 bid.[32]

Controversy erupted. The *New York Times,* sympathetic to the French engineer, had published an editorial backing him in a suit for patent infringement in April 1855.[33] In July, responding to an article that suggested that Maillefert had sent in the lowest bid, Husted & Kroehl wrote a brief letter to the editors of the *New York Times* and listed four bids, starting with Maillefert's $68,000 and ending with their $35,600 bid.[34] This was followed by an extensive letter in response to "various communications" in the *Times'* columns "evidently emanating from persons disappointed in not getting the contract."[35] Husted & Kroehl then went on to directly attack Maillefert and his business partner. "No persons bidding for that work knew better the extent of Diamond Reef than Messrs. MAILLEFERT & RAASLOFF. . . . Surely it comes with a bad grace from the *very highest* bidder to be so active in the matter."[36]

The attacks on the Husted & Kroehl bid intensified, spurred by allegations that the bid process was flawed, not only because the council allowed modification of the bid but also it had awarded the contract and not the Mayor, who alleged that he alone had the "executive power" to award contracts. Maillefert responded with his own letter to the *Times* a few days after Husted & Kroehl's letter appeared. "I beg leave once more to propose that personalities, which have nothing to do with the matter now before us, be left out of the discussion," he wrote, going on to further rebuke Husted & Kroehl, noting that he was certain his "interference" had disappointed them, "but nothing shall induce me to adopt such a system of argumentation."[37]

Maillefert went on to allege irregularities in the bidding process, flawed information about the amount of rock to be removed, and in particular, estimates that showed that his bid, per cubic yard, was cheaper than Husted & Kroehl's.[38] Husted & Kroehl replied the following day arguing that Maillefert's "repeated assertions were incorrect" and derided Maillefert's assessment and trial blasting of Diamond Reef a few years earlier as "a few charges fired as a sort of advertisement."[39]

The controversy was apparently resolved when Mayor Fernando Wood, no friend of the Whigs, vetoed the contract on August 7: "The Mayor considers the action . . . [of issuing the contract] of an executive character, and, consequently, improper. There was also a peculiarity in the form of the advertisement, which created much misapprehension on the part of those not initiated into the way by which contracts are sometimes gained, and which His Honor could not approve of. A new survey is recommended, on which bids for the work maybe based, and thus bidders understand exactly what is required of them."[40] If Benjamin Maillefert thought he would now get the job, he was mistaken. On September 12, the council again awarded the contract to Husted & Kroehl.[41]

In June 1856 the *New York Times* reported that Husted & Kroehl were prosecuting their work on the 300-foot-long, 40-foot-wide reef "with great vigor," blasting at it with 80-pound canisters of powder. The paper then went on to make an astounding comparison, and a noteworthy one given the firm's patent infringement problems with James Bogardus on the Mount Morris fire watchtower project. "The operations at Diamond Reef have been conducted on the plan of MAILLEFORT [*sic*]. By the old plan a great deal of time and labor were expended in drilling holes into the rock and then applying the powder. . . . By the plan used here, the expensive drilling apparatus and other tools being dispensed with, the powder is simply placed on the rock with canisters."[42]

A month later, Husted & Kroehl, perhaps with an eye to politics and public relations, especially after the controversy surrounding their contract, hired the steamboat *Ajax* to convey New York's aldermen to the reef to watch them blast. The *New York Times* described the work: "Six discharges were fired, two of one-hundred pounds, one of two-hundred, and two of five hundred. The water displaced . . . was not thrown to so great a height as on former occasions, owing to the greater depth of that portion of the rock on which the canisters were placed. . . . The last two charges, containing five barrels of gunpowder each, were the largest which have been fired on sunken rocks since the invention, in 1839, of this mode of blasting underwater."[43]

In August 1856 the *Scientific American* reported that the reef, covered by 16 feet of water at low tide, was in the process of being shaved down six feet by Husted & Kroehl, and "there is every prospect of these contractors accomplishing their object, with promptitude and profit," as their blasts acted "powerfully on the reef in a downward direction, and laterally, thereby riving and disintegrating it with rapidity."[44]

Husted & Kroehl must have provided some "history" to the *Scientific American's* reporter, aware that they were either infringing on Maillefert's patent, or at least skirting very close to it. The reporter described the blasting as following the 1830s work of Colonel Pasley, "who first applied it some years since. . . . Mons. Maillefert first introduced it, we believe into our country, and he obtained a patent for it, although, as we then pointed out, the invention was quite old."[45]

If by any stretch of the imagination, Maillefert was not already a committed enemy as well as a rival, this would have cemented the animosity. Maillefert did not sue Husted & Kroehl for patent infringement, however, despite an earlier lawsuit against another rival.[46] Instead, a lawsuit came from a disgruntled taxpayer "who claimed the City of New-York had no right to remove the reef."[47] The court slapped Husted & Kroehl with an injunction. It took two months to remove the injunction, slowing the project. When the winter of 1856 arrived, Husted & Kroehl were not done. In December, after "two or three vessels . . . drifted upon Diamond Reef during a single day," Husted & Kroehl wrote a defensive letter to the *Times,* noting that were it not for the lawsuit and delays, "our work would have been completed on the 1st of September last." "While we regret that any accident should occur," they noted, "we cannot be expected to superintend the navigation of vessels in and out of the Port . . . or to replace lost or broken buoys" placed by the Port Commission.[48] At the same time, Husted & Kroehl were also pursuing other work, a report in the *Boston Post* noting that the colonial government of Barbados had awarded them a contract to blast the coral reef "obstructing the entrance to the Careenage at Bridgetown. The work will be prosecuted this winter."[49]

Kroehl was clearly hard at work, as was Husted, trying to secure sufficient contracts to continue work, not only in New York but in other harbors, as submarine engineers. It was at this stage in his life that Julius Kroehl found a wife. On November 25, 1858, he married Sophia Rosa Leuber in Washington, D.C., at the Holy Trinity Church of Georgetown.[50] The 26-year-old bride was the daughter of deceased merchant Francis Leuber of Frederick, Maryland, and Helen Marie Simpson Leuber, a native of Georgetown. Francis Leuber, an Austrian, had immigrated to the United States in 1819, arriving in Baltimore. He married Helen Simpson in 1828, and they had seven children, four of them daughters. Sophia Rosa, their second oldest child, was born in Frederick on August 27, 1832.[51]

After Francis's death, the family had moved back to Georgetown to live near family. Among the family in Washington was Helen's sister Henrietta, who was married to Samuel Hein, a fellow Prussian and a prominent member of the US Coast Survey. Hein was probably the person who introduced Julius Kroehl to the Leubers. A friend of Kroehl's cousin Otto Sackersdorff, who worked as a surveyor for the City of New York, Hein was the disbursing officer for the Coast Survey and served as its first librarian, and as such would have provided access to reports and charts.[52] It is probable that Julius Kroehl journeyed to Washington between 1855 and 1858 to inspect and purchase Coast Survey charts for the work in New York Harbor as well as other possible job sites for Husted & Kroehl. He may also have sought Coast Survey work.[53] There, in the Coast Survey's offices on New Jersey Avenue, near the US Capitol building, Kroehl would have met up with his cousin's friend, perhaps with a letter of introduction, and might even have stayed with Hein and his family. Later in life, Kroehl would cite Samuel Hein as "my friend" and remember Hein in his last will and testament. It is probable that Hein took a liking to the affable Kroehl and introduced him to the extended family. Matchmaking may have played a part; in January 1858 another Prussian immigrant member of the Coast Survey, Albert J. Rolle, married Sophia Leuber's younger sister Helen. The office was dominated by German-speaking scientists and technicians for whom the *Küstenvermessungsbehörde* (Coast Survey) was a way of life, and so matchmaking as well as professional affiliation by Hein is very likely.[54]

Courtship and eventual marriage notwithstanding, Kroehl had work to do and a difficult job to finish in New York. Back at Diamond Reef, despite the initial hope of completing the job with "promptitude and profit," the task proved too difficult, and work dragged on for the next few years. The method they were using, adopted from Pasley and Maillefert, laid the charges on the rocks to blast. This worked when projections and outcrops could be blasted free, but once the reef was leveled and relatively smooth, surface charges had little to no effect. In order to successfully blast the reef down, Husted and Kroehl realized that they would have to drill into the rock, place charges, and blast. This would cost more money. In January 1857 New York Senator Hamilton Fish introduced a bill (S. 489) in his final months as a senator in the 34th Congress to blast and remove Diamond Reef and another harbor obstruction, Coenties Reef, at a cost of $40,000 "to be expended under the direction of the Secretary of War." With the additional funds, Husted & Kroehl continued work in 1858 but with a new approach and different equipment, adding a diving bell invented that year by Van Buren Ryerson of New York.[55]

VAN BUREN RYERSON AND THE "SUBMARINE EXPLORER"

Van Buren Ryerson was a member of the sixth generation of one of Brooklyn's founding Dutch families, the Ryerzsens. Van Buren was born on his father's farm at Pocquanq in 1809.[56] Despite his proud lineage, Van Buren was the seventh son of the fourth son. He did not have much, nor could he expect much, especially when Abraham died young and intestate in 1820 when Van Buren was 11 years old. But what he lacked in fortune, young Ryerson made up for with ingenuity. Known to his family as "the Professor," Van Buren had a knack for tinkering, inventing, and patenting. Inventing did not bring in much money, so Van Buren worked as an "agent" out of an office on William Street in New York.[57] But he kept at his "tinkering." The diving bell he created in 1858 was his most ambitious project to date, and his greatest hope for fortune.

Ryerson's inspiration was Henry Sears and Edgar Foreman's Nautilus bell, which he (and most likely Kroehl) had seen displayed at the Crystal Palace in 1854. But he felt it had three faults—it was linked to the surface by an air hose, which could break, it was completely dependent on a separate surface chamber for air, and it was difficult to balance, "arising from inability to adjust the point of gravity."[58] Ryerson's bell, which he called his "Submarine Explorer," merged the compressed air chamber and a water-filled ballast chamber into a single, albeit complex machine:

> It is formed of two very substantial wrought-iron cylinders, one of which is contained within the other. The space between them forms a compressed air-chamber. The inner chamber is divided into two compartments, which can be completely separated from each other by closing the intervening man-hole or trap whenever separation is necessary. . . . It communicated both with the compressed air-chamber and the external water, by means of pipes and stop-cocks. Into this ballast-chamber water or air may be admitted at pleasure by the workmen within the Bell, and the machine can ascend or descend; and the equilibrium is so nicely adjusted that it is absolutely impossible to upset the machine even when it may rest on only one point of rock.

The air for the dives was "condensed into the compressed air chamber at first, by an ordinary force-pump" before descending:

> The machine is now perfectly buoyant, but by an ingenious arrangement . . . water is admitted into the ballast-chamber; and the machine then sinks, and after it has reached the bottom it remains

ready for the proposed work. . . . The man-hole between the two
compartments of the inner cylinder is opened, and the workmen
begin their operations in the lower working chamber, and can
continue them without interruption, even for days, either in laying foundations of breakwaters, sea-walls, piers, permanent bulkheads (the Bell itself supersedes all ordinary coffer-dams), in raising
sunken vessels, treasure or anything valuable in them, in diving for
pearl, and sponge. . . . In short, this machine is applicable to every
branch of submarine engineering and exploration.[59]

Ryerson patented the "Submarine Explorer" on October 19, 1858.[60] At that
time, Husted & Kroehl were still struggling to complete the blasting of Diamond Reef, and even with a liberal use of the Pasley (or Maillefert) method,
could not dislodge enough rock. The time had come to resort to drilling and
blasting. The only way to do it was with a diving bell. The only two bells potentially available for the New York project were Sears and Hallett's *Nautilus,*
then in London, or a newly patented bell developed by Benjamin Maillefert.
Maillefert's "Aerostatic Tubular Diving-Bell" was a boat-shaped craft with a long
tube at its top—essentially a free-diving caisson. Maillefert built and tested his
bell in late 1858, and subsequently sold it to investors who formed the "New
York Submarine Engineering Company" in March 1859.[61]

For obvious reasons, Husted & Kroehl had no one to turn to until Van
Buren Ryerson patented his bell. Not long after reading of Ryerson's patent
in the *Scientific American* in October, the "submarine engineers" struck a deal
with Ryerson to use his bell at Diamond Reef. Between March and September
1859, "Submarine Explorer" went to work on the reef, operated by Thomas A.
Harley, and carried workmen Edward Farrell, Peter Coffee, John McMannus,
Charles McMannus, and Augustus Goetz down 28 feet to drill into the rock
of the reef, set charges into the holes, rig the wires, and then ascend to the
surface.[62]

At the same time, the *New York Times,* always sympathetic to Benjamin
Maillefert and no doubt tired of Husted & Kroehl's argumentative letters,
published a critical article on the lack of progress in the reduction of Diamond
Reef, noting that the work seemed to have stalled and that the only visible
sign of the contractors was "an old sloop, having attached to her bows an old
diving bell."[63] Husted & Kroehl were in debt, and assigned their payments to

a creditor, Jonathan Pettigrew, who received $10,000 in 1859 and $7,040 in 1860.[64] As for the new craft they were using, it was more than an "old diving bell." A month after the article, the American Institute awarded a gold medal to "Ryerson and Huested [sic]" for their "Submarine Explorer."[65]

Work on the reef would struggle along until 1862. During this time, the partners tried without success to contract both the bell and their own services to the US Navy. In 1855 a warship, USS *Water Witch*, had been fired on by Paraguayan forts and an American sailor had been killed while surveying the region. When the dictator of Paraguay refused US demands for an apology and compensation, in 1858 Congress authorized a fleet of warships to steam south and extract satisfaction, at gunpoint if necessary.[66] Because of news that the river was blocked to keep out the invaders, Husted & Kroehl proposed, and the navy agreed to evaluate their "renowned submarine blasting apparatus," which "underwent a thorough scrutinizing examination at the Brooklyn Navy Yard a few evenings since, previously [sic] to its being put on board the Memphis, and which is designed to operate on the sunken vessels and river snags, that report says Lopez has placed in the rivers on the border with Paraguay."[67] While the bell was found to be a worthy craft, when the squadron sailed, somehow it did so without "Submarine Explorer."

The bell remained attached to the bows of its support sloop, diving in New York Harbor for the next three years as Ryerson tried to market it beyond Husted & Kroehl. Ryerson's attempts never came to pass, and he turned his attention to mining. Traveling to California, Ryerson patented a centrifugal steam amalgamator to extract mercury from ore.[68] In addition to the workers, Kroehl made dives in "Submarine Explorer," primarily to test the bell and to oversee experiments with its air-replenishment system: "By a very simple expedient the air is restored to perfect purity in a few minutes, not as in all previous machines by deriving fresh air from above, but by driving (by means of a small forcing-pump within the machine) through a very minutely drilled rosette, resembling that of a common-watering pot, water from without, in the form of very fine spray or mist for some minutes. By this simple and easy process, the carbonic acid and other noxious gases . . . disappear, and the previously vitiated air recovers its oxygen."[69] The "Submarine Explorer" of 1858 did more than introduce Julius Kroehl to submersibles. It inspired him to take his experience in working with iron—and bending it into curves—and consider experimentation with underwater craft. In time, Kroehl would take the

Ryerson patent farther, perhaps inspired by the inventor's assertion that "it is important to know that the principles of the Bell can be successfully adapted by a submarine boat, propelled by a screw propeller worked by hand."[70] This assertion, tested by Kroehl, ultimately led him to develop an improved version of Ryerson's invention, Kroehl's own "Sub Marine *Explorer*" of 1864–65. After years of struggling to fit into the competitive worlds of iron manufacture and submarine engineering, the timing to perfect such a craft was seemingly ideal. National tensions, soon to erupt in the Civil War, might at last give Kroehl an opportunity to develop, and profit, by merging both into a new career.

4

A Submarine Engineer at War

In cases of danger you have exhibited
the coolness necessary to carry out your perilous calling,
and the Government may always rely on you
to perform that kind of service.

—David Dixon Porter, May 1862

WITH the outbreak of the Civil War in April 1861, the talents of men
like Julius Kroehl were required by both sides. A limited number of opportunities existed, however, and the key to securing a
contract, or a commission, was perseverance and self-promotion, as well as
having friends or family in positions of influence. Working through the émi-
gré community in New York, Kroehl tried to join the war in June 1861. That
month, Sándor (Alexander) Asboth (1810–68), a prominent Hungarian exile,
proposed to form a New York brigade. Half of the brigade would have been
composed from the 39th New York "Garibaldi Guards," and the other half
would have been Colonel Adolph von Steinwehr's 29th Infantry, the "Astor
Rifles," which von Steinwehr had recruited from the German American community.[1] Among those said to be destined for the brigade was a corps of "pioneers" (engineers) "led by Major Fornet, an excellent Hungarian officer," and
pontonniers (bridge builders) "under Capt. Kroehl, who has for several years
been engaged in excavating rocks in New-York harbor."[2] The brigade was not
formed; the two units, however, did form and operated separately, although
without the pontonniers and Kroehl.[3] The reason for Kroehl's failure to join
the 29th Infantry may have been that he was engaged in a money-making
endeavor in Washington.

A locomotive being ferried by barge across the Potomac to Alexandria sank in a squall on Sunday, June 16. The locomotive was intended for the Alexandria & Orange Line at Alexandria, which had just been reoccupied by federal forces. On June 21, the *Philadelphia Inquirer* reported that a $1,000 contract to raise the locomotive had been signed on June 20.[4] Husted and Kroehl received the contract and successfully raised the locomotive and its tender on July 8.[5] The time and effort spent in the raising of the lost locomotive probably not only cost Kroehl a commission with von Steinwehr, it also did not assure Kroehl any additional government work, at least not immediately. Undeterred, Kroehl approached both the army and the navy later in 1861. He was no stranger to federal government bids. He had previously, and unsuccessfully, bid on the installation of an iron roof for a warehouse at the Norfolk Navy Yard in Virginia in 1858, only to lose when underbid by $3,995.[6]

When he did not get the contract, Kroehl in typical fashion did not give up, and offered to manufacture "Grundt's Iron Nesting Pontoons," upon which a floating bridge could be quickly erected across a river.[7] The concept not only involved Kroehl's familiarity with iron, and his previously intended role in Asboth's brigade, but also his maritime experience. Iron pontoons had been used in marine salvage as well as waterfront construction projects since the 1840s in both Great Britain and the United States. The Grundt pontoons were a Prussian-patented invention that Kroehl either learned about from a personal or professional connection, or simply because they were being imported into New York. The firm of Hess, Kassel & Co. of New York was the importer, and in February 1862, they received a provisional US patent for Grundt's pontoons.[8] Grundt's pontoons may have been the equipment Husted and Kroehl had used to raise the locomotive from the Potomac. On January 16, 1862, Secretary of the Navy Gideon Welles wrote to Kroehl, then in Washington, that the navy's examining board had rejected his proposal because it was a "matter pertaining to the movements of troops" and was not of interest to the navy.[9]

This did not dissuade Kroehl, for he was determined, if not stubborn. He persisted in his correspondence to convince the navy of his expertise in underwater explosives. It was around this time, 1861, that Kroehl also designed plans for a "cigar-shaped" submarine, which he was not successful in selling, and which he ultimately abandoned.[10]

On February 27, 1862, still in Washington, he was notified by Secretary Welles that the navy had hired him "upon the following conditions":

You will leave for New York the 28th inst[ant] and report to Commodore Paulding, Commandant of the New York Navy Yard, for passage to the Gulf of Mexico in any man of war going to that station. You will take with you a 28 plate galvanic battery, and 20 torpedo cans capable of holding 200 lbs. of gun powder, and 20 cans for 600 lbs., and sufficient wire for exploding them at a distance of 1000 yards. Directions have already been given to prepare these things for your use. As soon as they are ready you will take passage for the Gulf of Mexico, and upon your arrival report to Commander D. D. Porter, US Navy, commanding the Mortar Flotilla, and place yourself entirely under his orders. Your compensation will be ten (10) dollars per diem, commencing the 28th inst. and terminating ten days after your services are no longer required in the Gulf.[11]

Commander David Dixon Porter was no stranger to underwater explosives, nor was he unknown to Julius Kroehl. Porter had worked with "Captain" George Taylor during the Mexican War, towing obstructions out of the way after Taylor blasted them on the Tabasco River.[12] After the war, Porter had surveyed Hell Gate, leading the way for Maillefert's efforts. As one of the navy's officers with a background in underwater work, he may have met Kroehl before the Civil War. Kroehl and Porter developed a mutual respect that carried through and beyond the conflict. Kroehl's employment by the navy may have also come about through his family connection to Samuel Hein and the Coast Survey, and Hein's good relations with the navy.

BAD NIGHT ON THE RIVER

To report for duty, Kroehl left Washington on the February 28 and arrived in New York on March 1.[13] He sailed for the Gulf on USS *Oneida* on March 9. On March 26, *Oneida* arrived at the "South West Pass, Mississippi River," where the Union Fleet was massing to prepare to strike up the great river and begin a campaign to control that strategic waterway and begin to strangle the Confederacy.[14] By controlling the river and its ports, notably New Orleans, 70 miles up the river, the Union could strike the Confederacy a mighty blow, effectively extending the Union blockade of Confederate ports to the river, surrounding and strangling trade and the resupply of Confederate troops. However, the way to New Orleans was blocked at the mouth of the Mississippi by two old brick forts, Fort Jackson and Fort St. Philip, which, positioned on opposite shores and fitted with cannon, offered a gauntlet of deadly crossfire to an invading fleet. To compound the problems of the Union fleet, the Confederates had blocked the channel between the forts with several dismasted schooners held together by heavy chains. Porter, sitting downriver with a group of ships mounting heavy mortars, was lobbing shells into the forts to silence their guns and clear the way for the fleet waiting off the river's mouth. That 24-ship force, the West Gulf Blockading Squadron, was under the command of Porter's foster brother, David Glasgow Farragut.[15]

Porter's mortar flotilla moved into close range of the forts and opened up what would become a seven-day bombardment, firing several thousand shells that arced into the sky and then burst on and around the forts, setting buildings on fire, damaging the parapets, and scattering the defenders.[16] The furious shelling of the forts did not have the desired effect, however, and both Farragut and Porter grew increasingly impatient. Porter decided to turn to Julius Kroehl to try to break the impasse, remembering an earlier experiment the two had made out on the river.

Following Kroehl's arrival in late March, Porter had assigned him to USS *Westfield,* and on April 2, Kroehl reported aboard. There, Kroehl "prepared submarine charges of 180, 90, 50 and 5 pounds of powder, and reported to Captain Porter that I was ready for service."[17] On April 13 the navy steamers *Oneida* and *Varuna* and the Coast Survey steamer *Sachem* had reconnoitered the forts and surveyed the chain-linked hulks that stretched across the river between the forts. Selecting a large wooden raft that had drifted loose and lodged on the bank downriver, Kroehl and Porter set a 50-pound charge on the hulk, which was "completely shattered, and by the next day had disappeared."[18] While sure of his boast that the mortars would force the forts to fall within 48 hours, Porter "tucked the experiment away in his mind, knowing that sometime soon the chain would have to be broken for good."[19]

Kroehl made another survey of the hulks in two small open boats on April 18, the same day that Porter's mortar bombardment commenced. Kroehl formulated a plan to clear the obstructions and submitted it to Porter on April 19: "It was decided to go up with a sufficient number of boats to board the hulks, if necessary, and either break the chains with chisels or hammer, and slip the anchors, or to place a 180-lb. torpedo under the bow of each hulk, about 10 feet below the surface of the water, and sink the hulks by exploding the torpedoes."[20] It was this plan that Porter submitted to Farragut when news reached Porter on April 20 that the admiral's patience had run out. Unfortunately for Kroehl, Farragut did not have his foster brother's trust of the German engineer or his ideas. The admiral instead sent his most trusted officer, Fleet Captain Henry H. Bell, to command the expedition. Bell, a 40-year veteran of the navy, had been personally selected by Farragut as the squadron's flag captain, having previously served with Farragut as an ordnance officer in the early 1850s.[21]

Porter, despite having worked closely with Bell in fitting out his mortar flotilla, did not like the flag captain, and with a well-known disposition to indiscreet comments about other officers, more than likely shared his opinion with Kroehl. It did the German engineer no favors. Perhaps spurred by Porter's attitude, as well as his own, Kroehl, irritated over what he perceived as a delayed departure, went on board Farragut's flagship "and had a consultation" (in his words), which more than likely was an argumentative confrontation between the obstinate civilian contractor and the two veteran naval officers.[22] Farragut dismissed Kroehl's concerns and reiterated that Captain Bell was in command. Bell, meanwhile, while noting that Kroehl was an "an experienced submarine torpedo man," objected to Kroehl's participation in the mission "as rather an experiment in so swift a current."[23] Experience would prove Bell right.

On the evening of April 20, an unhappy Kroehl and a most probably irritated Bell set out with a small force of men aboard the gunboats *Pinola* and *Itasca. Pinola,* with Bell and Kroehl aboard, approached the west end of the line of hulks, while *Itasca* approached the east end. Men from the gunboats were to swarm aboard the hulks at the two ends, set Kroehl's explosive charges, and back away, running out the electric firing wires, to blast the hulks to the bottom, their chains running out and into the soft mud of the river bottom. Nothing went as planned, however.

Despite the darkness and a drizzling rain, lookouts at the forts spotted the gunboats as they approached the hulks. A signal light flashed, and a signal rocket shot up from Fort St. Philip and burst in the sky. Lt. George Bacon, on board *Itasca,* later wrote that "in a moment a sharp fire was opened upon us," but fortunately "nearly all the shots" passed overhead.[24] Under fire, the two gunboats separated and made a run for the hulks. As *Itasca* struck one, her crew threw grapnels onto the hulk and stopped their engines. Strong currents tore *Itasca* free, and restarting the engines, the crew finally made fast to the hulk closest to shore. Setting their charges, the crew discovered that they could knock the chain loose. Without thinking, they did, and the dismasted hulk drifted loose, sending *Itasca* crashing into the mud bank. Stuck and under fire, the crew made preparations to abandon ship.[25]

Meanwhile, across the river, *Pinola's* crew had their share of difficulties. After crashing into a raft and missing the hulks, Lieutenant Crosby, commander of the gunboat, made a run for the hulks and grappled with the second one from shore. Kroehl and some of the crew scrambled aboard, set the charges, and stepped back onto *Pinola* with the wires for detonating the charges stretching between the two vessels. As they cast off, the gunboat's anchor snagged the hull of the hulk; Bell gave the order to gun the engines as the crew slipped the anchor and its chains free, and with a jolt, the two vessels separated.[26] Bell reported that it was then that "I called for the operator [Kroehl] to explode. He replied that his conductor was broken. I called for him to explode the second, and, after a little while, it was answered that that was also broken."[27]

Kroehl later complained that it was not his fault, and blamed Bell: "Instead of dropping downstream by a hawser attached to the hulk, as I requested, Captain Bell gave the order to back the engine. This, together with the rapid current, made it impossible to reel the wires off fast enough, and before we were the proper distance from the hulks the wires parted and I was unable to explode the charges."[28] The first attempt to blast the hulks had failed, and Kroehl raced to ready two more charges. That changed as Bell spotted *Itasca* and ordered *Pinola* to head for her. As the stranded gunboat's crew was about to jump on a hulk and ride it down the river, *Pinola* approached out of the darkness.

Tossing a line to pull *Itasca* off, *Pinola* backed away, but the line snapped. Rushing downriver to get another, they returned under fire, fastening another thicker line as the Confederates set a raft ablaze and pushed it downriver to destroy the Union ships. Racing their engines, *Pinola* again pulled, and once more the line snapped. A third line, now a 13-inch-thick hawser, finally held, and *Pinola* yanked *Itasca* off the bank. Both gunboats passed the barrier, and hugging the shore in driving rain, passed under the guns of the forts, and then turned and ran back downstream. Ramming the hulks at full speed, the two gunboats succeeded in snapping the chain.[29] Still under fire, the brave crews of *Itasca* and *Pinola* returned to the security of the fleet with Bell and Kroehl, neither impressed with the other.

The next morning revealed that the channel was partially cleared, as some of the hulks had drifted out of position, but as Kroehl bitterly complained, "Had Captain Porter's [and his own] plan been carried out, the chains would have been completely broken and all the hulks would have been out of the way of the vessels passing the forts."[30] On the evening of April 24, when Farragut made his run, the remaining hulks still blocked part of the channel, and the Union fleet ran through a gauntlet of fire that resulted in the loss of one ship, 37 dead, and over 100 wounded. Farragut then pushed on to New Orleans, which surrendered.[31]

While his casualties had not been as great as Farragut's officers had prophesied, and this gave the admiral some measure of contentment, he also felt displeasure over the battering his ships and men had taken, and he blamed Julius Kroehl, who remained behind with Porter as Farragut continued on. Porter's schooners continued to blast the forts until they surrendered on April 28. During that time, Porter kept Kroehl busy. On the morning of the 25th, in the aftermath of the fleet's run upriver, he blasted "what remained of the mortar schooner *Maria J. Carlton,* sunk by a shell April 19."[32]

Kroehl then assisted the Coast Survey's *Sachem* in charting the adjacent region including Lake Ponchartrain and the Pearl River. On that assignment, Kroehl demonstrated coolness and brave action. Departing Ship Island on May 13, the tiny steamer two days later was making what a *New York Times* correspondent termed a daring reconnaissance up the Pearl River when *Sachem* came under fire from Confederate sharpshooters. While trying to turn the vessel around in the narrow waterway, Coast Survey officer John G. Oltmanns was hit in the chest by a musket ball. "In the confusion," everyone on board forgot they carried heavy guns, but then "Mr. J. H. Kroehl, the submarine engineer, who was on board, mustered a crew to the broadside gun, and discharged first a shot and then a round of grape into the woods," driving off the sharpshooters.[33]

Brave actions by Kroehl notwithstanding, on May 20, Porter released the engineer from service with high praise, knowing no doubt that the engineer needed to be out of Farragut and Bell's sight and that his future employment depended on friends higher up the navy hierarchy:

> Sir: As there will not likely be any further necessity for your services
> out here, I think it would be the desire of the Navy Department
> to have you return home, and the *Baltic* offers you an opportunity

of doing so. I regret that your mission has not been more satisfactory to yourself, which, however, is no fault of yours, you having held yourself in readiness always to perform that what you came to do, and you have shown a commendable zeal in carrying out what was required of you. You had better report yourself to the honorable Secretary of the Navy immediately on your arrival, and make a report of your proceedings to him. Had you been permitted to carry out the plan arranged between us, the chains would have been broken thoroughly the night before the fleet started up, and no obstacle would have been left in the way. In cases of danger you have exhibited the coolness necessary to carry out your perilous calling, and the Government may always rely on you to perform that kind of service. I hope the honorable Secretary of the Navy may allow you to come out here and raise all the valuable property that has been sunk, and which can be easily recovered.[34]

Porter privately wrote to Assistant Secretary of the Navy Gustavus Vasa Fox on May 24, complaining about Bell—"He is pigheaded and slow and has a bad influence on Farragut, wanting to cover himself with glory gained by other people's energy and intelligence," and went on to defend Kroehl's actions on *Pinola:* "Bell had not made his mind how the chains were to be cut, though that really clever man Krouhl [*sic*], had matured all his plans, had his apparatus in my boats, and a dozen other boats to carry him through, and had as many gallant *young* men to back him; He was ignored as a charlatan—I presume I was also."[35]

Kroehl sailed in the US steam transport *Baltic* on May 23 and arrived at New York on May 31. The *New York Times,* reporting the steamer's arrival, noted Kroehl was a passenger and identified him as a "civil engineer."[36] Making his way to Washington, Kroehl reported to Secretary Welles on June 2. His four-page report, when Welles routed it back to Farragut, did nothing to endear Kroehl to the admiral or to Captain Bell, soon to be promoted to commodore. Kroehl's report laid the blame for the fiasco at the forts firmly on Bell and by extension, Farragut.[37]

Perhaps realizing his tenuous position, Kroehl ended his report to Welles with an entreaty. "I shall always hold myself in readiness to serve our Government in any capacity I am able to fill, and hope that soon an opportunity may offer itself."[38] The opportunity came soon. On July 19 Welles sent Kroehl to the James River Flotilla "on public service."[39] The engineer had valuable experience, and the James River was a long way from the Mississippi and Admiral Farragut.

INTERREGNUM ON THE JAMES

The James River, running inland to the Confederate capital at Richmond, was blockaded at its mouth at Hampton Roads. While the blockade kept ships from accessing Richmond, it did not guarantee Union control of the strategic river. Riverbank fortifications, ironclads, submarines, and "torpedoes" made the James a highly contested highway.[40] By the end of May 1862, however, the Union had gained control of the lower reaches of the river, and had steamed to Drewry's Bluff, eight miles outside Richmond, with orders to shell the Confederate capital into surrender. At the same time, troops commanded by General George B. McLellan had landed on the Virginia Peninsula and were marching toward Richmond.

The Union advance halted at Drewry's Bluff. The Confederates had blocked the river with "sunken ships, barges, large crates of stones, and old scrap iron."[41] Above the bluff, the Confederates had mined the river with a variety of "torpedoes." Stalled, the Union Navy decided on a new tactic. They would send the submarine *Alligator,* invented by Brutus de Villeroi up the river, to blast the obstructions. One characteristic of the submarine was a small chamber that could be pressurized to the ambient water pressure at depth, allowing a diver to leave and reenter the craft to lay explosive charges or do other work.[42] Commissioned as the US Navy's first submarine, *Alligator* arrived on the James on June 24, just as a climactic series of battles between forces commanded by Robert E. Lee and McLellan resulted in a Union withdrawal from the area. *Alligator* was hauled back to the mouth of the James, and on July 5 she was towed to Washington, D.C.[43]

But as *Alligator* reached Washington, so too did intelligence from a captured Confederate gunboat on the James. Found on board were plans for a new Confederate ironclad and maps showing the locations of the underwater mines. The threat of the new ironclad spurred Gustavus Vasa Fox to order *Alligator* readied for another try at the James, making an underwater run to the Confederate capital to destroy the new ironclad. But as the navy

assembled and trained a new crew for the mission with a newly selected commanding officer, Lt. Thomas Oliver Selfridge, defects in *Alligator* became
apparent. The mission was delayed as the submarine was modified, and then
finally the mission was scrapped at year's end.[44] But in the summer of 1862,
while the crew trained with *Alligator,* the navy continued with preparations
to clear the James River, and two weeks after *Alligator* arrived in Washington,
Secretary Welles sent Julius Kroehl to the James River Flotilla. Regardless of
Admiral Farragut's opinion, the Navy Department obviously thought highly
of Kroehl.

In addition to his contacts at the Coast Survey, whose chief, Alexander D.
Bache, had good personal and professional relationships with many naval officers, Kroehl also knew Samuel Francis Du Pont, one of the Navy's most senior
officers (and soon to be appointed rear admiral in July 1862). Du Pont had met
Kroehl 1853 when Du Pont, on temporary leave from the navy, had managed
the Exhibition of the Industry of All Nations and in that capacity had also
overseen the construction of its major hall, the Crystal Palace, in New York.
Du Pont was also no stranger to technology, and was an early advocate of iron-
cladding warships, and as commandant of the Philadelphia Navy Yard, had
been impressed by and ordered the evaluation of Brutus de Villeroi's submarine in May 1861. The new assignment of Julius Kroehl to a new arena of the
war is no surprise in this context.[45]

Kroehl's mission was to blast the obstructions and open the James River.
Throughout the summer, he reconnoitered the obstructions and prepared charges in New York. By September, though, as the navy began to reconsider the
task, the plans were shelved. On September 16 acting master Henry J. Rogers,
a "telegraphic engineer" assigned to Kroehl's project, wrote to his superiors:
"Commodore Wilkes, lately in command of the James River Flotilla, recently
proposed using the magneto-electric machine for the purpose of firing torpedoes or magazines, to remove the obstructions in James River in the vicinity
of Fort Darling. The torpedoes to be used for the purpose were made by Mr.
Julius H. Kroehl, of New York, and are now on hand at the navy yard, New
York. The magneto-electric apparatus was manufactured under the direction
of the undersigned by order of the Navy."[46] Concerned that blasting would
not completely clear the obstructions in the river, Captain John Rodgers noted
that he was "unwilling to try gunpowder," and this was enough for Admiral
S. P. Lee to concur and write to Secretary Welles that despite Kroehl's obvious

enthusiasm, "nothing at present can be done by the latter with his machinery" and that Rogers does not "see how he [Kroehl] could apply his apparatus elsewhere in the James River."[47] With that, Kroehl's service on the James River ended, and he returned to New York. Ironically, and no doubt to his dissatisfaction, his place was taken by his old rival, Benjamin Maillefert. Maillefert would remain on the James, clearing obstructions and gaining praise from the navy throughout the next few years, eventually shifting his operations to Charleston Harbor, where he joined the efforts of Admiral John Dahlgren to clear obstructions and mines and take the fortified Confederate port.

CAPE FEAR

It appeared that fortune was about to shine on Julius Kroehl. On December 1, 1862, assistant secretary Gustavus Vasa Fox wrote to Kroehl, then in New York, that Admiral S. P. Lee, then probing the defenses of the Cape Fear River's mouth in preparation for a planned conquest of the port of Wilmington, North Carolina, "would like to secure your services, and if your present engagements will permit you to accept the appointment of Acting Lieutenant in his squadron at a salary of $1,875 per annum, you can have it. If you accept, you will without delay report to Rear Admiral Lee at Hampton Roads."[48]

Kroehl immediately accepted, and on December 4 the navy appointed him an acting volunteer lieutenant.[49] The next day, Rear Admiral Lee wrote Kroehl in New York.: "I want your apparatus put in safe condition on board the 'Monticello,' Lt. Commander Braine. . . . You will take passage in the 'Monticello.' Show this to Lt. Comr Braine and have no conversation with anyone else on the subject of your appointment or orders."[50]

Kroehl spent the next weeks preparing more "torpedoes" and retrieving the ones he had assembled for the James River. On December 10 Welles telegraphed Kroehl in New York to let him know that the commandant of the Navy Yard "has been authorized to purchase any articles required by you in the preparation of your torpedoes, also to allow you to go to Ellis Island to obtain those prepared by you in July last."[51] Kroehl responded, asking for a "Birdsley Electro Magnetic Machine" to fire his charges.[52] On the 11th, Gustavus Fox wired back that acting master Henry J. Rogers was en route to Hampton Roads with one and "a quantity of insulated wire" for Kroehl's use, but that "the machine belongs to the Government."[53] Kroehl asked for more, and

Fox agreed.[54] On December 15 Kroehl wrote Fox that 12 machines were being delivered to him the following week:

> Last Friday and Saturday I was on Ellis Island and found all the torpedoes in good working order. The *Monticello* is expected to be ready next Wednesday, and I have orders to join her on that morning before she leaves the Yard. Captain Brain[e] will take aboard as many torpedoes as he can safely stow away, from the space which he allowed to them, I believe to be able to take with me 30 large torpedoes, 12 small ones, and 18 medium size, and I shall request to ship the balance, 24 large torpedoes, by the first vessel. Before closing I wish to make the request that, as soon as I have finished my work in a designated place, the Navy Department will give me an opportunity to do similar work in another place.[55]

Monticello departed for Hampton Roads with Kroehl and his torpedoes. As he prepared to join Admiral Lee's North Atlantic Blockading Squadron, operating in the waters off Virginia and North Carolina, Kroehl's services were again requested by David D. Porter.

On December 17 Porter, now an acting rear admiral, wrote to Secretary Welles: "I shall want the services of Mr. Julius H. Kroehl for the purposes of removing the rafts in the Yazoo and Red rivers. I would be much obliged if I could get him with all his apparatus."[56] The Navy Department responded to Porter on December 24: "Mr. J. H. Kroehl is acting with Acting Rear-Admiral S. P. Lee, but he can be sent to you in about three weeks, if you require his services at that time."[57] Kroehl, meanwhile, had answered Porter the day before: "Admiral: I have been in Hampton Roads since last Sunday, and should have sailed again had not part of the machinery of the vessel given out. Where I am going I do not know; what I have to do [I] believe I know; still, I may be mistaken. Admiral Lee only told me to be prepared for any emergency."[58]

Lee, meanwhile, was busy ordering his ships to reconnoiter the mouth of Cape Fear and had specific ideas about what Julius Kroehl could do. On December 29 he wrote to one of his senior captains that he wanted a close survey of obstructions in the "rips under Fort Caswell. . . . It is important to know what these obstructions are and if they can be removed. . . . Cannot Lieutenant Commander Braine and Mr. Kroehl approach these obstructions under favor of night, ascertain their character, and report if they can remove them?"[59] Lee also wanted Braine to take USS *Monticello* and plant spar buoys to mark the channel: "Can not Lieutenant Commander Braine in the *Monticello* plant these with the aid of the pilots? Where the *Monticello* is exposed to the chances of fire from the batteries, her torpedoes (of which Mr. Kroehl seems to have too many filled) ought to be on one of the other vessels or one of the schooners. I have sent Mr. Kroehl's spare torpedoes from the *Connecticut* to the ordnance vessel at Beaufort. Inform him. If he can use them, you may get them down and dispense of them as above mentioned."[60]

On January 7, 1863, Braine reported to Lee that because *Monticello* had been set to Shallotte Inlet to blockade, "I have not been able to give Mr. Kroehl an opportunity to visit the obstructions off Fort Caswell."[61] On January 19 Braine wrote Lee that Kroehl had, on "several occasions, been sent in to examine the supposed obstructions off Fort Caswell, but he has never yet deemed the weather propitious to go there, although passing part of several nights lying within a half mile of Fort Caswell. The nights have either been too light or the weather too boisterous to accomplish what he desired."[62] Kroehl was clearly exhausting Braine's and perhaps Admiral Lee's patience. At this juncture, however, he was saved from another disappointment by a change in orders.

On January 8 Secretary Welles ordered Kroehl to "proceed to Cairo, Illinois and report to Acting Rear Admiral D. D. Porter for duty in the Mississippi Squadron. You will take with you the Electro Machine and apparatus complete."[63] It took 10 days for the orders to reach Kroehl, who prepared to return to New York and then to Cairo. Captain B. F. Sands, senior officer at Cape Fear, gave Kroehl the responsibility of transporting four prisoners taken off the captured blockade-running schooner *Pride*. Kroehl was to deliver them to the district judge of Washington City "on his way North."[64] On January 26 orders were issued to the captain of the steamer *Baltimore* to give Kroehl and his prisoners—the supercargo, cook, and two seamen—"a passage on your boat to Baltimore free."[65] As Kroehl prepared to depart, he left 17 torpedoes, wires, and batteries behind with Braine in case the Cape Fear squadron needed them.[66]

RETURN TO THE MISSISSIPPI

Kroehl's assignment to Porter's squadron was intended to do more than blast obstructions. Even before the assault on the mouth of the Mississippi and the taking of New Orleans, the Union had built armored, shallow-draft gunboats under the superintendence of James B. Eads. These were intended to push down the river toward the Gulf, taking river ports and Confederate ports, all part of the overall plan to divide the Confederacy and blockade the Southern states to the east. After the fall of New Orleans on April 29, 1862, both Farragut and General Benjamin Butler had orders to push up the river to meet the army troops and naval gunboats heading down. Following the fall of Memphis on June 6, only the heavily fortified town of Vicksburg, Mississippi, remained as an obstacle to the Union's control of the river. By late June, two fleets had converged to spots above and below Vicksburg, and there they remained in a stalemate as Union forces tried feints on various side channels and tributaries, including the Yazoo, which emptied into the Mississippi ten miles north of the town. In July, Congress passed control of the gunboats to the navy, and on September 30, 1862, under Porter's command they were designated as the navy's Mississippi Squadron.[67]

In response to the Union Navy's growing presence and control of the rivers, the Confederacy had seeded the water with torpedoes, and at the end of December, as Kroehl answered Porter's request, he added a helpful hint: "I see by the papers that one of your steamers, the *Cairo,* was destroyed by torpedoes sunk in the [Yazoo] river. . . . I believe it would be advisable, if you had some torpedoes of 500 to 600 pounds each prepared, and when you run into the neighborhood where you expect torpedoes placed by the enemy, to fire yours, and the concussion in the water will set every torpedo below you, even if a mile off, leaking, and wet the powder."[68] Kroehl reached Cairo at the end of February. He had spent most of February in Washington, thanks to his contacts at the Coast Survey, learning how the survey practiced photography. This was because Porter had asked for a photographer to document "the places which might be reached" by his gunboats.[69] Kroehl left Washington with a Coast Survey–issued photographic apparatus, part of a dual assignment to use his abilities to assist the navy not only through his blasting skills but also through surveying. The superintendent of the Coast Survey noted that Kroehl "by steadiness in service was well fitted for usefulness in the fleet by Vicksburg."[70] By early March Kroehl was on the river aboard Porter's flagship, USS *Black Hawk.* On March 5 Porter had ordered Kroehl to report to the flagship and "bring with you, whatever photographic apparatus you have with you."[71] Kroehl, working with Coast Survey officers Clarence Fendall and Alexander Strausz, was employed in surveying the river in the ironclad gunboat USS *Carondelet* on an expedition up the Confederate-controlled Yazoo River.

In March, Porter and a small force of gunboats headed into Steele's Bayou, Black Bayou, and then up the small tributary to reach Deer Creek, a route by which Porter hoped he could send gunboats and troop transports to reach the upper Yazoo. There they would land troops to "embarrass the enemy's Vicksburg position" by flanking the town's northern defenses.[72] On March 14 Porter entered Steele's Bayou with the ironclads USS *Louisville, Cincinnati, Mound City, Pittsburg, Carondelet,* four tugs towing mortar boats, and coal barges to fuel the fleet. On March 15, 1863, as the fleet began its slow trek, *Carondelet's* logbook mentions that at "6:30 p.m. laid to and sent picket ashore with Acting Ensign Amerman and Lieutenant Kroehl. 8:30 p.m. strengthened the picket force ashore."[73]

The expedition reached Deer Creek on March 16 and pushed along the narrow waterway as curious civilians lined the levees to watch the gunboats pass what historian John Milligan calls a narrow, winding creek and what Porter termed "a ditch."[74] By the 18th the Confederates were using slave labor to fell trees and drop them into the creek to trap the Union gunboats. After sailors were sent ashore to work with local blacks, the trees were cleared, but the next day the fleet met with Confederate troops who opened fire on them. After a day of action, even as the troops withdrew, Porter learned that the enemy was cutting trees behind him to block him if he withdrew. Finally, on the evening of March 21, Porter gave the order to retreat.

As the gunboats, tugs, and mortar barges drifted back, their position was "precarious" as they were "desperately slow" and constantly harassed by Confederate fire.[75] On the morning of the 22nd, the retreat suddenly halted when one of the coal barges, formerly in the rear but now in the lead, sank and blocked the channel. "Under continuous sniper fire, it was impossible to remove the obstacle," and so Porter issued orders to cut rations, repel boarders, and blow up the ships to prevent capture.[76] Fortunately, the army was close at hand, and as they engaged the Confederates, *Carondelet's* log records that on "March 22nd, 3 a.m. Lieutenant Kroehl returned on board, having exploded and sunk a coal barge. . . . A sharp skirmish took place between the rebel sharpshooters and the infantry on shore. Fired several effective shots at the retreating enemy."[77]

The removal of the coal barge allowed the fleet to continue, and with more assistance from the army, the gunboats successfully left Deer Creek after a few more tedious but intense days. Kroehl's work with explosives on the barge is an example of how his time spent surveying did not halt his enthusiasm or his opportunities to apply his skills in underwater survey and demolition.

And yet Kroehl was not entirely celebrated. Following the withdrawal from Deer Creek, Porter wrote Farragut on March 25 that the sunken Union iron-clad gunboat *Indianola* was lost to Confederate action on February 24, adding that the wreck might still have guns and other items that the Confederates could salvage: "I have a diver here who will find out all about it, if you like. Mr. Kroehl is not ready to blow up the *Indianola.* He wanted so many things to do with it that I told him to let it alone."[78]

Farragut's response was short, an indication that he did not hold the engineer in high esteem: "I am glad Kroehl has given it up. I think we can do the work well enough with barrels of powder."[79] Clarence Fendall, the Coast Survey officer attached to Porter's squadron and no friend of Kroehl's, wrote that Kroehl was "a perfect butt on board. Farragut insulted him at dinner today. . . . The old Admiral don't like failures, neither do I."[80] At this stage, Kroehl had been reassigned from blasting to survey and photographic duties, using the Coast Survey–provided daguerreotype "apparatus." His relative (by marriage) and friend Samuel Hein most likely had come into play.

One of Kroehl's photographs, of the gunboat USS *Cincinnati,* was engraved by *Harper's* and published on June 20 with a letter from Kroehl that explained how the gunboat had been sunk by enemy fire off Vicksburg on May 27.[81] Working with Fendall and Alexander Strausz, whom he befriended, Kroehl stayed with Porter on several feints, including a diversionary attack between April 29 and May 1 against Confederate fortifications at Haynes' Bluff on the Yazoo River, all part of a larger strategy to "hasten the fall of Vicksburg."[82] The attack was the keep the Confederates occupied while Grant attacked Grand Gulf below Vicksburg. Strausz and Kroehl went ahead to survey the approaches to the bluff. Fendall remained no friend: "I am sorry to say that neither Kroehl nor Strausz was hit yesterday. They will have another chance today."[83]

Porter reassigned Kroehl and the Coast Survey officers to the army on June 6: "Sir, You will report yourself to Maj. Genl. U. S. Grant for duty."[84] The battle for the control of the rivers had come down at last to the defenses of the last Confederate outpost, Vicksburg. Besieged, the river port city was holding out but was encircled by troops under the command of Major General Ulysses Grant and Porter's fleet on the river. Grant needed engineers to survey the fortifications and various approaches to the city, and Porter had ordered Kroehl and the two Coast Survey engineers to join Grant's staff.

On June 8 the army's chief engineer, Captain Frederick E. Prime, who on May 25 had been placed in charge of an effort to "start mines, trenches or advance batteries,"[85] wrote from the army's headquarters of the Department of the Tennessee to Brigadier General Jacob G. Lauman: "General: Captain Kroehl, of Admiral Porter's staff, and the Messrs. Strausz and Fendall, of the Coast Survey, having been assigned to duty with the army, will for the present assist Captain Freeman, aide-de-camp, engineer of your division. Messrs. Strausz and Fendall will commence the survey of the enemy's works and our approaches from your extreme left, until they connect with the surveys now in progress. Captain Kroehl has served in the artillery abroad, and can be of assistance to Captain Freeman in the trenches and in reconnoitering."[86] On June 13 Porter also wrote Grant directly about Julius Kroehl and his abilities: "In case you should want any blowing up of works done,—one of the officers I sent you, Mr. Kroehl, has been engaged in that kind of business for some years, and that is his duty in the Squadron. You will find him very expert in all such matters."[87]

The nine-day survey was critically described by Fendall in a June 16 letter to F. H. Gerdes. Working with an acting ensign named Farrell, Strausz, Kroehl, and Fendall set out to quickly map the terrain with a plane table, compass, and survey chains and an ambulance and three saddle horses. Fendall complained that Strausz not only took the horses, along with Kroehl and Farrell, leaving Fendall to labor alone, but also worked too quickly, estimating distances while the meticulous and slower Fendall surveyed. Strausz "took the whole work in his hands," wrote a frustrated Fendall, "instigated by Kroehl who from the beginning had thrust himself forward as the leader of the expedition." While the map had been completed, Fendall fussed that "of course Strausz' map is worthless."[88] Kroehl, who had befriended Strausz, a fellow German immigrant, was clearly caught up in the personality dispute between the two Coast Survey officers. The campaign was winding down, however, and the three men were soon to be separated. Vicksburg fell on July 4, although Kroehl was in no position to celebrate the victory. Stricken with what his doctors diagnosed as malaria, Kroehl went back aboard USS *Black Hawk* under the care of the ship's surgeon.

When Kroehl finally left *Black Hawk*, on July 27, it was with his health broken, and he headed back to New York to recuperate.

THE "FEVER"

Kroehl was not alone in his illness; during the Civil War years of 1861–66, 1,315,955 Union troops were diagnosed with malaria.[89] Probably as he slept, Julius Kroehl's body was infected by malarial sporozoites injected into his bloodstream by an infected female anopheles mosquito. Within days, parasitic merozoites developed from the initial sporozoites and fed off Kroehl's red corpuscles, filling his body with dead and dying red blood cells that blocked the flow of blood to his internal organs. The symptoms of his infection were chills, nausea, the shakes, an enlarged spleen, and a fever that hit either daily or every three days depending on the parasitic cycle of one of four types of malarial infection. The fevers, or "paroxysms," weakened and could even kill a patient.[90] Recovery from an intermittent fever did not guarantee health; the fevers could return, as subsequent infections were often the case in heavily mosquito-infested areas. Physicians were unaware of the role of mosquitoes, believing instead that an imbalance in the body's "humors" ("blood, phlegm, black bile, and yellow bile") caused diseases and that malaria was particularly caused by "bad air" or "miasmas" caused by swamps and decaying animal and vegetable matter.[91] "Curing" a patient involved quinine, if the patient was lucky, or turpentine plasters, hot mustard baths, and doses of castor oil, calomel (mercury), and "spirit of nitre" (nitric acid, which is both corrosive and toxic).

Testifying in 1889 in support of her application for a widow's pension, Sophia Kroehl said that her husband had first caught malaria aboard ship and that it had been aggravated while in the trenches with Grant's army: "He was driven out of his tent during a frightful thunder storm, lost all of his instruments and his clothes and was obliged to ride in his underclothes several miles to the Quartermaster to provide another suit which made him very ill, but in spite of all he remained before Vicksburg until the surrender of the city, then got a sick leave and was the first person who brought the news of the capture of Vicksburg to Cairo."[92]

Kroehl requested a furlough and used it to return to Washington. There, instead of leave, he was mustered out of the navy as an invalid on August 8, 1863. "Your services no longer being required," wrote Secretary Welles, "your appointment as an acting volunteer Lieutenant in the Navy of the United States, on temporary service, is hereby revoked."[93]

The same day, Porter, writing to the head of the Coast Survey about the engineers and survey officers, also mentioned Kroehl. "I have always found them prompt and ready to execute my orders, never for a moment taking into consideration the dangers and difficulties surrounding them."[94] Julius Kroehl had paid a price for that service, as had Alexander Strausz, as both left with malaria that broke their health. Ironically, a few weeks later, Admiral S. P. Lee, then seeking assistance on the Roanoke River, had written asking for "torpedoes" and suggested that "Mr. Kroehl or some other person with suitable torpedoes and apparatus" be sent to him.[95] But Julius Kroehl's war was over, and he would never return to duty. That thought tormented him as much as his malaria, especially with Benjamin Maillefert and the New York Submarine Engineering Company now assuming preeminence as the navy's submarine experts. As he slowly and painfully recuperated, Kroehl returned to Ryerson's bell, perhaps as a means to influence his return to the navy's favor.

~ 5 ~

The Pacific Pearl Company

Your only chance of making anything by your invention
is to get some person of capital and influence interested with you
by giving him a good share [and] take a patent.

—Editors of *Scientific American,* February 7, 1863

ISCOURAGED and sick, Julius Kroehl left Washington and made his way to brother Henry's home at 42 Seventh Avenue in New York. Henry's business was thriving, and he and Cornelia and their children turned a bedroom over to Julius. With the help of his physician, Alexander Clinton, Kroehl battled malaria through the winter of 1863–64.[1]

Kroehl soon turned to drafting plans for a new, improved *Explorer.* Unlike the earlier bell, this would be a different type of craft, capable of operating on its own without connection to the surface. Working from Van Buren Ryerson's original concepts of ballast and compressed air to make the craft sink and rise, Kroehl redesigned the bell, stretching it out into a 36-foot-long craft that could face into a current. Its form was not unlike the bottom of Maillefert's bell. Another possible design influence was Hermann Grundt's iron pontoon, which bolted together to form a flat-bottomed, boat-shaped hull. Kroehl may also have been influenced by Alexandré's copy of Payerne's "Submarine Explorer" and its egglike shape. Meanwhile, his old rival, Benjamin Maillefert was busily manufacturing his patented "aerostatic tubular diving bell." Maillefert's New York Submarine Engineering Company was thriving under contract to the US Navy for submarine clearance, blasting, and salvage, with both Maillefert and his business partner, Levi Hayden, on the battlefields of the James River and Charleston Harbor, conducting operations that Kroehl had once been active in.

Kroehl's motivation for the new craft may have been his own desire to build a submarine that would enable the Union Navy to continue the work of torpedo and obstruction clearance. However, the funding for Kroehl's work came from a group of investors who had been introduced to the concept of a submarine by none other than Van Buren Ryerson. Ryerson was then living in the Holcomb Valley, the site of an 1860 gold discovery in the San Bernardino Mountains outside Los Angeles. At one mine, the Greenleaf, Ryerson was working with partners to process the quartz gold being dug out of the ground.[2] The ore, crushed by stamp mills, was then processed through the use of a mercury amalgamator, which operated on the principle that mercury attracts gold and retains it. In June 1861 the ever-inventive Ryerson patented a barrel-shaped amalgamator that used steam to assist the process of removing the mineral from the quartz.[3] The "Ryerson Amalgamator" was in use at another California mine, the Coe, in Nevada County, and in the Bear Valley mills on the Mariposa Ranch, also in Northern California.[4]

The Mariposa Ranch, ostensibly owned by former army officer, explorer, and presidential candidate John Charles Frémont, was actually owned by his banker, Mark Brumagim. Brumagim, born in New York's Montgomery County in 1826, had gone to California in 1849. In 1850 he opened California's first bank north of San Francisco in Marysville. Prospering, he founded the San Francisco banking firm of Mark Brumagim & Company in 1858. Brumagim continued in business with his partners in until 1863, when he left to become the chief cashier of the Pacific Accumulation Loan Company.[5] Brumagim widely invested, including a directorship in the Citizen's Steam Navigation Company, which ran steamers between San Francisco and Marysville. In this capacity he had become the creditor of Frémont.[6] Most probably in his capacity as owner of the Mariposa Land and Mining Company, Brumagim met Van Buren Ryerson when he purchased Ryerson's amalgamator for the Bear Valley mills.

Several years earlier, Samuel Hallett, the president of the Nautilus Submarine Wrecking Company, had sent Sears's Nautilus diving bell to Baja California to investigate the possibilities of using it in the pearl diving business. A New York banker with a variety of business interests, Hallett was known to Brumagim's circle of friends and associates. Just a few years earlier, General Frémont had invested with Hallett to take a controlling interest in the Leavenworth, Pawnee & Western Railroad (later the Union Pacific's Eastern Division) to gain a piece of the action in the transcontinental railroad. Even though Frémont had withdrawn from the partnership with Hallett, as Frémont's attorney, Mark Brumagim would have had even greater reason to know about the Nautilus bell and the Mexican pearl expedition. Finding that the engineer he was working with on a new process of amalgamation also had a patent on a diving bell, he undoubtedly talked with Ryerson about the inventor's "Sub Marine Explorer."

Yankee interest in the mineral and natural resources of the former and current Mexican territories was high—thanks to the discovery of gold in conquered California in January 1848 and tales of rich mines in the new American Southwest as well as in Mexico. Interest in the pearls of both Baja California and Panama occasionally surfaced, and like other natural resources in the region, they were considered ripe for the plucking. As the editors of the *San Francisco Daily Alta California* opined, "The Yankee Nation having had a rather satisfactory experience in the business of mining for silver and gold is now about to turn itself to the pearl fishery."[7] In the spirit of the age, many American entrepreneurs believed that all that was needed was American drive, determination, and technological prowess to reap the riches of lands and waters hitherto left incompletely tapped by people who were either indolent or indifferent. While applying American "can-do" energy and technology to his mining, Brumagim, ever the speculator, saw potential in Pacific pearls and arranged to license the patent for the bell from Ryerson. He then had to find someone to build it—or an expanded, improved version. That person was Julius Kroehl, and he was likely introduced to the project by Ryerson.

If Brumagim was the instigator of the project, by the fall of 1863 he had interested a group of investors join together to form the "Pacific Pearl Company." Julius Kroehl also joined as a trustee with a large number of shares that he had either purchased or obtained as "sweat equity" for building the submarine. They incorporated it in New York on November 18, 1863, the day before Abraham Lincoln delivered the Gettysburg Address overlooking the battlefield that would later be seen as the high-water mark of the Confederacy.[8] While the investors may have been attracted to the idea of also selling the submarine to the US Navy, especially in a city where a number of entrepreneurs were making fortunes because of the war, they modeled their business plan on harvesting pearls and shells from the sea.

The founding directors all had strong links to New York, some of them through the American Institute of the City of New York. Some were politically connected and others were members of the Masonic Order and the Odd Fellows, but their principal connection was through California and the West's mineral resources. All had experience in banking, mining, invention, and selling arms to the government. Some, like Brumagim, had familiarity with both Mexico and Panama, the company's intended fields of operation, and one new director had excellent connections to the government as a federal commissioner.

That director was 41-year-old Charles D. Poston, superintendent for Indian affairs in the new territory of Arizona. The Kentucky-born Poston had worked as a clerk in the county clerk's office in his native Hardin County and then moved to Nashville to clerk for the Tennessee Supreme Court while earning a law license. Following the California gold discovery, Poston headed west in 1850 to make his fortune. Instead of mining, however, he worked for three years as clerk for the US Custom House on the San Francisco waterfront.[9]

In January 1854 Poston left San Francisco, sailing to Guaymas, Mexico, with 30 men intent on exploring Mexico's silver mines. Shipwrecked and stranded, the expedition a failure, Poston had instead struck out over land with one other man, Herman Ehrenberg, to Fort Yuma and from there to Arizona's fabled silver mines. After prospecting in the Cerro Colorado area, Poston returned to San Francisco and booked steamer passage to New York via Panama. Lining up investors in New York, back home in Kentucky, and in Washington, D.C., Poston headed to Cincinnati, where he met up again with US Army officer Samuel Heintzelman, whom he had met on the frontier in Arizona. Heintzelman in turn introduced Poston to two printers from Albany, New York, Thomas and William Wrightson, publishers of the *Railroad Record*, who were strong advocates of building railroads to link the West to the rest of the country. In March 1857 they jointly formed what would become the Sonora Exploration and Mining Company, which they incorporated with other investors in August 1857.[10]

Finding it difficult to raise the funds they needed, the company was saved by a timely investment from firearms manufacturer Samuel Colt (1814–62), who provided $10,000 in cash and $10,000 in guns that the company could sell to raise capital.[11] The company then set up a mining in the Cerro Colorado, contending with distance and Apache attacks, including ones that killed Poston's brother John in 1861 and William Wrightson in 1865.[12] The company reorganized in 1859–60, shifting out of Ohio to New York and acquiring new directors, among them Colt's trusted aide and the secretary of the Colt Arms Company, William M. B. Hartley. Born in Montreal in 1821, Hartley was a Yale-educated and literary-minded lawyer with diverse interests and experience.[13]

He became the vice president of the Sonora Exploration and Mining Company after it reincorporated in New York on February 9, 1860.

Poston, after setting up the mining operation, had returned to New York in 1857, taking an active role in business but also making frequent visits to Washington, lobbying for Arizona to become a territory. With the onset of the Civil War, he moved to Washington to work as a civilian aide for now General Heintzelman and to continue lobbying for Arizona. He was rewarded for his efforts in 1863, when President Abraham Lincoln appointed him superintendent of Indian affairs for Arizona. Poston would go on to be elected as Arizona's first delegate to Congress in December 1864, serving as a Republican in the 38th Congress until March 1865.[14]

Poston was the most prominent and influential director of the new Pacific Pearl Company. He was joined by Hartley, and 28-year-old George J. Wrightson of New York, Poston's attorney.[15] George was the younger brother of Poston's partners in the Sonora Exploration and Mining Company, William and Thomas Wrightson.[16] The other two directors were New York financier William H. Tiffany, at that time a member of the jewelry firm founded by his brother, Charles Lewis Tiffany, and John Chadwick, merchant and entrepreneur from Newark, New Jersey.[17] The 44-year-old Tiffany, born in 1819 and an 1840 graduate of Yale, while a New Yorker, was no stranger to California; after working for his brother for several years, he had sailed there during the gold rush, arriving in San Francisco in June 1849. He remained in the State for 14 years, engaged in "mining, real estate, and other pursuits."[18] After a stint in San Diego, Tiffany had returned to San Francisco in 1854, remaining there for the next nine years, listed alternately as an attorney and then as a partner with James S. Wethered as agents for filing US patents and "oil and gas works."[19] Tiffany returned to New York in 1863 and rejoined Tiffany & Co. before branching out into his own pursuits.[20]

John Chadwick, born in New York in 1815, amassed a fortune as a manufacturer of patent leather and as an importer of silks. Prominent in the community, he had served as a member of the city's Common Council in 1846.[21] Chadwick helped found and was a director of the Newark City National Bank, its public library, and engaged in maritime trade with California.[22] Like Kroehl, Chadwick was a member of New York's American Institute and had won awards for his products at their annual fair.[23] Significantly, Chadwick had a family interest in submarines. His wife, the former Julia Halstead, was the sister of Oliver S. "Pet" Halstead. Pet Halstead had become involved in the American Submarine Company of New York, and in the last half of 1865, was taking it over.[24] The company in late 1863 had contracted with inventor Scovel S. Merriam to build an iron submarine, and the largely completed craft, later named *Intelligent Whale,* was acquired by Halstead and moved to the Newark machine shop of Hewes & Phillips. There, it is very likely that Chadwick, as Halstead's brother-in-law, saw the craft before its trial dives for the new owner in April 1866.

These men, all linked either by business association with Brumagim and Poston, or with ties to California and the Pacific, or in Chadwick's case, another submarine, would have seen an opportunity in Kroehl's improved version of Ryerson's *Explorer* to diversify their investments in yet another speculative venture to harvest the West's (particularly the Hispanic West's) abundant natural resources, with Tiffany perhaps particularly eager to obtain pearls for the family business, then America's premier jewelers.

They did not want to assume all the cost or the risk, however. Under Hartley, who served as the first president, the Pacific Pearl Company offered 10,000 shares of stock at $100 per share. According to their prospectus,

> THIS Company has been organized for the purpose of gathering pearls and pearl-shells on the Pacific coast. Their operations will be carried on by means of a *Sub-Marine Explorer* of an improved construction. The enterprise is not speculative, but as real, substantial, and legitimate, as the smelting of copper or the importation of ivory. It was suggested by the progress and inventions of the arts, and the caprices of fashion, which have made pearls and pearl-shells, or mother-of-pearl, essential among articles of luxury. The largely increased and increasing demand for these articles has prompted men of genius and enterprise to perfect some mode of gratifying this demand, more reliable than the uncertain and dangerous process of searching for them by divers.[25]

The partners appointed Kroehl, also a shareholder, as chief engineer. One of the investors was Van Buren Ryerson, who apparently retained a key role even though he was not a trustee, particularly in regard to Kroehl's position within in the company. In January 1864 Ryerson, still in California, had written his attorney in New York on the sale of a half interest in his amalgamator to an interested investor, Samuel Butterworth of the Quicksilver Mining Company of New York, and asked the attorney to "say nothing about what I am doing here or who are the parties [involved in] the purchase of the submarine. If you see Kroehl see what he will want hereafter. I mean what wages he will want to take charge of an expedition to the pearl fishery on this coast."[26]

With the backing of the Pacific Pearl Company's investors, Kroehl turned to retired shipbuilder Ariel Patterson. They began work at Patterson's old shipyard on the banks of the East River in Williamsburg, directly across from Manhattan and adjacent to Brooklyn.[27] The yard stood at 273 First Street (now renamed Kent Avenue), near North Third Street. The site is now a recycling yard for Greater Manhattan, surrounded by derelict buildings, its former ways paved over and the rocky shores strewn with garbage.

ARIEL PATTERSON: SUB MARINE EXPLORER'S BUILDER

Work on *Explorer* required not only access to an industrial facility such as Patterson's Yard; it also required a working partnership with Ariel Patterson in the design and fabrication of the submersible. Kroehl, trained as an engineer with experience in iron casting and fabrication, was not a naval architect or shipbuilder. Patterson, a veteran New York shipbuilder, had operated New York's fourth largest shipyard, Perrine, Patterson & Stack, between 1845 and 1853. The yard built a number of merchant vessels, clipper ships, and steamships, including a number of vessels employed in the steamer routes to and from Panama during the California Gold Rush. In one 1852 project, the yard built the experimental "caloric ship" *Ericsson* for inventor John Ericsson, which utilized hot air engines for propulsion.[28]

The firm dissolved in 1853, and the principals operated separately until 1854, when the shipbuilding boom collapsed. Patterson's last major vessel, a 209-ton schooner, was launched in August 1854. Through 1865 Patterson remained at the site of the old yard of Patterson, Perrine & Stack at First Street near North Sixth. City directories list him as a "shipbuilder" as a "ship joiner" (carpenter) in 1861–62 and again as a "ship builder" as of 1864–65, when he was working with Kroehl. An advertisement in the Brooklyn directory at that time advertises Patterson's services as a "ship builder and ship smith," and noted his work in both wood and iron; "planing [*sic*], sawing, re-sawing, and scroll sawing" as well as "heavy iron planing [*sic*], turning, punching, and cutting."[29]

Patterson's work with Kroehl involved his facilities as well as the shipbuilder's experience as the submersible progressed through design and into fabrication. The vessel's lines, metacentric height, stability, and trim required naval architectural experience, and certain construction features on the submersible, as noted archaeologically, suggest experienced marine engineering craftsmen were employed. For example, the bracing of the compressed air chamber employed what appear to be modified stays or braces from a marine steam boiler. As well, the experienced foundrymen also played a key role. They knew from their experience how to determine the final weight of the submarine, based on the weight of their wooden patterns. A simple formula converted the weight of pine or mahogany to cast iron because the weight of each per cubic foot was a known quantity (cast iron, for example, weighs 450 pounds per cubic foot).[30]

The construction sequence began with initial drawings, completed by or with Kroehl and Patterson, for every aspect of the submersible. Then the vessel's mould lines and preliminary offsets were laid out at Patterson's yard. The complex castings for the submersible's lower hull and components required the completion of wooden patterns for each piece of the lower hull, including the valves, frames, and hull plates. To build *Explorer,* hundreds of drawings, and subsequently hundreds of patterns, were fabricated out of white pine, mahogany, or cherry. Each pattern was likely completed in Patterson's carpenter shop. The work would have kept a carpenter busy for an extended period of time. Building the submarine involved very little use of "off the shelf" components. Once the patterns were fabricated, however, numerous castings could be made, and presumably, an unlimited number of submarines could be manufactured.

The casting probably did not take place at Patterson's. Casting required specialized facilities, and it is possible that Patterson and Kroehl turned to Patterson's old shipbuilding partner, William Perrine, who operated a nearby foundry.[31] To cast each smaller piece, a large wooden flask with a two-sided drag (or bottom) and a cope (or top) contained a water-moldable sand composite that held the impression of the wooden pattern. Small castings, with metal melted in crucibles, were handled in this fashion. Larger castings were done through "loam molding," the loam being the matrix that formed the casting mold and reacted well to the higher heat of furnace-heated iron. The matrix formula was a carefully kept trade secret of each iron-founder, and involved mixing the sand with clay, straw, manure, and other organic materials to help bond it.[32] After being formed, the mold was rammed to pack the sand, and the larger molds were capped with brick to hold the matrix ready for the pour. Assembled and gated (meaning that access holes were created to pour the molten iron into the empty cavity), the mold or cope was then ready for casting. Other castings were done in sandboxes or in sandpits.

Pig iron was melted in blast furnaces or cupolas by means of a coal fire that heated the metal rapidly—furnaces of various types could melt anywhere from half a ton to three tons in an hour.[33] When the cast iron (which was an impure combination of iron, carbon, and silicon) reached 1,150° to 1,200°C, it melted. A group of men then carried the liquid metal to the mold in pots that could hold a few hundred pounds; an overhead crane was used to dip and carry larger pots to the mold.

Poured from crucibles into troughs and then into the molds, the lengthy, hot, and tiring process of casting the parts of the submersible, large and small, was doubtless similar to that described by a visiting reporter to New York's Novelty Iron Works in 1851:

> The workmen carry the molten metal in ladles, which, though they do not appear very large, it requires *five men* to carry. . . . These ladles are filled from the various furnaces, the iron throwing out an intense heat, and projecting the most brilliant scintillations in every direction, as it flows. In the case of the largest castings, it requires sometimes four or five hours, to get together from the furnaces, a sufficient supply of metal. . . . The flowing of the metal from the reservoir to the mould, in a great casting, forms a magnificent spectacle. The vast mass of molten iron in the reservoir, the stream flowing down the conduit, throwing out the most brilliant corus- cations, the gaseous flames issuing from the upper portions of the mould, and the currents of melted iron which sometimes overflow and spread, like mimic streams of lava, over the ground, present in their combination quite an imposing pyrotechnic display.[34]

The casting then had to cool before being cleaned and finished. Small castings required a few minutes to cool, but larger castings took longer. A five-ton cast- ing took between 24 to 48 hours to cool.[35] Once the casting could be handled, but before it had completely cooled, skilled workers broke clear the excrescences that formed at the joints and at the gates through which the metal was poured into the mold. The casting was then finished with chisels and files and polished. Only then could the workers begin the assembly process for the submarine.

The time-consuming, meticulous, and labor-intensive pattern work, molding, casting, and finishing of hundreds of parts consumed the attention and energy of the yard through most of 1864 and 1865. However, work on *Explorer* was well under way by June 1864, when Kroehl reinitiated contact with the navy.

LOBBYING THE NAVY

On June 14, 1864, Kroehl wrote to Gustavus Fox. He apologized that "a contagious sickness, the Western fever, which I contracted while attached to the Mississippi Squadron, has detained me so long in writing you." Kroehl went on to relate that it was with a "sad heart" that he had read about "the destruction of our gunboats by torpedoes." Kroehl explained that he considered "very easy to destroy the rebel torpedoes without picking them up," and offered to assist "with the little ability I have, to make them harmless." Kroehl ended with the sentiment that "I shall not be able to go out in the service myself, but shall give you my plans, on the condition that the latter be acknowledged by the Navy Department."[36]

The same day, Kroehl wrote a letter to Admiral Joseph Smith, chief of the Bureau of Yard and Docks: "I sent you last week a pamphlet issued by the Pacific Pearl Company, for whom I am now building a submarine boat, constructed on the same principal as the diving bell, which I have used for six years in the harbor of New York. . . . In the operations against some of the rebel forts and harbors I have no doubt the Navy Department will require submarine boats, and I think it would be advisable to bring this to the attention of the Honorable Gideon Welles, and have the plans examined by a proper board."[37] Kroehl's letter was sent the same time that George Wrightson, now serving as the president of the Pacific Pearl Company, wrote to Secretary Welles that "I am engaged in building a submarine boat for wrecking purposes":

> As this vessel has advantages over all other submarine boats I wish to call the attention of the Navy Department to its merits. The boat now being built is of a size to hold twenty four men & its construction is such to require no communication at all with the surface so that the enemy will be unable to discover its movement below water as is the case with all other submarine boats. In other boats the enemy can cut the necessary supply of air from the parties

inside the boat, thereby endangering the lives of its occupants. It is independent of hose, float or anything connected with the surface of the water, & by a simple process of purifying the air when it has become vitiated by respiration it enables the men to remain for 24 hours or in fact an indefinite period of time. The boat now building will be propelled by hand as we intend to work it at a depth of from 100 to 150 feet, but if we should build a boat for war purposes we propose to place an engine in the vessel to be propelled by compressed air. Should the Navy Department wish to examine the plans of our submarine boat I shall be happy to give all necessary information with drawings, patterns, & such parts of the boat as we have already put together. The boat will be finished in say 6 weeks, when I shall be able to show its practical working.[38]

While Kroehl was still pursuing his relationship with the navy to remove "torpedoes," the new submarine project was also on the table—or another built on its model—for sale to the US Navy. Given Kroehl's connections and an apparently excellent reputation, Wrightson's letter to the secretary of the navy was immediately answered, and within four days the navy's general inspector of steam machinery, W. W. W. Wood, was assigned to inspect and evaluate the submarine.[39] Welles wrote Kroehl on June 17, the same day he assigned Wood to inspect the submarine, to let the engineer know of his decision.[40]

On June 18 Kroehl wrote Welles that he would "lay the plans of the same" before Wood by the following week. He went on to offer his opinion that an underwater explosion, from "1000 to 200 yards" could rupture torpedoes and make them "entirely useless" by "wetting the powder." Kroehl hoped the navy would experiment with the method and "please inform me" of the results.[41] Welles answered immediately and assured Kroehl that tests would be made "and you will be informed of the result of the examination."[42] Welles also let Kroehl know that his letter had been forwarded to the navy's senior admirals, and the same day wrote to Admirals Farragut, Dahlgren, Lee, and Bailey to "call your attention to the accompanying extracts from a letter of J. H. Kroehl relative to the explosion of torpedoes."[43] Julius Kroehl may have been out of the navy and out of the fight, but his opinion still mattered for Welles to send his letter on to the admirals poised off the Confederacy's harbors.

BUILDING SUB MARINE EXPLORER

During the summer and fall of 1865, work continued on the submarine. When Kroehl and Wrightson had written to the navy, Kroehl explained in his letter to Admiral Smith, "I have the Patterns for one boat all finished and nearly all the castings made."[44] The first work to be completed would have been the casting and assembly of the keel plate on an elevated platform, followed by the casting and assembly of the ballast tanks. The boat-shaped lower hull, once assembled, represented months of casting, fitting, and bolting.[45] The upper hull, including the dome and the top of the working chamber, as well as the turtleback shell that would enclose the compressed air chamber, required boiler iron, a difficult to obtain, expensive commodity during wartime.

In mid-June 1864 Kroehl was confident that "it will not take much to finish this one boat. . . . [However,] I have to wait for the Boiler Iron to make all the necessary compressed air and ballast chambers."[46] Work on the submarine, delayed by the lack of the boiler iron, dragged through 1864 and into early 1865. As boiler iron became available, the sections to be fabricated were the working chamber and dome. The iron required bending, punching, and riveting, with the most complex work being the forming of the dome. With this done, the next step was the acquisition, cutting, and forming the bends and curves, followed by assembling the turtleback cover. This work required the use of huge mangles to roll the heated strakes, which then would be hammered into final shape. The overlapping plates were punched for rivets, and then the turtleback was riveted. A hole was precisely cut to allow the top of the dome to penetrate the turtleback and yet form a tight fit so as not to allow the air to escape. The assembled turtleback would then have been lifted and fitted atop the lower hull, with the sleeve that fitted over the top of the dome (forming a "conning tower" or turret atop the hull) riveted into place to help form the seal. The seal would not be complete with riveting, however. A rust joint or seal was required.

Rust joints, a nineteenth-century practice employed in the manufacture of iron steam machinery and boilers, were formed by caulking the metal to be joined with a formula of 1 pound weight of iron filings with 1 ounce of sal-ammoniac powder and water. "Some persons add about half an ounce of flowers of brimstone and a little sludge from the grindstone trough."[47] After standing for a few hours to commence the process of oxidization, the mixture was applied to the surfaces of the metal joint, which had been cleaned with nitric acid. The rust joints, once formed, would have formed the final seal for the compressed air chamber. A rust joint can be broken and re-formed, and so if necessary (as will be seen later) it was a reversible feature.

The braces inside the compressed air chamber now required fitting and fastening. Working inside the compressed air chamber by crawling through the access port in the dome, probably no more than a pair of workers hand-fastened the braces one at a time, bolting the top and then the bottom to the angle-iron ribs and angle-iron mounts. With the turtleback firmly bolted in place, the external portions of *Explorer* were completed.

By late January 1865, work on the craft had progressed to the point where Inspector Wood could finally make his report. Wood's 18-page report, dated February 2, 1865, was sent to Secretary Welles along with a rudimentary plan of the submarine. Wood ended his report with this summary:

> The uses to which a boat, such as is above described can be applied, in Naval Warfare, would be the removal of submerged obstructions in the channels of rivers and harbors. Approaching hostile fleets at anchor and destroying them by attaching torpedoes to their bot-toms and exploding such localities as are commanded and covered by the guns of an enemy. The importance of a successful applica-tion of the principles involved in such a vessel for such purposes are of much importance and can not be too highly estimated. . . .
> In conclusion I would respectfully suggest that practical tests of the Submarine Explorer be made on its final completion, that a correct report may be made conclusive of the merits and value for the pur-poses proposed.[48]

Kroehl wrote immediately to ask for a copy of Wood's report. On February 15 Gustavus Fox wrote that the navy had no problem with Wood giving Kroehl a copy if it was "expedient."[49] Delighted with the report, Kroehl wrote back 10 days later asking for permission to publish it.[50] Fox responded on March 2 that the Navy "has no objections."[51]

Despite publication of the report, the Navy Department did not agree to take *Explorer*. Poston's influence had apparently waned (his term in Congress was coming to end, as his bid for reelection was a failure, and he was about to embark on a European tour). The Navy Department forwarded Wood's report to Rear Admiral Francis H. Gregory, superintendent of ironclad construction, for review. Gregory's shortsighted review, appended on the back of Wood's report, was the death knell for the navy's acceptance of *Explorer*. "This report recommends that this vessel be examined again when it is completed—I do not think the Navy has any use for such a vessel, but parties exploring sunken vessels or engaged in wrecking may find it useful if it be found to answer."[52] Welles and Fox did not overrule the admiral's recommendation. The war was within a few months of ending, and they perhaps viewed *Explorer*'s arrival on the scene as coming too late to be used effectively against the remaining Confederate strongholds. In the navy's professional circles there was a prevailing sentiment of reaction against the technological advances of the Civil War period, notably against steam power but also other new applications, including submarines, which took the navy four more decades to accept as part of the fleet. The rejection of *Sub Marine Explorer* by the navy most likely happened because of this myopic view. It is another example of how the US Navy was relegated by its leadership to the backwaters of naval development following the Civil War.[53]

A TRIUMPH OF "TRUE SCIENTIFIC PRINCIPLES"

Kroehl and his backers carried on, either hoping that a public demonstration of the craft might shift official opinion, or that a navy "stamp of approval" of their design might help secure investors. Wood's report noted that many of the internal systems were not completed in January 1865; indeed, it took much of the rest of 1865 to complete the submarine. Workers commenced the installation of the internal systems, which included the fitting of the propulsion machinery, the installation of the piping systems for transferring compressed air into the working chamber and ballast chambers, and the installation of the dive manifold for regulating the egress of air from the ballast chambers as they filled with seawater. The hatches on the bottom of the submersible may have provided easier access and working conditions on an elevated platform than access through the dome.

Once the internal systems were fitted, the final details would have included fitting the propeller, rudder, and steering system and the final painting of the interior and possibly the exterior of the craft (the interior was probably painted white to reflect the light of the spermaceti candles Kroehl employed). Other final details would have included fitting the rubber gaskets for the hatches and manhole and installing and fitting the glass deadlights in the dome collar sleeve (turret) and bow. The construction crew would have transferred *Explorer,* probably by the yard's marine railway, to the dock at the foot of North Third Street and launched her into the East River, sometime around or after the reported completion of the submersible in November 1865. On the 12th the *Brooklyn Daily Eagle* reported the

> COMPLETION OF A SUBMARINE NOVELTY—a submarine
> explorer, which has been in course of construction for the past
> eighteen months . . . is now finished, and will be submerged for a
> trial of its capacity in the East River early next week. It is of non-
> descript shape, constructed partly of wrought and partly of cast
> iron, and contains three chambers. It was constructed by the well-
> known submarine engineer, MR. JULIUS H. KROEHL, at a cost
> of $40,000, for the Pacific Pearl Company, and is intended to be
> taken to the Pacific coast, to be used in gathering pearls and pearl
> shells. MR. KROEHL claims that this explorer will be able to
> traverse the bed of the ocean without difficulty, and that the men
> working it (there are accommodations for six) will be as free to
> labor there as in the streets of the city. Several eminent engineers
> have examined this novelty and expressed their confidence in its
> success, among their number the Chief Engineer of the United
> States Navy.[54]

Despite the announcement, the launch did not immediately take place. A month later, on December 13, the *Brooklyn Daily Eagle,* in an article summarizing local shipyards, reported that Patterson "has not been in the business for some time" but that "at his yard, the celebrated Submarine Explorer was built. . . . The Explorer is for the purpose of searching for pearls on the Pacific coast, but whether it is a success remains to be seen. The Company, by whom the novelty was constructed, intend, it is said, to launch it, this week, but this is only rumor. They are very secret in their action as regards this enterprise."[55]

Following the initial test dive, other trials took place over the next six months, delayed perhaps as problems were sorted out and leaks dealt with, and possibly by winter conditions on the river. They culminated in a fourth "private trial" in front of the Pacific Pearl Company's officers and investors on May 30, 1866. At that stage, Mark Brumagim had taken over as president, replacing Chadwick, who had served in the role in 1865.[56]

The next day, the New York *Times* reported:

> Yesterday afternoon there was a private trial of the Pacific Pearl Company's Submarine *Explorer,* in the dock foot of North third-street, Eastern District. The officers of the company and a few friends only were present. At 1:30 o'clock Julius H. Kroehl, engineer, with Frederick Michaels, August Getz and John Tanner, entered the explorer through her man-hole, which being finally closed and the signal given the boat was submerged, and for an hour and a half she traversed the bed of the dock. During the submersion the friends of those onboard the boat exhibited considerable anxiety for their safety, but then at last when she rose to the surface and Engineer Kroehl and his companions emerged from her chambers, (the former leisurely smoking his meerschaum), they gave vent to their feelings in repeated cheers. These were again and again repeated, when the engineer held up a pail of mud which he had gathered at the bottom of the dock, showing conclusively the success of the experiment. This boat is 36 feet long, was built under the immediate supervision of Engineer Kroehl, and cost about $75,000. Those who went down in her say that with the exception of a slight tingling sensation in their ears they felt quite comfortable and could remain submerged for days. This is more remarkable as the boat is air-tight, and the men depending on the fresh air "manufactured" in the chamber of the boat assigned to them, and they live on the surplus of oxygen gas in the water, on the principle that fishes live. The boat is worked by a propeller worked by hand. The hull is of peculiar shape, constructed partly of wrought and partly of cast iron, and is divided into three chambers. The experiment yesterday, which was the fourth made, was highly gratifying to the officers of the company present. A public exhibition of this novelty will take place in the course of a few days, at which the Government will be represented by a board of competent engineers. Although this boat was designed for pearl-fishing in the Pacific, her success as an engine of naval warfare is looked upon with favor by the Navy Department, Chief Engineer

W. W. W. Wood, of the United States Navy, having made an elabo-
rate report to Secretary Welles to that effect.[57]

On June 11, less than two weeks after the trial, Wood wrote privately to Kroehl
to "congratulate you most sincerely on the success of your sub-marine boat.
You deserve all the success claimed for this valuable and most remarkable pro-
duction of engineering skill, founded as it is on true scientific principles. The
result of this trial is peculiarly gratifying to me as well, as I have felt great interest in this invention, and should be glad to render you any assistance in my
power."[58] Wood was absolutely right. The new craft was a technological marvel.
Despite the sincerity of Wood's words, however, there was nothing more he
could do, given the intransigence of his fellow officers and superiors. The time
had come for the Pacific Pearl Company to move on, as always planned, and
take the submarine into the Pacific.

OFF TO PANAMA

In 1866 Mark Brumagim was president of the Pacific Pearl Company, having
replaced John Chadwick, who had served the year before. Under Brumagim,
the company republished its advertising brochure and used the opportunity to
announce that it had increased the number of shares from 10,000 to 30,000 ultimately to raise $3 million in capital. Obviously the costs of construction and
the intended operations of the submarine were now calculated to be higher
than first expected. The $75,000 cost of *Explorer* was higher than its initial
budget estimate of $40,000. In modern terms, the cost of *Explorer* jumped
from just under $900,000 to $1,749,000.

> The Pacific Pearl Company also explained that they wereabout to
> send the *Explorer* to the Pacific Coast. To furnish the means to do
> this, and to sustain the enterprise until the receipt of ships of shells
> and pearls, they propose to issue 7 per cent. Coupon bonds of the
> Company, to the amount of $50,000, to be issued at par, the interest
> payable annually at the office of the Company in the city of New
> York. These bonds being the only indebtedness of the Company,
> have the security of all its property, among which may enumerated
> the *Explorer* itself . . . and which has been built wholly of iron, at
> a cost nearly $100,000; a lease of the valuable fishing grounds at

Tiburon Island, in the Gulf of California, a location famed for the abundance and fine quality of its pearls and pearl-shells; the fishing rights of the Bay of Panama, conceded by the Government of the State of Panama; and the entire ownership and control of the exceedingly valuable patents under which the boat has been built. The security for those bonds, it will thus be seen, is most ample.[59]

The brochure also enumerated the business plan for the company. In an average year, they estimated, *Explorer* and its crew would work 250 days, raising 12 tons of oyster shells per day in 10-hour-per-day dives. That would total 1,800 tons of shell, which would then sell at $120 per ton, to make $216,000. They estimated as well that they would recover $250,000 worth of pearls each year.[60] In modern dollars, the company *expected to make a gross profit of over $10 million a year.* After subtracting the "cost at opening" of $1 per thousand of the $3,150 and $15,000 they estimated it would cost to freight, insure, and store *Explorer* in Panama, the company would net $447,850 in gold. Operations would cost $33,500 per year; $2,500 for Kroehl as the salaried submarine engineer, $7,500 for the submarine's captain and crew, $5,000 for the captain and crew of the submarine's tender boat, $7,500 for provisions, $2,500 for coal, $3,500 for insurance, and $5,000 for "office and contingent expenses." That left an amazing $414,350 ($9.6 million in modern dollars) in potential annual net income.[61] Not surprisingly, enough shares were sold to send Kroehl and *Explorer* to Panama. One investor, Charles A. Morris, bought 25 shares at $2,500, a considerable sum.[62]

Before shipping the vessel away, the Pacific Pearl Company registered *Explorer* as an American-flagged "screw steamer" (a misnomer) of 14 tons, home-ported in New York, with official number 8803.[63] Partial disassembly of the submersible by the yard was necessary to prepare to ship it as cargo. This probably took a few months. The only portions of the craft readily accessible for disassembly without punching out rivets (an unlikely, expensive, and potentially damaging process) would have been the external plates sealing the ballast chambers, the rudder, propeller, and potentially the entire turtleback, all of which, if removed and separately crated for shipment, would have reduced the total weight of the submersible by one-third.

After disassembly and crating, *Explorer* was loaded onto a Panama steamer in New York in late August or early September 1866. With perhaps a few workers on board, the steamer pulled away from the docks on the East River, headed out the Narrows, and entered the Atlantic for the two-week run to Aspinwall, the Caribbean depot for the Panama Railroad. Julius Kroehl followed on December 11, steaming out of New York on the Pacific Mail steamship *Henry Chauncey* to rendezvous with his submarine on the isthmus.[64] A few days earlier, he had completed and filed a last will and testament in New York, with his signature witnessed by Mark Brumagim and Van Buren Ryerson. The will was an essential piece of business for a man in less than perfect health leaving on an extended trip to a country notorious for fever; it was also, in hindsight, a chilling portent of what would soon follow.[65]

6

Panama

Sceptics are now tolerably well satisfied that the
EXPLORER can perform all that her builder has promised,
and few of them would be willing to risk a bet
against her thorough success.

—*Panama Star and Herald,* May 1867

LONGSTANDING American interest in dominating the natural resources of the Pacific, as well as an innate Yankee desire to extend American hegemony into the Pacific, had both inspired and abetted the Pacific Pearl Company's decision to send Julius Kroehl and the *Sub Marine Explorer* to Panama. In that vein, Panama had first come to prominence in competing British and American schemes to revitalize the Isthmus of Panama as an oceanic shortcut to the Pacific Ocean.

Panama is the crossroads of the Americas. Only 47 miles wide at its narrowest spot, Panama had flourished as a link in Spain's far-flung maritime empire between the 16th and early 19th centuries, only to decline in prominence as Spanish power waned. During the struggles for independence from Spain, South American patriots attempted to use the isthmus as a political bargaining chip to gain foreign support. Venezuelan General Francisco Miranda offered a Panamanian canal concession to Britain in exchange for support, but nothing came of it. When Panama itself became independent from Spain in 1821, it joined the new republic of Gran Colombia, with Bogotá as its capital, but within two decades Panamanian patriots made four separate but short-lived attempts to take control from the central government in Bogotá. Gran Colombia split into three smaller states in 1830, with Panama remaining part of Nueva Granada, with its capital remaining in Bogotá. The Panama route languished, in the view of European critics at least, because of these "frequent revolutions . . . and the consequent poverty and want of enterprise in the Spanish part of the population."[1]

Panama returned to international attention when British and American entrepreneurs in Chile and Peru founded the Pacific Steam Navigation Company. Their plans were publicized in 1838 when the Honorable Peter Campbell Scarlett published an account of his South American and isthmian travels and included a prospectus for the company in his book. "The establishment of steam navigation along the southern shores of the Pacific Ocean, in connexion with the Passage of the Isthmus of Panama to the Atlantic, has created much interest," the prospectus read, "since the trade of the countries whose shores are washed by that sea has been thrown open; and, as commerce and intercourse have increased, a still greater interest has been manifested."[2]

The Pacific Steam Navigation Company built two steamers, *Chile* and *Peru,* and sent them into the Pacific via the Straits of Magellan. It was not until February 1842 that the first of them, *Chile,* finally reached Panama City after a year and half of operation farther south. Regular connection with Panama was not again achieved until 1846, however, when the company placed another ship, *Ecuador,* into service and received a contract from the British government to transport the mails via Panama. By 1847 the company placed a fourth steamer in service and was able to advertise joint sailings linking with Royal Mail steamers calling at Chagres, on Panama's Caribbean shore. It remained in service for several years. This route revitalized the isthmus as an international link.[3] It also attracted renewed American interest, which coincided with the recent conquest of California by the United States during the Mexican War.

AMERICANS IN PANAMA

Initial US interests in the isthmus date to the 1780s. In 1842 the US position was clearly enunciated by acting secretary of state Fletcher Webster to the US consul in Bogotá, William M. Blackford: "It is of great importance to the United States that the railroad or canal . . . should be constructed, and that we should have free use of it upon the same terms as the citizens or subjects of other nations."[4] In 1845 Secretary of State James Buchanan instructed

Benjamin Bidlack, chargé d'affaires at Bogotá, to collect information about any foreign schemes for a railroad or canal across the isthmus because the United States had "strong motives for viewing with interest any project which may be designed to facilitate the intercourse between the Atlantic and Pacific oceans." Buchanan also reminded Bidlack that it was important that "no other nation should obtain an exclusive privilege or an advantage," and that "you will use your influence . . . with the government of New Granada, to prevent it from granting privileges to any other nation which might prove injurious to the United States."[5]

To help secure American privileges, the United States signed a treaty with Colombia at Bogotá on December 12, 1846. The treaty was a step forward, but it also concerned Secretary of State John M. Clayton, who wrote to chargé d'affaires Thomas M. Foote, that the rights it gave the United States were laden with responsibilities, not the least of which was a guarantee of neutrality and sovereignty. Speculating that British financial interests on the isthmus might lead the British government to "seize the isthmus of Panama" to settle debts, Clayton felt that this might bring "an inevitable war" between the United States and Britain.[6] Just the previous year, the two nations had settled their differences over the northern border, with the United States gaining the Oregon Territory and a boundary 300 miles north of the Columbia River. Tensions remained, however, thanks to the imperial expansionist ambitions of both nations.

War did come in 1846, but with Mexico, not Great Britain. The conquest of California during that war only heightened American interest in Panama. With its new Pacific possession firmly in hand in 1847, Congress subsidized the creation of two steamship lines to operate on the Panama Route and link the eastern seaboard with California and Oregon. Chartered in 1848, the United States Mail Steamship Company and the Pacific Mail Steamship Company built steamers to connect New York with Chagres, on the isthmus's Caribbean shores, and Panama City with San Francisco. Both companies expected to lose money on passenger and freight service, but the discovery of gold in California in 1848 and the resultant rush brought hundreds of thousands of eager gold seekers to Panama's shores. The two steamship lines flourished and expanded, building major bases of operation on both sides of the isthmus.

While Panama City's population swelled monthly with thousands of Yankees transiting through town, and then declined as they left, a number of

Americans remained behind to establish businesses that changed the character of the isthmus. These enterprises started small. In April 1849 Joseph Crackbon stopped in Gorgona, where "several Americans have taken huts here & at Chagres and gone into business furnishing provisions & liquor and are making money as fast as they would probably dig it in California. The American people will soon revolutionize this Country."[7]

This was not viewed with universal delight by the Panamanians. In 1851 J. D. Borthwick wrote that "in establishing their hotels at different points at the Chagres River, the Americans encountered great opposition from the natives, who wished to reap all the benefit of the travel themselves; but there were too many centuries behind the age to have any chance in fair competition, and so they resorted to personal threats and violence, till the persuasive eloquence of Colt's revolvers, and the overwhelming numbers of American travelers, convinced them that they were wrong, and that they had better submit to their fate."[8] Albert Wells, in Panama in December 1849, wrote home about the changes in the city: "Restaurants are plenty here and are coming into existence fresh every morning. In fact our Countrymen are taking the business into their own hands here." He also felt that "if the California fever rages for only a few years many of our Enterprising Countrymen will be located permanently in this hot region."[9]

By early 1850, when British traveler Frank Marryat passed through Panama City, he found that "the streets present a vista of enormous sign-boards, and American flags droop from every house."[10] Panama City's newspapers, the *Panama Star,* the *Panama Herald,* and the *Panama Echo,* were founded by American gold seekers temporarily delayed on the isthmus.

German miner Carl Meyer, passing through Panama in 1850, found that "a ray of revival and of new creation shines in the heart of the city. On Main Street, which has already lost its original Spanish name," new shops and restaurants had opened. "That great nation which seems destined to elevate lands and nations from their decay and lethargy has also achieved astonishing results here in a short time. The citizens of the United States have been able to make a new stopping place in Panama for the world of commerce and trade." The City of Panama, opined Meyer, "will flourish again like her old demolished predecessor, only it is not the Castilian but the Yankee who assures her progress."[11]

Journalist Bayard Taylor, also in Panama City in 1850, found that "the city was already half American. The native boys whistled 'Yankee Doodle' on the streets. . . . Nearly half the faces seen were American, and the signs on shops of all kinds appeared in our language."[12] By 1854 traveler R. G. S. Ten Broeck still found the city "ruinous and decayed, 'the mere shadow of its former self,' everything about it shows a woeful lack of energy and enterprise, 'los Yankis' however are building it up again and when the Rail-Road is completed, it will once more be a place of considerable commercial importance."[13]

SPANNING AND DOMINATING PANAMA

Ten Broeck was referring to an ongoing endeavor to establish a railroad to reopen the isthmus as a highway of commerce. In December 1848 a group of New York entrepreneurs headed by William Henry Aspinwall, the president of the Pacific Mail Steamship Company, signed a contract with Nueva Grenada's officials to construct an isthmian railroad. The Panama Railroad Company was chartered in 1849, and in June 1850 the Nueva Grenadian legislature ratified the contract.

Work began immediately but progressed slowly. The builders contended with malarial swamps, dense jungle, steep mountain passes, and high fatalities. Gold rush traffic in the thousands spurred on construction, with passengers disembarking now at Aspinwall, the Caribbean terminus. This new American town rose as a rival to Chagres, while Panama City filled with American-owned businesses. All were built, said Frank Marryat, "with American money and for American purposes." In Panama, "the advantages of the California emigration are entirely reaped by foreigners."[14]

When it was completed in January 1855, with the last link to the Pacific opened, the railroad began to reap tremendous dividends. Nueva Granada had granted the Panama Railroad exclusive rights for 49 years in return for 3 percent of the net profits. The profits between 1853 and 1905 totaled $37.8 million, but Nueva Granada settled for less. A financially strapped Bogotá government concluded a new contract in 1867 for a $1 million payment and a $250,000 annuity, while the Panama Railroad had its concession extended by 99 years.[15]

The Panama Railroad, the first transcontinental railroad in the Americas, had an impact beyond a financial one. The rapidly developing Pacific Coast of the United States, particularly the principal port, San Francisco, made good use of Panama. Pacific Mail steamers running from Panama City linked every major American port on the West Coast, as well as steamers running across the

Pacific to Asia after 1867. The majority of passengers bound to and from California crossed the isthmus; in all, 808,769 persons transited Panama between 1848 and 1869, when a transcontinental railroad was completed in the United States. Tremendous treasure, often in excess of $1 million per biweekly voyage, was shipped from California's mines across Panama to waiting steamers bound for New York.[16]

By the end of the Civil War, Panama was an important link in America's growing empire. Steam and iron had conquered Panama's jungles and swamps, and to some expansion-minded Yankees, Panama by right of enterprise and ingenuity should become part of the United States. American interests were also apparent in the schemes of entrepreneurs seeking other opportunities in addition to servicing the route's needs, notably the Pacific Pearl Company's interest in the pearl fishery.

REVIVING THE PEARL FISHERY

Ships sailing to Panama City in the late-eighteenth century, as they came in sight of land, were guided by an unusual aid to navigation, the twin spires of the city's cathedral. On bright days, the tips of the spires flashed in the sunlight, pinpointing the way as surely as a lighthouse. The source of that illumination was an amazing array of hundreds of oyster shells, the shiny mother-of-pearl that caught and reflected the sun's rays. The shells, symbols of wealth pulled from the sea, were a fitting reminder to those who entered the magnificent church that Panama was a source of potential fortune for those who sought to wrest pearls from the waters of the Bay of Panama, and that the sea had yielded harvests of oysters, mother-of-pearl, and pearls since before Panama was born. Many a bended knee and fervent prayer beneath those spires had doubtless sought divine assistance in finding enough pearls—or that special pearl—that would transform a poor man into a rich one.

The pearls came from an archipelago a day's sail out of Panama, a cluster of more than a hundred islands inhabited since the first century CE. Like many coastal islands, these are the tips of mountains that once dominated an ancient coast, a shoreline drowned by rising seas after the last great ice age 10,000 years ago. Valleys and slopes, now submerged, became a rocky seabed, host to a diverse range of marine life. On the rocks of the seabed, colonies of oysters clustered, their flesh providing sustenance, their shells and the occasional pearl

providing decoration to the people who arrived in the islands 9,000 years after the islands were surrounded by the sea. Archaeological evidence from the
islands includes pearls from burials, among them pearls drilled to be strung as
necklaces and bracelets.[17]

When Columbus set out from Spain in 1492, among the instructions he
received from his monarchs was that he also seek out pearls. During his first
two voyages, Columbus failed to encounter pearls, despite questioning the
natives and showing them pearls he carried with him from Spain. It was not
until his third voyage, in 1498, that he succeeded. On the voyage, as Columbus
headed farther south than he had gone in his two previous voyages, he reached
the island of Trinidad and pressed on to the Gulf of Paria, on the northern
coast of South America (now Venezuela), arriving in August. There, the admiral collected gold and pearls—so many that he named this the "Cabo de las
Perlas," or the "Pearl Coast," a name that would inspire others to follow and
give rise to the first European pearl fisheries in the New World.[18] When news
of Columbus's discovery of a land rich in gold, pearls, and potential slaves
reached Spain in December 1498, fortune seekers mounted several expeditions
to the Pearl Coast. Between 1499 and 1504, these Europeans explored the coast,
"discovered" new lands and rivers, including the Orinoco, and landed on Mar-
garita Island, named by Columbus, where they traded for pearls.[19]

When the Spanish adventurer Vasco Nuñez de Balboa finally crossed the
Isthmus of Panama, ostensibly "discovering" the Pacific, his inspiration was to
avoid arrest in Spain and garner riches for himself and his sovereign. Balboa
wrote to the king about what he learned from the natives he encountered on
his travels on the isthmus. He had been told that beyond the mountains of the
coast there was another sea, easily navigated by canoes. "I believe that there are
many islands in that sea. They say that there are many large pearls, and that the
caciques have baskets of them. . . . It is a most astonishing thing and without
equal, that our Lord has made this land."[20]

When he finally crossed Panama and reached the Pacific in 1513, Balboa
and his men took to canoes and followed the islands down to a village by the
sea. Storming into the village, Balboa took control. He was able to convince
Tumaco, the fleeing cacique, or chief, of the village, to return. Tumaco gave
Balboa gold and a basin of pearls, 240 of them "of extraordinary size. This was
indeed something worthy of an Oriental India."[21] Tumaco was surprised at
the Spaniards' reaction, because for him, the flesh of the oysters was far more

valuable to his people as food. When Balboa understood that the natives considered the pearls to be of lesser value, and that the pearls were often spoiled by being roasted inside the oysters over an open fire, he instructed his hosts in how, in the future, the Spaniards would prefer the pearls.

Returning with a larger force of men, the Spaniards enslaved the people of the islands, which they renamed the Archipiélago de las Perlas. For the next century, the islands were the setting of terrible misery as the natives slowly died out from disease and overwork. As divers depleted the shallower oyster beds of their pearls, the natives were forced to go deeper. The Spaniards tied heavy rocks to the feet of their slaves, handed them a sack and a knife, and dumped them over the side of the boat. Plummeting to the bottom, holding their breath against the tremendous pressure, the divers searched for oysters, stuffed them into the sack, and then cut the rope to rise again to the surface. On the boat, the crew pried the oysters open to search for pearls. No pearls meant another trip to the bottom for the diver, while success brought a temporary respite. Often men surfaced with blood streaming from their noses, ears, and mouths. The life span of a native diver, owing to these conditions and to European diseases, was painfully short. By the sixteenth century the natives of the islands were extinct, and the Spaniards imported large numbers of black slaves to replace them. The descendants of these slaves still populate the Pearl Islands.[22] The desire for additional pearls spread Spanish pearl-diving enterprises north to the oyster-rich waters of Mexico's Baja California peninsula.[23]

By the early-nineteenth century the fishery had declined due to overexploitation, although most observers did not see that. They assumed the timeless tradition of breath-holding divers was limited or inefficient, even while admiring the divers' skills. In 1838 Captain Edward Belcher of the Royal Navy visited the Pearl Islands and described the diving operations:

> The depth on which they usually fish, is about five or six fathoms, the bottom uneven and rocky, or stony. The boat, in the present instance, being anchored in a tideway, the padron commenced by repeating prayers, in which he was joined by the rest of the crew, amounting to seven. This ended, they divested themselves of superfluities, and almost simultaneously inhaling a long breath, dived feet foremost. The average time of immersion ranged from forty to forty-two seconds, and on reaching the surface, they had generally

seven or ten oysters each, about the size of a cheese plate, packed from the left hand to the left shoulder, four being firmly secured between three fingers and thumb; all this is effected under water. Upon offering rewards for those who could remain longest under water, we were only able at first to witness seventy-six seconds. But after a little practice, the padron remained beneath the surface ninety-six seconds, bringing up seven oysters from the depth of seven fathoms. From what we witnessed of his exhaustion, and the reports of others who repute him their best diver, I am strongly inclined to doubt the suspension of breathing, with power of exertion, for a longer period. The fishery is carried on at their own expense and risk; they either sell the oysters, and open them in the presence of the purchaser, at a real or less per dozen, or take the risk themselves; in fact, a novel species of gambling has arisen, in which many of us indulged without adding to our wealth; completely the reverse, for many of us, ashamed to have nothing to show, purchased pearls. One exception, however, occurred in the consul's servant, who turned up a prize worth, I was told, about forty dollars.

I examined the collections of several dealers in these articles, who reside here in readiness to purchase during the diving season. Some were enormous, as large as nine tenths of an inch long, by five tenths diameter, but pear shaped, and of bad colour. Indeed, none that I saw would be reckoned fine in England, and amongst some thousand large ones, very few were perfectly round. The Yslas del Rey cover about four hundred square miles, and comprise numerous islets, and probably thirty or forty fishing villages. The quantity of pearls estimated at the season, is about two gallons.[24]

Even during the height of the gold rush and the bustling crowds that regularly and hurriedly crossed the isthmus, the old pearl beds of Panama attracted attention. Carl Meyer, the literate and history-minded German gold seeker, wrote in 1849 that the Pearl Islands were "rocky and bleak, partly encrusted with sea salts by the waves and partly covered with guano." The pearl fishery had declined because the price of pearls had dropped. "Several companies have attempted to stimulate and enlarge the business but without the desired result. It will not be easy to bring back to the pearl fisheries near Panama such happy times as those of which the most striking monuments are the pearl shell deco-rated towers of the cathedral."[25]

In July 1852 an article in the *San Francisco Daily Alta California,* quot-ing from the *Panama Herald,* explained that following Panama's independence from Spain, Spanish control over the fishery had ended, and also the duty, "pearls being considered as the natural products of the sea, and like all other fish, free to all. There is, now, no duty required—every man enjoys the same privilege in common with another, and is entitled to all the results of his labor. He can dive anywhere in the waters of the bay, and is protected in the posses-sion of all he can in this way acquire."[26]

The article went on to describe the Pearl Islands. "There are, at this time, from twelve to fifteen hundred persons engaged in the pearl fisheries of these islands." The pearl divers recovered between $80,000 to $150,000 in pearls each year, and from 900 to 1,000 tons of pearl shells, averaging in value $40,000. "These shells were formerly esteemed as worthless, but recently they have be-come the chief article of export from this country, being worth from thirty to forty dollars per ton."

The recovery of the pearls and shells, however, was a "dangerous pursuit." The divers worked in three to seven fathoms of water to bring up six to twelve shells at a time, diving at low tide to go deeper into the beds since the shallower areas had been picked clean of oysters. They worked 2½ to 3 hours, diving 12 to 15 times:

> The best divers remain underwater from fifty-eight to sixty-one
> seconds, but the most of them can only remain under from forty-
> five to fifty seconds. It is altogether a mistaken idea that has gone
> abroad, and is now currently believed, that pearl divers can remain
> under water ten and fifteen minutes. We have conversed with a
> distinguished gentleman of this city, who has been engaged in the
> pearl trade upwards of thirty years, upon this point. And he assures
> us that the very longest time he ever knew a diver to remain under
> water was sixty-one seconds, and that he was induced to do so by
> the promise of a reward at two or three ounces doubloons.[27]

What was obvious was that great wealth lay beneath the water, "though at so great a depth as to defy the skill of the diver." But technology provided an an-swer, the *Daily Alta California* stated. "By means of a submarine armor, or by the use of a proper machine constructed for the purpose, in connection with a submarine armor, we have no doubt that that a fortune could be realized in a very short time."

The article continued, "The shells alone which could be thus obtained, would defray any outlay for such an apparatus and all the expenses attending such an operation," and "that the best and largest pearls are found in deep water." To try and harvest these, an unnamed English company "some years since obtained a privilege to fish with diving-bells; but the enterprise proved a total failure in consequence of the unevenness of the bottom. Since then no attempt of a similar character has been made, nor has any machinery or apparatus ever been used to bring up the shells."

Despite the potential for profit, and the article's assurances that the Pearl Islands were "considered remarkably healthy" and that "the inhabitants, who are mostly black, are kind, hospitable and inoffensive," no diving suit and helmet apparatus had yet worked the archipelago's beds, and Henry Sears's Nautilus bell, while shipped out to the Pacific, had ventured only into the waters of Baja California.

A decade later, in 1862, the *Scientific American* published an article on "The Pearl Fishery of Panama" and noted the arrival of diving equipment introduced by "enterprising merchants" to "prosecute it on a more extensive scale than ever before" with "submarine armor imported from London by Mr. Steffins." "We hope that in their submarine explorations of the 'unfathomed caves' they may find many a gem."[28] At that time, the American Civil War was still raging, but a year after the article's publication, an invalided Julius Kroehl was in New York soliciting funds for his submarine, and mindful of the potentials in Panama, perhaps with the *Scientific American* clipping in hand, he and his investors formed the Pacific Pearl Company.

The potential for profit lay not only in shipping pearls to the United States but also to Europe. In 1861 an article in Britain noted that pearl shell imports from Panama had been increasing "in late years," with four ships carrying 650 tons of shell arriving in the United Kingdom, while in 1859, 957 tons of shells had arrived at British ports. All of the shells had been collected "at the islands in the Bay of Panama."[29]

Four years later Julius Kroehl and *Sub Marine Explorer* landed at the steamship dock in Aspinwall, where dockside steam cranes hoisted the crated submarine parts onto the railcars of the Panama Railroad for the day-long ride through the jungle, across the rivers and ravines, and down the mountains to the Pacific shore in Panama City.[30]

REASSEMBLY, TESTS, AND DISASTER

Kroehl unloaded the submarine at the railroad station, on the edge of Panama Bay, and set to work. In December the *Panama Star and Herald* reported: "A new diving apparatus, intended for Pearl fishing in this bay has been recently brought out from New York, and is now in course of construction at the Railroad Station. It is a boat about 36 feet in length, constructed in such a way as to be capable of propulsion at a depth of several fathoms under water, and persons can remain working below for several hours in succession. The apparatus will be complete within two months, and in the mean time we shall be enabled to furnish our readers with a full description of it."[31] Hopes were high for the submarine and its engineer. In January 1867 a news report in Cleveland noted that "a New York company of wealth have sent a party to the Pearl fisheries, in the Bay of Panama, equipped with a submarine boat. Many persons think the company will secure untold wealth."[32]

Three months passed without the full reassembly of *Explorer*. This may have been due to the loss of one of Kroehl's men. In January 1867 the *New York Daily Tribune* reported that a recent outbreak of yellow fever in Panama City had claimed three lives, among them "Mr. Kuster, late of New York, who is connected with the Pacific Pearl Diving Company."[33] In early March a Panama-based correspondent reported to the *New York Times* that Kroehl, who "has spent $30,000 or more in Panama in constructing a boat for pearl-hunting, has come to a halt from lack of funds—the company in New York having come to the conclusion that men are willing, or ought to be willing, to work for glory in Panama."[34] Apparently trying to help, the *Brooklyn Daily Eagle* reported on March 4 that "a wealthy New York company have sent a party to the pearl fisheries, in the Bay of Panama, equipped with a submarine boat. Many persons think that the company will secure untold wealth."[35]

Three weeks later, however, the *Panama Star and Herald* wrote that "we are glad to see that the work on the Pearl Diving Boat, which was temporarily suspended was again resumed last week, and the top, a piece weighing 13 tons was successfully put on. There is comparatively little now to be done to finish the work, and we trust in a few weeks to see the boat launched."[36] It was not until the end of May, however, that the *Star and Herald* announced the launch: "The sub-marine boat *Explorer* was most successfully launched from the Railroad Company's works on Wednesday, the 29th instant, under the superintendence of her builder, Mr. Kroahl [*sic*], and can now be seen afloat off the wharf. In a few days she will be taken to the Pacific Mail Steamship Company's islands, where the experiment of submerging her will take place. Sceptics are now tolerably well satisfied that the *Explorer* can perform all that her builder has promised, and few of them would be willing to risk a bet against her thorough success."[37] A year had passed since Julius Kroehl had submerged *Explorer* on her well-publicized trial dive in the East River, surfacing with a pail of mud to cheers.

The trials that followed the launch in Panama, based out of Flamenco Island, approximately four miles offshore from the railroad depot, were successful. On June 22 the *Panama Star and Herald* reported:

> The Pacific Pearl Company's submarine boat *Explorer,* the launching of which from the Railroad Co.'s works we announced some days ago, made a most successful trial trip under water on the 20th inst. Mr. J. H. Kroehl, the builder, took her to Flamenco and went to a depth of 22 feet, remaining below about an hour. Every thing worked most satisfactorily, except that it was impossible to procure a sufficient pressure of steam from the boiler of the *Panama*[38] to enable Mr. Kroehl to make as extensive experiments as he would have wished; however he is fully satisfied of the perfect success of the boat, and has invited a few friends to witness a second trial this afternoon, when he will be happy to take down with him any ladies or gentlemen whose curiosity or love of novelty may induce them to take a peep at the bottom of the ocean.[39]

Two days later, the *Panama Star and Herald* commented that

> Another experiment was made on Saturday [June 22] by Mr. Kroahl, with the Pacific Pearl Company's submarine boat Explorer, which proved most successful. Mr. Kroahl went to a depth of about twenty-five feet and remained below about fifteen minutes; he was accompanied by Captain Stone, as volunteer, and four assistants. The experiment was witnessed by the President of the State, General Olarte; the Secretary of State, Mr. Bermudez, and some twenty other invited guests, all of whom are now fully satisfied that the *Explorer* is competent to perform everything in the way of submarine

labor that her builder has represented, and we trust that as soon as
Mr. Kroahl can complete his arrangements he and his associates
may reap a rich harvest from the enterprise."[40]

Another correspondent, writing to the *New York Times,* took note and reported
in June that "Mr. KROEHL's new submarine iron boat Explorer intended to
hunt out pearl shells and pearls from the bottom of the ocean, has made two
successful trips down among the fishes, and will go to the Lower California
coast as soon as the Company in New York fit out a steam tender for her."[41]

At this time, the US consul in Panama, Thomas Kilby Smith, wrote home:

> The pearl oysters abound near the Pearl Islands of Panama, some
> forty miles distant. I have not visited them as yet, but expect to
> shortly. There are now employed upon these islands an average
> of four hundred and fifty native divers. A boat, or submarine ex-
> plorer as it is called, has been invented, and is now here, by means
> of which it is expected that larger and finer pearls and shells than
> have ever before been brought to light, will be fished up. The usual
> method of fishing is attended with many disadvantages and dan-
> gers. The divers cannot go beyond a certain depth, about seven
> fathoms. They are at all times in danger of an attack from the
> Tinteros ground sharks and Macugos. They can only work three
> hours per day, just before and after low slack water, on account of
> the heavy currents. These difficulties, it is expected, by the use of
> new and improved machinery, will be overcome.[42]

At the same time, the Pacific Pearl Company took steps to patent the submarine. In August 1867 George Wrightson hired British patent attorney Alexander
Melville Clark to file a provisional patent for their "apparatus for submarine
communication." The provisional patent was granted on August 29.[43]

Then disaster struck. The *Panama Star and Herald* reported on September 12:

> It is with painful feelings of regret we record the death of Julius H.
> Kroehl, who died in this city on the afternoon of Monday, the 9th
> inst., after a brief illness of fever. Mr. Kroehl was born in Germany,
> but early in life emigrated to the United States, of which country
> he became a naturalized citizen in 1840. He was a submarine en-
> gineer by profession, and brought an excellent education and rare

intelligence and talent to its practice. When the war broke out he entered the naval service of his adopted country, and was engaged in the Gulf squadron, and took part in the actions which resulted in the capture of New Orleans from the Confederates. He retired from the service after the close of war, taking with him very flattering testimonials of respect and esteem from his superior officers, and again engaged in the private practice of his profession, which brought him to Panama about twelve months ago, where he was engaged by a company of New York gentlemen to construct the pearl diving machine now lying in our harbor. In social life Mr. Kroehl was much esteemed for his many genial qualities and genuine warm-heartedness, and his loss has cast a deep gloom over our community, in which he was widely and favorably known. He leaves a wife and children in the US to mourn their loss, to whom we offer our very sincere sympathies and condolence. The remains of the deceased were interred in the Foreign Cemetery with Masonic honors.[44]

On September 21, 1867, Consul Smith wrote from Panama City that Julius Kroehl, "a naturalized American citizen . . . superintendent and chief engineer of the Pacific Pearl Company, and [who] was attending their works here" had died "on the ninth of September from fever. His funeral was conducted by the Masonic fraternity here."[45] The consul's letter also reported that "[Kroehl] also has a large interest in a submarine boat here amounting it is said to some $10,000, but this is in connection with the Pacific Pearl Co. of No. 38 Broad Street, New York. His wife Sophia R. Kroehl resides in Georgetown, D.C. I have written her by this mail."[46]

In February, probably spurred by Brumagim or another California investor, the *San Francisco Daily Alta California* reported on *Explorer,* a "submarine boat, made of boiler iron . . . open at the bottom."[47] The article commented on the technology involved in replenishing the air inside the craft, noting it was the "invention or application . . . we believe, by Mr. Ryerson, a Californian inventor." The "boat and apparatus have been tried in New York harbor with the most satisfactory results," and after having been "taken apart, shipped to Panama, and there put together," the submarine was about to depart for the Pearl Islands. The article then commented enthusiastically about the chances for profit. The San Francisco article, uncritical and uninformed, was the subject of comment by the *Panama Star and Herald* at the end of February:

> The Alta of San Francisco has an article on the enterprise of the Pacific Pearl Co. in the bay of Panama, the little submarine boat which was built and successfully launched here some eight or nine months ago. The Alta says in regard to the boat: "It is expected that she will soon start on her pioneer expedition to the Bay of Pearls fifty miles from Panama, where 450 native divers get pearls enough to pay them for their labor. The Pacific Pearl Company, of which Mark Brumagim is President, and in which a number of Californians own stock, is incorporated in New York, and has published a pamphlet, in which the annual expenses are estimated at $33,500, the gross income $197,850 from shells, and $250,000 from pearls, leaving a net income of $414,350. Of course, the enterprise is hazardous in its nature, but it is not too wild to deserve the attention, interest and encouragement of the press. It is understood that if they succeed at Panama, they will soon send a boat to the Gulf of California."

The *Star and Herald* went on to note:

> It is very probable that if the Company had used ordinary energy and judgment in completing the boat, and supplying the necessary means for sending her to the Pearl Islands and working her there when she was finished, the speculation should have turned out a success, but it is very evident that nothing remunerative can ever be expected from her as she now lies neglected and apparently abandoned, on the sand beach at the island of Flamenco, some three miles from Panama, where no pearls exist. If the Company either wish or hope to realize anything from this speculation beyond a dead loss, they had better send a suitable steamboat and competent men here and get the machine to work at once. That is the only way of ascertaining its usefulness.[48]

With Kroehl gone, *Explorer* languished. In August 1868 an article in the *Philadelphia Inquirer* asked, "What has become of the Pacific Pearl Company? Their little submarine boat, which cost one way or another nearly one hundred thousand dollars, has been lying neglected on the sand beach at one of the islands in the Bay of Panama for almost a year past. When its unfortunate builder, Mr. Kroehl, was alive there was a fair prospect of its being a success if funds had been supplied to him to work it, but now it looks as if the boat were entirely abandoned, or if it is not it will very soon, if not already, prove entirely useless."[49]

THE LAST DIVES

Another year passed before the press made another mention of *Explorer*. The Pacific Pearl Company obviously employed a sympathetic editor or two, as a flurry of newspaper accounts suddenly appeared. On August 13, 1869, the *Panama Mercantile Chronicle* reported on *Explorer,* then working on an "experimental expedition of the Pacific Pearl Company to the island of St. Elmo, in the Bay of Panama":

> The *Explorer* is 36 feet long, 12 feet high, and 13 feet broad, its bottom is perfectly flat, and has two hatches 4½ feet and 6 feet long respectively. These hatches, as the machine approaches the bottom, are opened for the purpose of gathering the oysters, the water being kept at bay during the submersion by the air contained within the machine. Through these apertures, when the machine rests on or near the bottom, the oysters are collected and stowed away by the men within. The shape of the machine resembles somewhat the upper segment of a short, thick cigar, with a turret in the middle of the top part for the entrance of the men who descend in it. The machine, when under water, is moved over the bottom in search of oysters by means of a small propeller, three feet in diameter, worked by hand by the men inside.

In the only known description of a dive in the submarine, the *Panama Mercantile Chronicle* account went on to explain:

> The manner of working the *Explorer* is as follows: Before going down a powerful air pump, having a cylinder of nine and half inches diameter, and driven by an engine of thirty horsepower, forces air into the compressed air chamber until it is compressed to the density of about sixty pounds; the men then enter the machine through the turret at the top; the cap or top of this turret is securely

screwed down, and as the water or ballast chamber is allowed to fill, the machine gradually sinks and approaches the bottom. When once fairly down a sufficient quantity of air is let into the working chamber from the compressed air chamber, until it has gained sufficient volume and force as to counter-balance the tremendous pressure of the water from without; when this is done the hatches in the bottom of the machine are opened, and the men proceed to take in the oysters, the air within the working chamber completely checking the ingress of the water. When the men have been down a sufficient length of time, and having collected all the shell within reach, air from the compressed air chamber is let into the ballast or water, and as the air slowly forces out the water, the machine as slowly and surely rises to the surface.

The *New York Times,* in an August 29, 1869, story on the submarine, reported on "the actual working of the vessel at St. Elmo" taken from a recent account published in the *Panama Journal:*

> Inflated with forty-six pounds of compressed air, then partially filled with water, it went down at 11 a.m., remaining under water four hours, when it rose to the surface with 1,800 oysters, or about seven-eighths of a ton of shell. The machine afterward made one downward trip each day for eleven days, at the end of which all the men were again down with fever; and it being impossible to continue working with the same men for some time, it was decided, the experiment having proved a complete success, to lay the machine up in an adjacent cove and to convey to the Company the gratifying intelligence. We understand Mr. DINGEE proceeded to New York on the 31st ult. with the proceeds of the experimental trial—some 10½ tons of pearl shells and pearls to the value of $2,000, more or less.

"Mr. Dingee" was New York entrepreneur, arms dealer, and yachtsman Henry Augustus Dingee, a business associate of William M. B. Hartley and a man with enough familiarity with machinery to oversee *Explorer*'s operations.

Dingee, therefore, was *Explorer*'s last submarine engineer, a title he retained in the last contemporary reference to *Explorer,* appearing in the *Georgia Weekly Telegraph* in 1871. Citing an article in the *New York Commercial Advertiser,* the account described what appears to have been the first tests of *Explorer* off San Telmo: "At the first trial the thing struck a rock forty feet below the surface and lodged, and then slid off, taking a second plunge thirty feet further. The seven men who were inmates of the machine do not appear to have been in the least discomfited by this occurrence, as they spent six hours serenely surveying the ocean world around them, and at pleasure quickly rose to the surface. This happened ninety miles from Panama, near the Island of St. Elmo."[50] The account went on to describe how the submarine then made dives to recover a quantity of pearl oysters and return to New York. "The engineer of the 'Pacific Pearl Company' by whom this success was achieved, is now in this city, and his submarine iron diver is safely moored at St. Elmo."

The *San Francisco Daily Alta California,* ever sympathetic to the Pacific Pearl Company, also commented in their August 29 edition on how "American ingenuity" had developed the craft that would "sink down to the pearl bed . . . open underneath, so that workmen can walk about on the bottom of the sea, pick up the shells and put them into baskets, to be lifted up by the boat when it rises to the surface."[51] The *Daily Alta California* noted that the dives of the "submarine boat, called the Explorer" had, according to "the latest advices . . . commenced in a most satisfactory manner. Large quantities of shells and *some* [my emphasis] pearls have already been collected and a cargo has arrived at Panama."

The August 29, 1869, *New York Times* article mentioned that Dingee had returned with only $2,000 worth of results, which the *Boston Journal* noted was comprised of 12,700 pounds of pearl shells and "several hundred pearls" as the "first invoice of materials" of the Pacific Pearl Company.[52] It was the first and the last invoice. The 1871 *Georgia Weekly Telegraph* account made it clear that the Pacific Pearl Company's investors, while expending a great deal of money, had "made their experiment—but not their fortunes." An earlier, 1869 mention in the *Boston Journal* that the "company are talking of building additional boats and sending one to each of the main pearl fisheries of the world" had come to naught.[53] The old hope of a sale to the navy, however, still beckoned, although the *Georgia Weekly Telegraph* account less than accurately reported on its history: "The United States Government having made overtures some time ago for the purchase of the American pearl diving apparatus above described (to be used as a torpedo-boat or sub-marine ram), we may not hear of it again in the employment for which it was intended, but American enterprise is not subdued by temporary difficulties, and searches in the Pacific may be resumed ere long with renewed energy."[54] They were not. The same article commented that the engineer of the company (Dingee) was "now in this city" (New York) "and his submarine iron diver is safely moored at St. Elmo." This is the last known contemporary reference to *Sub Marine Explorer.* The Pacific Pearl Company was listed in the New York directory at 34 Wall Street in 1870, and then it vanished, never to be listed again.[55] The company died with a whimper, not a bang, quietly dissolved by the New York registrar of companies in 1924.[56] The US government canceled *Explorer*'s official registry as a US-flagged vessel in 1878 with the note "nature of loss unknown."[57] The submarine had been abandoned, the company had closed, and in that same year of 1878, the bankruptcy proceedings of one investor, William Headlam Jr. of Chicago, listed among his assets a number of shares of the Pacific Pearl Company, "all worthless."[58] All that remained of Julius Kroehl's dreams and his backers' ambitions were a few faded stock certificates, a mention of *Explorer* in a naval architectural journal, and a rusting submarine, its identity forgotten, emerging from the tidal surf each day on an isolated beach.

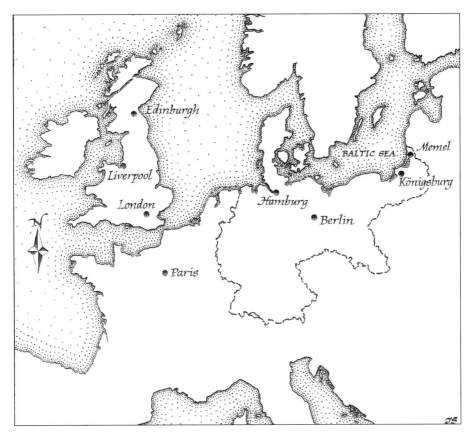

Figure 1. Prussia at the time of Julius Kroehl's birth, showing East Prussia and Memel on the Baltic Sea. (Map by Jack Scott)

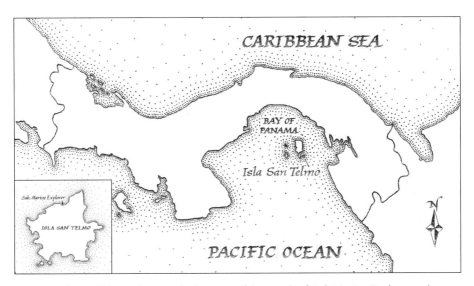

Figure 2. Isla San Telmo, showing the location of the wreck of *Sub Marine Explorer;* and (inset) Panama, showing the location of Isla San Telmo. (Maps by Jack Scott)

►Figure 3. Julius Kroehl's passport, August 31, 1854. (Courtesy National Archives)

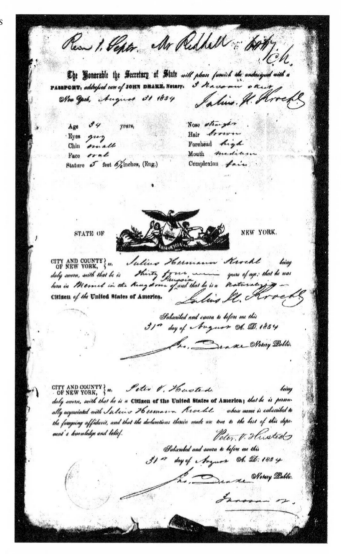

▼Figure 4. German map of Memel, Julius Kroehl's birthplace, in 1880. (From author's collection)

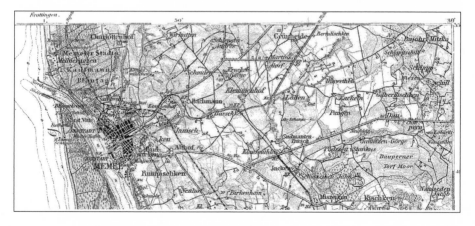

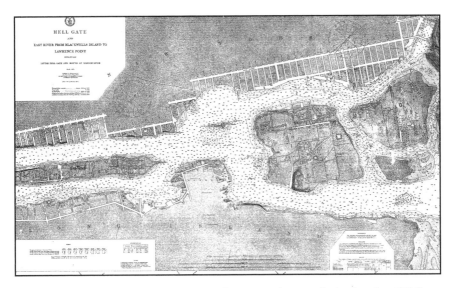

Figure 5. Detail of a chart of the East River, from 1903, showing the landmarks of Hell Gate, the setting for Kroehl, Husted, and Ryerson's blasting operations prior to the Civil War. (Courtesy National Oceanic and Atmospheric Administration, Historical Map and Chart Collection, Silver Spring, MD)

Figure 6. Interior of the Crystal Palace, showing its intricate cast iron construction. Julius Kroehl supervised the construction of the massive dome in the center of the fabled New York exhibition hall. (Courtesy New York Public Library Digital Collection #801379)

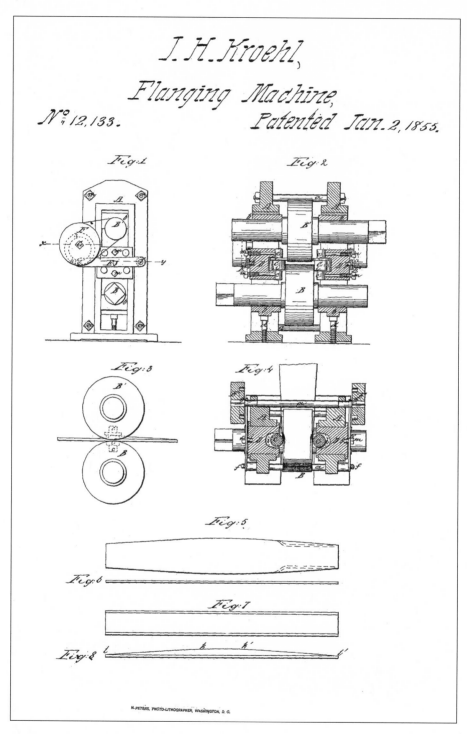

Figure 7. Julius Kroehl's patent for bending iron flanges, 1855. (Courtesy United States Patent Office)

Figure 8a–c. Modern views of
Kroehl's fire tower in Marcus
Garvey Park (formerly Mount
Morris Park) in Harlem.
(Photographs by author)

Figure 9. "Professor Maillefert and Naval Officers at Torpedo Station on James River," photograph by Matthew Brady. Benjamin Maillefert, shown in uniform, is holding court at a captured Confederate torpedo depot at Dutch Gap, April or May 1865. Maillefert and Kroehl were fierce competitors before and during the Civil War. (Courtesy National Archives, III-B-219)

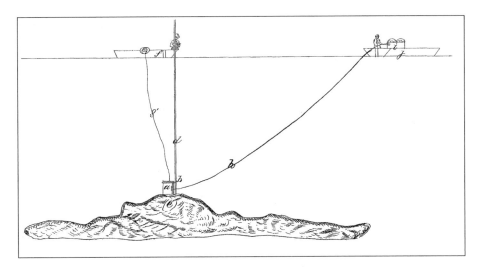

Figure 10. Benjamin Maillefert's patent for improvements in blasting rocks under water. His "torpedo" was inspired by Col. Charles William Pasley's, and the same method was also used by Peter Husted and Julius Kroehl in their underwater work. (Courtesy United States Patent Office)

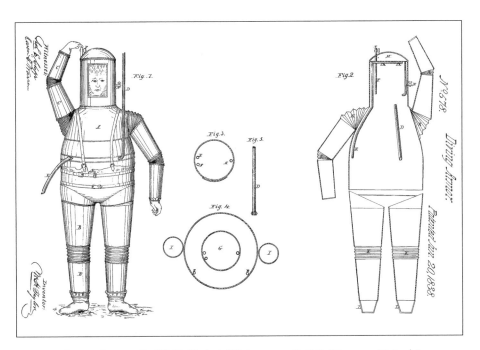

Figure 11. Patent drawing for W. H. Taylor's "diving armor," 1838. (Courtesy United States Patent Office)

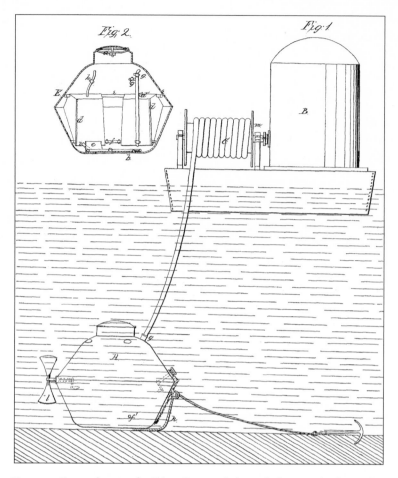

Figure 12. Patent drawing for Edgar Foreman's diving bell, 1853. The form of the "bell" is more like that of a submersible. (Courtesy United States Patent Office)

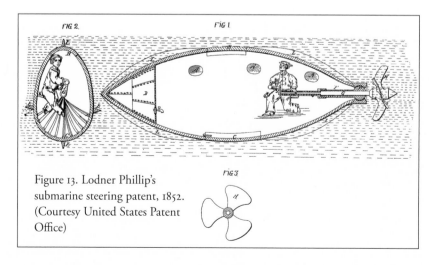

Figure 13. Lodner Phillip's submarine steering patent, 1852. (Courtesy United States Patent Office)

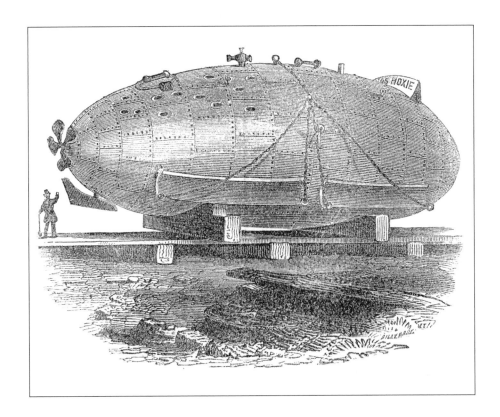

▲ Figure 14. The "New York submarine" of 1853, a locally built copy of the successful submersible diving bells of Dr. Prosper Antoine Payerne. (From author's collection)

◀ Figure 15. Alexander Dallas Bache, superintendent of the US Coast Survey, another Kroehl supporter and the supplier of his photographic apparatus for the Mississippi River campaign. (Courtesy National Oceanic and Atmospheric Administration)

▶ Figure 16. David Dixon Porter, Kroehl's staunchest supporter in the US Navy. Photograph by Matthew Brady, ca. 1864. (Courtesy US Naval History and Heritage Command, NH 47394)

▼ Figure 17. Julius Kroehl's manuscript map of the obstructions below Forts Jackson and St. Philip on the Mississippi River. (Courtesy National Oceanic and Atmospheric Administration, Historical Map and Chart Collection, Silver Spring, MD)

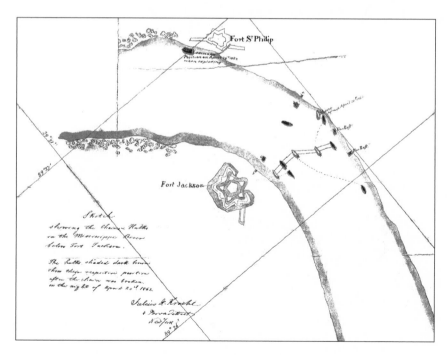

18. Gunboats *Itasca, Kennebeck, Winona,* and *Pinola* (with Kroehl aboard) reconnoiter the obstructions below Forts Jackson and St. Philip on April 20, 1862. The original engraving was published in *Harper's Weekly.* (Courtesy US Naval History and Heritage Command, NH 59066)

Figure 19. USS *Carondolet* on the river during the campaign to force open the Mississippi and capture Vicksburg. Kroehl is probably the photographer who captured this scene of the ironclad. (Courtesy US Naval History and Heritage Command, NH 63376)

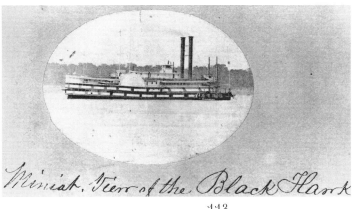

◀ Figure 20. USS *Black Hawk,* Kroehl's "home" while serving with Admiral Porter. (Courtesy US Naval History and Heritage Command, NH 63376)

▶ Figure 21. The Honorable Charles D. Poston, ca. 1865. Photograph by Matthew Brady. (Courtesy National Archives, 111-B-3183)

Figure 22. Charles D. Poston's shares in the Pacific Pearl Company. (Courtesy Sharlot Hall Museum and Archives)

Figure 23. Mark Brumagim (*seated to the left*) in Masonic regalia, ca. 1880. The Masonic order and the Order of the Odd Fellows were a common link binding the various members of the Pacific Pearl Company. (Courtesy Meriam Library, California State University, Chico)

Figure 24. William Henry Tiffany (Courtesy Yale University Library)

Figure 25. William M. B. Hartley. (From author's collection)

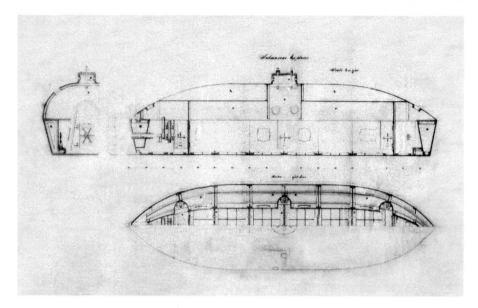

Figure 26. The only known original plan of Kroehl's *Sub Marine Explorer,* appended to W. W. W. Wood's report on the submarine. (Courtesy National Archives)

Figure 27. Profile drawing of *Sub Marine Explorer* published by the Pacific Pearl Company. (Courtesy Henry E. Huntington Library and Archives)

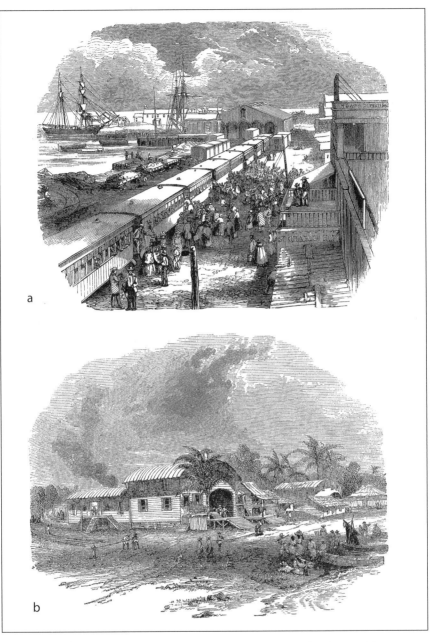

Figure 28. (a) The Aspinwall (Colon) terminal of the Panama Railroad, 1867. This is where Julius Kroehl and the partially disassembled *Sub Marine Explorer* landed to start their journey by rail across the isthmus; and (b) the Panama City terminal of the Panama Railroad, 1867. This is where Julius Kroehl and the partially disassembled *Sub Marine Explorer* landed at the end of their journey by rail across the isthmus. It was in these buildings that Kroehl reassembled his submarine. (From Otis, *History of the Panama Railroad,* 1855; author's collection)

▲ Figure 29. Aerial view of the cove and the wreck of *Sub Marine Explorer* at Isla San Telmo, 2008. Photograph by Lance Milbrand. (Courtesy Waitt Institute for Discovery)

▶ Figure 30. Doug Devine and Carlos Velasquez lidar-scanning *Sub Marine Explorer,* 2004. (Photograph by author)

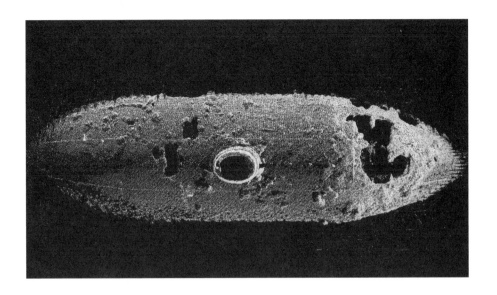

▲ Figure 31. Lidar
scan of *Sub Marine
Explorer*'s pressure
hull and dome, 2004.
(Image by EpicScan)

◄ Figure 32. Pearl
diver from La
Esmeralda, the closest
village to San Telmo,
2006. (Photograph by
author)

▲ Figure 33. James Delgado examines *Sub Marine Explorer* during an intermediate tide. Photograph by Marc Pike. (Courtesy Open Road Productions/Eco-Nova Productions.)

▶ Figure 34. Bert Ho of the National Oceanographic and Atmospheric Administration charts the waters off Isla San Telmo from a modified inflatable, 2006. (Photograph by Michael McCarthy)

▲ Figure 35. Todd Croteau and Bert Ho document the interior of *Sub Marine Explorer* at an intermediate tide, 2006. (Photograph by Michael McCarthy)

◀ Figure 36. Larry Murphy, Joshua Price, and Jacinto Almendra prepare for corrosion readings on *Sub Marine Explorer*'s starboard side, 2006. (Photograph by author)

▶ Figure 37. Donald Johnson measures corrosion thickness on *Sub Marine Explorer,* 2006. (Photograph by author)

▼ Figure 38. The 2006 *Sub Marine Explorer* archaeology team members (*left to right*): Todd Croteau, Joshua Price, Bert Ho, Michael McCarthy, Larry Murphy, Donald Johnson, James Delgado, Jacinto Almendra. Photograph by Todd Croteau. (Courtesy Historic American Engineering Record, National Park Service)

Figure 39. Erich Horgan assessing *Sub Marine Explorer*'s biological growth, 2008. Photograph by Lance Milbrand. (Courtesy Waitt Institute for Discovery.)

Figure 40. Fritz Hanselmann measuring damage to the submarine's port (offshore) side, 2008. (Photograph by author)

Figure 41. View of the starboard quarter at low tide, *Sub Marine Explorer,* 2008. (Photograph by author)

Figure 42. View of the bow, *Sub Marine Explorer,* 2008. (Photograph by author)

Figure 43. View of the stern, *Sub Marine Explore*r, 2008. (Photograph by author)

Figure 44. View of the conning tower, *Sub Marine Explorer,* 2008. (Photograph by author)

▲ Figure 45. View of the compressed air chamber, *Sub Marine Explorer,* 2008. (Photograph by author)

◀ Figure 46. View of the "dome" connecting the working chamber with the turret, as seen inside the compressed air chamber, *Sub Marine Explorer,* 2008. (Photograph by author)

Figure 47. View of the exposed intake valve, *Sub Marine Explorer*, 2006. (Photograph by Michael McCarthy)

Figure 48. View of the braces inside the compressed air chamber, *Sub Marine Explorer*, 2008. (Photograph by author)

Figure 49. View of the working chamber, showing the interior of the "dome" and the manifold, *Sub Marine Explorer*, 2006. (Photograph by author)

Figure 50. View of the working chamber, looking forward to the bow, *Sub Marine Explorer*, 2008. (Photograph by author)

Figure 53. The *San Francisco Call* on July 20, 1901, published this photograph of *Intelligent Whale*, falsely and unfairly characterizing the contemporary and close cousin of *Sub Marine Explorer* as a death trap. (chroniclingamerica.loc.gov)

Figure 51. Three views of equipment inside *Sub Marine Explorer*'s working chamber covered with concretions and marine organisms, 2008: (a) the high-pressure air line from the compressed air chamber into the working chamber; (b) an air line from a saltwater ballast tank; and (c) a ballast tank control valve. (Photographs by author)

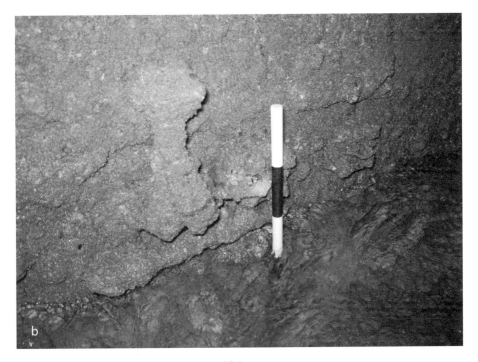

Figure 52. Damage to the stern plating of *Sub Marine Explorer*, 2008. (Photograph by author)

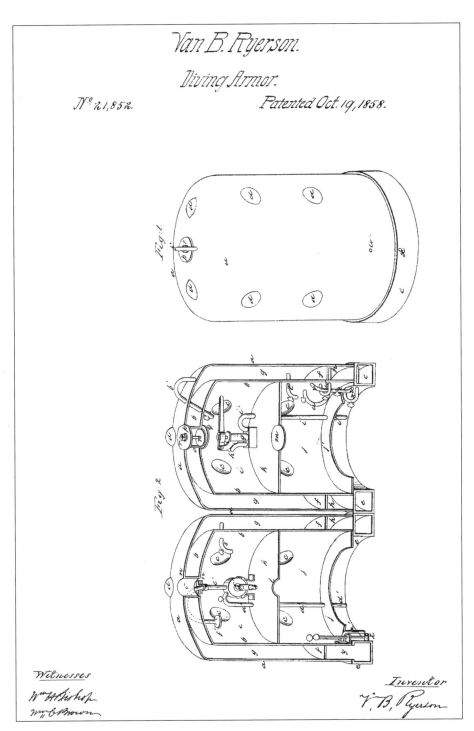

Figure 54. Julius Kroehl's design for *Sub Marine Explorer* was influenced by Van Buren Ryerson's patent for a *Submarine Explorer*. (Courtesy United States Patent Office)

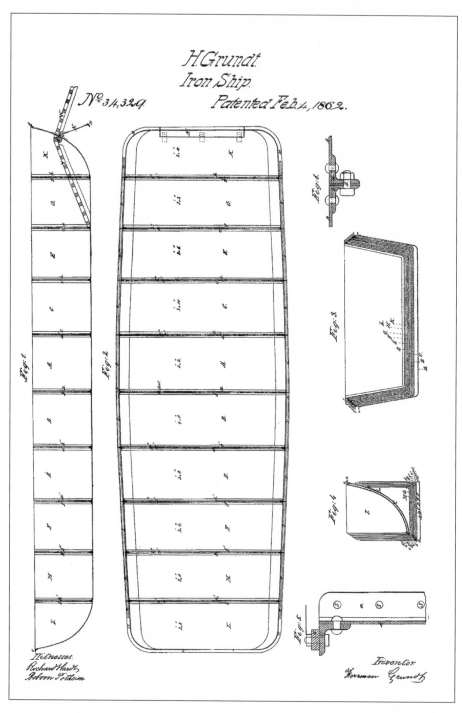

Figure 55. Julius Kroehl's design for *Sub Marine Explorer* was also influenced by Hermann Grundt's patent for an iron pontoon "boat." (Courtesy United States Patent Office)

7

Requiem

I always found him an efficient and gallant officer
ready at any time to sacrifice himself to the good of his country.

—Rear Admiral David Dixon Porter, February 8, 1868

FTER Julius Kroehl's death from fever on September 9, 1857, the US
consul in Panama, Thomas Kilby Smith, dispatched two consular
officers to inventory Kroehl's effects, which they did on the 10th.[1]
Consul Smith sent the inventory to Washington along with a letter on September 21, noting that "Mr. Kroehl made a will in December 1866, but it is
not among his papers here nor do I know who his executors are or where the
will is deposited." Julius had completed the will in New York just days before
setting out on the SS *Henry Chauncey* to join *Sub Marine Explorer* in Panama.

Consul Smith went on to report to his superiors that Kroehl also had "a
large interest in a submarine boat here amounting it is said to some $10,000,
but this is in connection with the Pacific Pearl Co. of No. 38 Broad Street, New
York. His wife Sophia R. Kroehl resides in Georgetown, D.C. I have written
her by this mail."[2] Hopefully Sophia had learned of Julius's death before his
obituary appeared in the German American newspaper, the *New Yorker Staats
Zeitung*, on September 26.[3]

Consul Smith wrote that he had "taken charge" of Kroehl's personal effects
and that he had notified the Pacific Pearl Company, who he hoped would
notify Julius's widow as well as his family in New York. The inventory lists a
substantial amount of material, a leather trunk full of papers, another trunk
full of books, a tin box of papers, drafting equipment, carpet bags, silver-plated

utensils, a teapot, coffee pot, sugar bowl and creamer, cigars, stamps, a $60 US gold piece and $4.30 in New Granadian money. In addition to his drafting tools, a steel rule, and a "surveying instrument," the other links to Kroehl's work would have been his books, papers. and a bottle of nitrate of silver for developing photographs.[4] In his will, Julius had left his gold watch and chain to his nephew, Frederick Kroehl, as well as "all my drawing materials and scientific books" except for his sets of Coast Survey reports and an encyclopedia that he left to his cousin Otto Sackersdorff. Julius also left instructions that Sophia was to select from his possessions "a suitable keepsake" for each member of his family, and his in-laws, noting all by name, including "my brother-in-law Albert Rolle and his wife Helen M. Rolle . . . and my friend Samuel Hein of Georgetown, D.C."[5] No one knows whatever happened to all of these possessions. They vanished into history. Julius left half of his estate to Sophia, and the use of the second half for any children they might have, suggesting that perhaps when Julius left for Panama, there was a possibility in his mind that he was departing with an heir on the way. If there were no children when Sophia died, and there was an estate, then Julius wished for it to go to nephew Frederick and niece Agnes Kroehl. He also made provisions for a $25 per month payment for his mother and stepfather. Kroehl appointed his brother, Henry, and his friend Charles A. Morris (a shareholder in the Pacific Pearl Company) as his executors.

The estate notwithstanding, Kroehl's death left Sophia in difficult circumstances. Sophia, the oldest daughter, lived with her mother, Helen M. Lueber, when she married Julius in 1858 and remained in her mother's home throughout Julius's absences, as did her sister Helen, married to hydrographic survey officer Albert Rolle. With Julius's death, Sophia stayed on permanently with her mother, as sister Helen would also do when Albert Rolle died. Unmarried brother Francis and sister Mary made up the rest of the family in a single house—a family that needed money to live.[6] Sophia, widowed at age 35, needed to find employment.

A logical place to turn was to the government. On December 28, 1867, Kroehl's old commander, Admiral David D. Porter, now serving as the superintendent of the US Naval Academy in Annapolis, wrote a letter of recommendation for Sophia:

> The friends of Mrs. Julius H. Kroehl have applied to me for letters
> to enable the widow of the deceased to obtain some employment

under the government. I always feel it a duty to those who served under me in the cause of the union, even at the expense of appearing importunate. I am told the widow of Mr. Kroehl is in depressed circumstances and is seeking employment in some Dept. of the government. Her husband served under me during the war. He was a good officer, & a fine man, and under any circumstance, would have sacrificed his life in the cause of his country. It would afford his numerous friends and myself much gratification to have his widow receive some employment under the government.[7]

Porter's intervention or perhaps that of brother-in-law Albert Rolle may have been the reason that Sophia gained employment with the US Treasury Department beginning in 1868 as a "lady clerk" in the office of the Fifth Auditor.

Sophia also tried to gain a pension based on Julius's naval service and the malaria she and the family firmly believed had come through his time in the trenches outside Vicksburg. In February 1868 Porter again picked up his pen to support Sophia, writing that Julius Kroehl had served as an "efficient and gallant officer . . . he contracted the disease of which he died while serving on the Mississippi River and had left a family in destitute circumstances. Under all circumstances I think his family have a strong claim on the government which he so ably and gallantly served."[8]

Sophia also gained an affidavit from Julius's New York physician, Dr. Alexander Clinton, who wrote in April 1868 that he had treated Julius in October 1863, "then ill with fever, contracted in the South, soon after the Battle of Vicksburg, while in the service of the United States."[9] Thus began Sophia Kroehl's long battle with the United States government for some form of compensation for Julius's fever, which she believed had finally killed him in Panama. She would press that point for nearly 50 years. Whatever claim for pension Sophia thought of making in 1868, it was apparently not pursued, perhaps because her supporters had found her the government job.

Twelve years after Julius' death, on September 27, 1879, Sophia finally filed an application for a widow's pension. Her employment with the government had come to an end around this time, probably necessitating her application. A large file of supporting documents began to attach to it—Admiral Porter's letter of February 1868 and testimony from former Coast Survey officer Alexander Strausz, who had served with Kroehl on USS *Black Hawk,* as well as Kroehl's brother, Henry, who provided an affidavit from his retirement home in Asbury Park, New Jersey. Henry explained that Julius "never recovered" from the fever with which he had come home from the war.[10] After several months of review, government examiner Lewis C. White completed the last entries on Sophia's claim form. Julius Kroehl died of "Fever (Panama) Malaria, Not due to US Service. Reject."[11]

It took another decade before Sophia, now age 57, fought back. With the assistance of Washington, D.C., lawyer Henry D. Nicholson, she petitioned the government under a new act for widow's pensions. In an affidavit prepared by her lawyers in December 1889, Sophia affirmed that Julius had not died of "Panama fever" but had caught what was loosely described as "malarial fever," sometimes just as fever, in the trenches outside Vicksburg.[12] Over the next few months, Sophia assembled her file of letters, documents (including some of Julius's copies of his service records), and affidavits. Alexander Strausz, Julius's wartime friend from the Coast Survey, wrote a lengthy letter to Sophia in March 1890, recollecting that when he first met Julius on March 3, 1863, he was "a healthy robust looking man, and I never heard him complain about his health until he was taken with malaria fever, like myself."[13]

Strausz noted that he had encountered Julius "about one year" after Vicksburg, or the summer of 1864. "He was looking very badly and still suffering from malarial fever, and as I was in the same condition, he told me of the various remedies (which I do not now recollect) he tried but of no avail. I did not hear of Mr. Kroehl again until after his death." Strausz went on to state that he had no doubt that Kroehl's "early death was due to the fever contracted during his service. . . . I say this, because I came very near dying from the same cause in 1867." With her paperwork assembled, Sophia formally filed for her pension on July 10, 1890.[14] On this occasion, the application, perhaps with the backing of a D.C. law firm, was successful, in that Sophia did receive a widow's pension "under the Act of June 27, 1890."

It was a watershed year. On December 5, Henry Kroehl died "suddenly" at age 72 in his home in Asbury Park.[15] His obituary followed a day later: "Henry Kroehl, one of the oldest and best-known bristle importers, died . . . last evening. . . . He was born in Memel, Prussia, and started in business in this city in 1851. He was one of the founders of the form of Dill & Kroehl of Pearl Street, which for some years controlled the bristle trade of this city. He leaves a wife and two children, Mrs. Agnes Seighhortner of New York and George Frederick Kroehl, President of the First National Bank of Asbury Park. Mr. Kroehl left a large fortune."[16] The death of Henry Kroehl apparently severed the last link Sophia had with Julius's family. Amazingly, Sophia's mother-in-law, Johanna

Philippine Dorothea Kroehl Heanes, had lived until 1883, dying in Brooklyn in September.[17] With Julius's mother and brother now gone, Sophia fades out of the Kroehl family's life. If any support had been coming from Henry, it also ended, meaning the pension, small as it was, made a critical difference for Sophia, now living with her siblings, as her elderly mother had also died.

In 1892 the government rejected Sophia's pension claim, again noting that Julius had died "from 'Panama Fever,' which had no connection with the service." Nicholson, Sophia's lawyer, appealed at the end of December 1892, arguing that the case had been proven that Kroehl left the service because of malaria and that "Panama fever" was a presumption solely based on the fact that "the officer died in Central America."[18] Sophia followed it with a letter of her own a few days later, asking that special attention be given to her appeal, noting that Archbishop John Ireland of St. Paul, Minnesota (then a center of German American immigration) was asking the Bureau of Pensions to give her case careful consideration.[19] It was for naught. A few days later, Sophia's appeal was rejected for the final time: "There is no evidence on file which shows or tends to prove that the fever of which he died was due to service. On the contrary, it appears that he was engaged in an important and responsible position at a place where, and at a season of the year in which he was exposed to the fever-breeding surroundings and malarial poison—to which the cause of his death may be ascribed, and with which his service in the Navy had no connection."[20] The rejection, a formal letter sent from assistant secretary of the interior Cyrus Bussey to the commissioner of pensions, noted that "it appears that the appellant is receiving a pension under the Act of June 27, 1890."[21] Fortunately, the government did not ask for the money back, and continued to pay Sophia $12 a month.

Sophia's long battle to convince the US government that Julius had died of his service-related malaria was finally over. She had failed to make her case. She did continue to receive her small pension, but a service-related death would have added more money to it, as well as a certain stamp of honor to Julius's death in Panama.

Sophia fades into history, occasionally listed in the Washington, D.C., directories as the widow of Julius, and cared for throughout her last years by her faithful younger sister, Mary Lueber, who remained with Sophia until the end. In September 1916 Sophia, now aged 81 and at 809 Twenty-first Street N.W., sent in a request for an increase in pension under a new act, approved on September 8. Sister Mary filled in the request for her, and in between her first and last names, Sophia marked an X, too infirm or ill to sign for herself.[22]

On October 1 Mary wrote the commissioner of pensions to say that Sophia had just received a supplemental certificate increasing her pension to $20 per month, but "Mrs. Kroehl, widow of Julius passed away September 29th (Friday) at midnight after a long illness. Sincerely yours—Miss Mary Lueber, sister of Sophia Kroehl."[23] A devout Catholic, Sophia was laid to rest in Holy Rood Cemetery in Washington, D.C.

Mary wrote again in December as "executrix for my sister's small estate," inquiring whether the $12 monthly check for the month of September, and the subsequent $20 check would be sent to her. "Please inform me as I have enclosed stamp for information."[24] The government's response was quick. On December 28 the commissioner on pensions wrote that "the estate of Mrs. Sofia [*sic*] Kroehl could have no possible claim against the Government," as survivor benefits went only to a widow, then to children under 16 years of age. "No other person is entitled to receive the accrued pension as a matter of rights, nor is it a part of the assets of the estate." The interdepartmental letter explained that "a copy of the Act" had been sent to Mary Lueber as her answer.[25] Mary lived on, alone, dying in Washington, D.C., in 1930.

With that, the books close on the Julius Kroehls and the Luebers. History was busy erasing memories and traces of Julius and Sophia. This process is often magnified when there are no children nor children's children to carry on a memory or save family possessions. Thus it is possible, with the death of Mary Lueber, that the last family treasures of Julius and Sophia, other than what may have been passed along to family and friends at the time of Julius' death, were tossed into a rubbish bin—Julius's letters, perhaps the drawings and records for his submarine, his uniforms, Sophia's dresses, their wedding certificate, the copies of letters Sophia had saved from her long fight with the government— all burned, thrown into landfill, or otherwise disposed of without a trace.

ERASED FROM HISTORY

Along with the inherent unfairness of the discarding of family papers and records and the seeming loss of the Pacific Pearl Company corporate archives also came the inevitable erasure of Julius Kroehl from memory as the last person dies who once knew someone. By 1933, when Julius' nephew and heir Otto Hein died, most likely the last person who knew Julius Kroehl was gone. His extended family, the descendants of Henry, ultimately only remembered Uncle Julius as a listing in the family bible, although even that document fails to record the actual date of his birth.[26]

What was left were a handful of scattered references in the mass of government files—the passenger list for Julius's arrival in America, his applications for citizenship and a passport, his patent application, the records of his military service—or W. W. W. Wood's report on *Sub Marine Explorer* and, thanks to Julius providing him with it, a 12-foot-long sheet of linen showing an incomplete *Explorer,* invaluable as the only known surviving plan of the craft—all enshrined with the navy's records at the National Archives. There were also scattered references in the press, but these were available only to dedicated researchers who would sit in front of huge volumes in dark basements or sift through boxes in an archive.

This is a truth incomprehensible to post-Internet researchers, who work in a time when digitized documents from nineteenth-century newspaper articles, census records, and obscure engineering journals are now readily available. For more than a century, the trail of documents that survived, like crumbs in a labyrinth leading to the story of Julius Kroehl, were not readily accessible. Even in a more accessible digital age, to trace the trail of crumbs through archives or the Internet requires a serendipitous discovery, a spark that sends one down the path. That spark would not come until the early twenty-first century and the chance rediscovery and identification of *Sub Marine Explorer.* That rediscovery was not easy, as the forces of time and history had done more than erase the memory of the small yet precious aspects of Kroehl's experiences contained in those lost trunks of books, papers, and photographs.

This is particularly relevant in terms of Julius's early life and family origins in Memel. The processes of recent history were particularly hard in Memel. Its long history of German settlement has been substantially erased. A bone of contention between Germany and Lithuania, Memel was made a "free city," separated from Germany under the terms of the Treaty of Versailles. Taken by Lithuania in 1923, Memel was a political battlefield that attracted the attention of Germany's National Socialists and Adolf Hitler, and in 1939, Memel joined the Third Reich as Hitler's last prewar territorial demand. A key center in the Nazi State, Memel suffered in the apocalyptic end to the war.

Occupied by the Red Army, Memel was swept into the Union of Soviet Socialist Republics as part of the Lithuanian SSR. As part of Stalin's postwar remolding of the region, its old churches were demolished, along with much of the older buildings and other traces of a German past the Soviets sought to erase. Among the other losses, of course, were the historical records of Memel, into the flames or perhaps carted off to the Soviet Union. The documents that record the life of the family Kroehl, the birth and baptism of Julius, and perhaps the reasons for the family's odyssey to Berlin, Great Britain, and finally America have not yet surfaced and perhaps never will. As a consequence, all that can be said about the early life of Julius Kroehl is what has been written in the first chapters of this book, riddled with necessary supposition.

The ravages of war also extended to Panama. Julius's Masonic brothers laid him to rest in the Cementario de los Extranjeros, the cemetery for foreigners and heretics in Panama City's Chorillo District, now one of the city's tougher barrios. The records of the cemetery are sparse, and while they show that Julius Kroehl is indeed buried there, they do not specify exactly where. That should not be a problem, for the position of a tombstone delineates a grave.[27] Julius's grave should lie somewhere among the many mid nineteenth-century monuments for California gold seekers and isthmian travelers of the pre-canal period, but there is no marker for Julius Kroehl. There are a number of graves marked by broken stumps of stones or by an occasional cast iron fence, victims of time, vandalism, or the events of December 1989.[28]

Those events, the United States' invasion of Panama to capture Manuel Noriega in "Operation Just Cause," involved headquarters of the Fuerzas de Defensa de Panama (the Panamanian Defense Force) just across the street from the cemetery. Local residents claim that in an attack on the headquarters, American tanks laid down heavy fire from an elevated position inside the Canal Zone, and the area was burned out in the battle.[29] Perhaps Julius's marker was lost at this time, along with many others, or perhaps it disappeared long ago, with no family or friends come to tend a lonely grave far from home.

The rest of the Kroehl family lay in Henry's family plot in beautiful Green-Wood Cemetery in Brooklyn—Henry, Caroline, his wife, their children, and his mother and her second husband, John Heanes. Sophia, meanwhile, no longer lies in her forgotten grave at Holy Rood Cemetery in Washington, D.C. The Catholic cemetery, which lies near Wisconsin Avenue, suffers from neglect and vandalization. It languishes, detractors say, because the church wishes to sell it off and develop the land.[30] The Leuber family crypt stands empty, its wooden door smashed and gone, its interior empty except for the iron rack that once held the coffins of Sophia and her siblings and parents.[31] Whether the bodies were removed and buried elsewhere, or were stolen by vandals, is a mystery. All other traces of Sophia's life are also gone save the Georgetown church where she married Julius, as is every address at which she lived now occupied by a modern building. The same holds true for all but one of Julius's addresses in New York.

The loss of history, however, is not always complete. That is because archaeology, especially archaeology of the recent past, comes into the picture to rescue history after it is seemingly lost. Historical archaeology inspires the type of dedicated research that gathers the fragmented records and documents buried in archives and attics and brings them together in a complex meld of digging through soil, sand, and paper to reconstruct the past. The record is never as complete as one would like, but in the end, much more is brought back into history and the remembered past by things such as the chance rediscovery of a lost submarine on a remote Panamanian island.

LOSING JULIUS KROEHL

By the early-twentieth century, Julius Kroehl was dimly remembered by some and forgotten by most, particularly in regard to the chronicles of the development of the submarine. Every account of American submarine development, with the exception of one, ignored him completely. Part of the reason for this is the fact that *Explorer* was completed in relative secrecy at the end of the Civil War, tested and publicly acknowledged briefly, and then shipped off to a distant country, out of sight and hence out of mind to most Americans. There is also the curiously nonpublic demise of the Pacific Pearl Company. As has been noted, it died with a whimper, not with a bang, not long after the company's last glowing public testimonials. Its demise left no lasting public relations legacy, only thousands of now worthless stock certificates (only a handful have surfaced so far in the twenty-first century) and at last count, five known copies of the company's pamphlet from 1865 (revised and rereleased in 1866).[32]

Typical of the accounts of early submarine development is a 1900 article by John Holland, the "father of the modern submarine." Holland's career had begun in the 1870s in the waters off New York. He developed a series of submarines that ultimately would result in a craft that was successfully adopted by the US Navy in the early-twentieth century, beating out his closest rival, Simon Lake. Holland's article, "The Submarine Boat and Its Future," presciently described the innovations that in short order would lead to the use of submarines not only as weapons but also, he hoped, for passenger travel and undersea salvage and survey.

He also described how safe they were, arguing against the public perception that submarines were inherently dangerous. He cited a prevalent New York "urban legend" of the "coffin boat" *Intelligent Whale,* a Civil War–era submarine that "for years has been on display at the Brooklyn Navy Yard."[33] Holland's account completely fails to mention *Intelligent Whale*'s contemporary, *Sub Marine Explorer,* or Julius Kroehl.

Holland's omission likely comes from the fact that when he arrived in the New York area in the 1870s, Julius was long gone, as was his boat, and the only "Submarine Explorer" was a modified and improved diving bell manufactured by William Mont Storm of New York for use in wreck salvage in the East River. Storm was working, ironically, with a modified version of Van Buren Ryerson's old patent.[34] Had he heard of the *Explorer* that went to Panama, and without access to it, Holland may well have thought that it was only an intermediate step in the progression of Ryerson bells of 1858 and 1868, when Storm patented his version and embarked on highly publicized dives to rescue a reported treasure from the Revolutionary War wreck of HMS *Hussar.*[35] Another factor in Holland overlooking the *Sub Marine Explorer* is that both it and *Intelligent Whale* were similar craft in terms of how they were laid out and operated. It is possible that Kroehl's craft was remembered, linked to the unfairly castigated *Intelligent Whale,* and hence was damned by the association and dismissed as another copy of a "failed" design. Some background on *Intelligent Whale* may shed light on the fate of *Sub Marine Explorer* in the literature on submarines.

The first detailed description of *Intelligent Whale* comes from a letter by an unnamed naval officer at the Brooklyn Navy Yard just prior to the navy's official trial of the submarine in September 1872:

> It is known at the yard as the "Intelligent Elephant." It certainly does not derive the name from its size in comparison with other vessels, it measuring about 30 feet [9.14 meters] long and 9 feet [2.74 meters] deep, though it is bulky in appearance and is built of iron, with air and water-tight compartments for its regulation and control. At the bottom of the boat, amidships, is a flat gate, the upper part and the ends being round and tapering. The water being kept from entering the vessel when it is open by compressed air. Out of this gate someone is expected to pass and place a torpedo under a vessel, an electric wire being attached and connected with a battery in the boat and thus fired. It is estimated that the air compartments will contain compressed air enough to last ten hours in use under the water. The water compartments are filled for sinking

the boat by opening a valve, and can be ejected by pumps or forced out by compressed air being let in, there being a connection between both compartments. The boat will hold thirteen persons and has been tried in the Passaic River with that number on board. Six men are sufficient for working it, its motive power being produced by part of them through the agency of a crank. Its speed would be about four knots an hour, or according to the amount of labor used. The lookout is an iron cupola on top, somewhat larger than a man's head. When underwater the boat is without other ventilation except the compressed air in her. When the air becomes foul it can be let out by opening thumb valves. Nothing more definite can be learned until she is tested.[36]

The navy trial on September 20, 1872, at the Brooklyn Navy Yard, in front of a committee of seven officers and a number of sailors, did not go well. As *Intelligent Whale* dived, it began to leak. "After sinking the boat, it was found the opening on top was leaking through defective packing and after remaining under water a short time, the leak was so bad it was found expedient to raise her, but in doing so she caught under the derrick, and signals were sent to those on board to hoist the boat out, which they did. In the meantime, those on terra firma were excited by the fear that some serious mishap would occur to the persons in the torpedo-boat, but after having been under the water sometime in the same spot, nor having traveled or accomplished anything, the boat was got out, and found nearly half full of water, her navigators unhurt, but we imagine, considerably frightened."[37]

The naval committee offered a damning verdict: "As a practical instrument of warfare it is utterly useless."[38] An 1877 letter from the navy's Chief of the Bureau of Ordnance noted that the "boat not having been successful, the Hon. Sec. of the Navy refused to pay any more money, since which time the whole matter has been abandoned."[39] *Intelligent Whale* remained for decades at the Brooklyn Navy Yard where over time it gained a sinister and unfair reputation.

In 1875 Lt. F. M. Barber of the US Navy, in an overview of submarine development to that time, reported on *Intelligent Whale*'s characteristics: it was built of ½-inch boiler iron, had a four-bladed propeller, its compressed air tanks were made of copper and could hold up to 600 psi, and the valve admitted water in a spray to refresh the air inside the craft. In a footnote, however, Barber stated, "In the course of the various attempts made to use this boat she sunk four times, destroying the lives of thirty-two out of thirty-six men who formed the four crews."[40] Barber was confusing *Intelligent Whale* with *H. L. Hunley,* the Confederate sub that had sunk three times with a loss of its crews.

In October 1897 the *New York Times* reported that the old submarine at the Brooklyn Navy Yard was "one of the most dangerous vessels built for the United States Government. . . . It has been there for more than twenty-five years. Its peculiar construction attracts the attention of visitors to the dock."[41] The article noted that the submarine, built "shortly after the war," was "the first vessel of its kind to be constructed, and it proved a failure. Early in the Seventies it was brought to the Brooklyn Navy Yard, and from there taken to the Passaic River for a trial. Several attempts were made to move the boat, and they not only resulted in failure but cost the lives of thirty-two men." This was not true, but *Intelligent Whale* had a bad reputation that now stuck. An article in the December 2, 1914, edition of the *New Outlook* stated that "nine crews had found their grave in her." These lies were repeated by a number of submarine historians, and only recently has the scholarly work of nautical archaeologist Peter Hitchcock restored *Intelligent Whale* to its proper place in the history of submarine.[42]

In the end, the only reference to Kroehl and *Explorer* outside the Pacific Pearl Company's pamphlet was made in a 1902 article by Civil War veteran George W. Baird, a former assistant of W. W. W. Wood and fellow Mason, who in his review of early submarines singled out for noteworthy mention the Confederate war craft *H. L. Hunley* and Kroehl's *Explorer,* which Baird called a link that connected "the diving bell with the dirigible submarine automobile."[43] It would be Baird's solitary reference to *Explorer,* and his republication of Kroehl's basic profile of the boat, that would lead to its ultimate identification in 2003. But in 1902, and in the decades that followed, no other mention was made.

In May 1937 Henry's grandson, Howard Kroehl, wrote to the US Navy seeking to learn more about his uncle Julius. Captain Dudley Knox, the head of the historical section, answered Howard with a brief synopsis of Julius's Civil War career, but he made no mention of *Explorer,* as "no record has been found here relative to the work of Mr. Kroehl outside of the Navy."[44] Unfortunately, in a sign of how much had been forgotten, a copy of the Pacific Pearl Company's promotional pamphlet, with an illustration of the submarine, lay just outside Knox's office in the section's library, but too much time had passed and no one knew to go to that shelf and pull the pamphlet out. All of that changed after 2001.

RESURRECTING JULIUS KROEHL

Following the rediscovery of the submarine and its identification in 2003 (with the ironic note from Gene Canfield that it looked like a cousin of *Intelligent Whale,* which it proved to be in more ways than one), the physical survival of the submarine served as both a touchstone and starting and ending point for what would become years of historical archaeological research. In addition to the original opportunities provided by Zegrahm Expeditions to initially assess the craft,, three field seasons of work followed in 2004, 2006, and 2008. At the same time, researchers Mark Ragan, Robert Schwemmer, John McKee, Hank Silka, Rhonda Robichaud, John Ulrich, and myself conducted considerable work in the archives, inspired by the incredible little craft's age and survival and the need to learn more about what had inspired its creation and abandonment.

Julius Kroehl's brilliant invention had been left behind, presumably because it was considered to be nothing more than scrap and therefore not worth the expense involved to remove it from Isla San Telmo or even to break it up. In time, the identity of the submarine was forgotten by the local inhabitants on the nearby islands, pearl divers and fishermen who knew what it had been used for—diving to pearl beds—but who believed it to be a Japanese submarine that had poisoned their beds and driven them out of the world market for pearls. Ironically, their disinterest, if not trepidation, probably helped the submarine's continued survival, albeit as a castaway derelict.

As will be seen, years of work, virtually autopsying and reconstructing the submarine, have given us a detailed sense of how it was built, how it worked, and why it failed. We know more about "what made it tick" than we do about Julius Kroehl, but of course we are talking about an iron craft, a machine without personality that simply performed in response to simple actions. A valve is turned, air is released, water floods in, a crank is turned, and a propeller spins. It is not so simple, however, particularly in the absence of personal correspondence or intimate memoirs, to say much about Julius Kroehl.

He inspired diverse feelings—Sophia loved him, as did his family. Brother Henry took him in after the Vicksburg campaign and saw Julius returned to a semblance of health. Julius's will speaks to close feelings for his nephew and niece and for his uncle-in-law and friend, Samuel Hein. Some of Julius's early business relationships ended without future connection—Husted disappeared from his life, but others, notably Van Buren Ryerson, remained. In his wartime career, he clashed with Farragut and Bell, and the Coast Survey's Fendall certainly joined the them in their critical assessment of Kroehl as a "failure." Fendall also criticized Julius's taking charge of the Coast Survey party in the fields of Vicksburg, but Kroehl was commended for showing that same initiative on the *Sachem* when he took charge of the gun crew that drove off the Confederate sharpshooters after John Oltmanns was shot. Kroehl was recognized by a warm, fond obituary in Panama. W. W. W. Wood, George Baird, Alexander Strausz, and David Dixon Porter remembered him fondly, and Porter and Strausz went above and beyond the call of duty to assist Sophia the best they could when Julius died.

What comes back to us through the years is the sense that Julius Kroehl had a friendly, engaging, independent, stubborn spirit that may have verged on the obstinate. His style was egalitarian, as researcher John McKee notes. McKee sees Kroehl as a nineteenth-century liberal,[45] a man committed to free ideas and to the ability of a man (limited literally to men in his time) to rise above the circumstances of his birth and family. Julius's known career certainly documents how he applied his engineering and scientific interests to the latest technologies to make breakthroughs in his life, from colored daguerreotypes to cast iron technology, from undersea blasting and diving bells to submarines. He came to the United States not only because it seemed to have no limits if you were a white man, even if you were a foreigner, as long as you could make money, but also because it had a government of, for, and by the people, something his homeland of Prussia had failed to develop, particularly after the abortive revolution of 1848. As evidence of his egalitarian tendencies that would not have been welcome back in Prussia, he could be familiar with his superiors Secretary Welles and Assistant Secretary Fox, argumentative with admirals and captains, and playful in correspondence with Porter.[46] He was also, apparently, a member of the Whigs, an American political party founded on the basic principle of its British predecessor, which was to oppose what the government wanted. And unlike Henry, who did follow successfully in Jacob Kroehl's footsteps as a merchant, Julius demonstrated his stubborn individualism in turning his back on the family profession.

We are left without even a photograph of the man. Other than Strausz's memory of him as "robust and healthy" in 1863, all we have on Julius's appearance is the description of him in his 1854 application for a US passport. Julius was then 34 years old, standing 5 feet 6½ inches tall. Passports then described a person's features since no photograph would be available for an official to consult, or fingerprints used for matching. Julius's passport notes he had gray eyes, brown hair, with an oval face, small chin, a straight nose, a high forehead, a medium mouth, and a fair complexion.[47] It is a brief, seemingly intimate, and yet ultimately unsatisfactory glimpse of such a fascinating man. What we are left with, therefore, are his creations.

In the merging of the surviving historical records and the physical evidence, we are left with two direct manifestations of Julius Kroehl's ingenuity, skill, and labor. Through them, we may utilize archaeology to render some sense of Julius Kroehl. He was highly intelligent, with the manifestation of his intelligence being adaptive, not creative.[48] He took the ideas or work of others and improved upon them. Shifting from silvered to colored daguerreotypes is one example, but more telling is the fire watchtower he built. Historians have noted that Kroehl followed James Bogardus's patent so closely that he was technically guilty of infringement—a fact that the court tacitly acknowledged in the nominal award it granted Bogardus when he sued the City of New York over his failed bid.[49] Not only was Julius was smart enough to realize that the rocky promontory of Mount Morris Park gave the watchtower sufficient height at lesser cost, enabling him to undercut Bogardus's bid, but he was also wily enough to copy Bogardus's patented design and get away with it. Julius was keenly competitive—recall that he did the same thing to Benjamin Maillefert, that is, he did everything he could through the press to put down Maillefert, only to blast Diamond Reef using a technique virtually unchanged from his rival's.

But Julius did not have the best luck. His "authorship" of the fire tower was forgotten, and for many years historians presumed it was the work of James Bogardus. It is ironic that Kroehl's tower gives modern architectural historians their best evidence to assess Bogardus's work.[50] In that, we have some indication of who Julius Kroehl was, or at least, how he operated in business. That also comes through when we look at the development of *Sub Marine Explorer*. Here, his genius lay in taking Van Buren Ryerson's original design and modifying it, perhaps by watching what others had done, including Grundt's patented iron pontoons, Alexandré's copy of Payerne's *Belledonne,* Maillefert's diving bell, and *Intelligent Whale,* which was being refitted in Newark by Oliver Halstead and his associates as Kroehl simultaneously labored on *Explorer* in New York. While there are several critical differences between *Explorer* and *Intelligent Whale,* there are also some amazing similarities.

The craft that emerged, *Explorer,* performed well, amazingly more so than *Intelligent Whale* seemingly did, although John Holland's comments on *Intelligent Whale's* undeserved reputation were correct, particularly his remark that while *Intelligent Whale* never took a life, "Heaven knows, she was handled carelessly enough."[51] *Sub Marine Explorer,* product of the adaptive genius of Julius Kroehl and his shipbuilder partner, Ariel Patterson, was not handled carelessly. Just the same, *Explorer* also failed. It is said that human strengths, when magnified, become weaknesses. *Explorer's* strength was its ability to handle pressure. Its weakness was that it handled too much and for too long a time.

Julius Kroehl and *Sub Marine Explorer* gained a modicum of fame in the first decade of the twenty-first century, in particular, thanks to the Internet. When research began in 2001, a Google search for "Julius Kroehl" yielded seven hits. There are now more than 7,000 hits.[52] The website for Klaipeda in Lithuania, the former Memel, now lists Kroehl as one its famous citizens, and various submarine websites and discussion groups include *Explorer.* A variety of articles can be found in the media, many of them erroneously reporting that *Explorer* was Jules Verne's inspiration, while others are more factual accounts. One of the better ones, by Sven Robel of Germany's *Der Spiegel,* resulted from the magazine's coverage of the 2006 archaeological expedition to Isla San Telmo. At the same time, *Der Spiegel* Television began work on an hour-long documentary on *Explorer* and Kroehl, which aired in 2009.

Explorer and the Pacific Pearl Company entered into the realm of popular fiction in 2005 when author Katherine Govier wove them into a six-page section of her best-selling novel *Three Views of Crystal Water.* In it, James Lowinger, a young man embarking on a career in pearls, visits Panama City and encounters several gentlemen from New York, among them Mr. Hartley and Mr. Tiffany, who speak to him of how a submersible could harvest pearls better than the native divers. Govier writes that "Hartley laughed at the general lack of imagination that had led all involved in the business until now to overlook this fine option. James laughed in turn. 'I think you've been reading too much Jules Verne.'"[53] The section ends with James investing in the Pacific Pearl Company and their submarine, which will allow six men to the do the work of 300, but as the "only investor. The submersible was never launched."[54] In 2010 British fantasy writer China Miéville also invoked Julius Kroehl and *Sub Marine Explorer,* describing an apocalyptic cult that believed that God had sent holy rains to flood the earth to reward his faithful, not punish humanity, and that Noah's ark had been a huge submarine. "The Communion of the Blessed Flood prayed for the restoration of the wet. Marge read of their utopias, sunk not in ruination but reward. . . . They honoured their prophets: Kroehl and Monturiol, Athanasius, Ricou Browning, and John Cage's father. . . . They gave thanks for the tsunami and celebrated the melting of the satanic polar ice." One wonders what a serious engineer like Kroehl would think of this aspect of his twenty-first-century "fame."[55]

8

Archaeological Examination of
Sub Marine Explorer

THE archaeological evidence suggests that sometime in the fall of 1869, *Sub Marine Explorer*'s last crew pulled it up on the beach in a small cove at Isla San Telmo, as they had most likely done the year before. It was standard marine practice in the nineteenth century to lay up or "mothball" vessels for extended periods of inactivity. Preparations would have been made to protect the submarine, a valuable asset of its owners, the officers and shareholders of the Pacific Pearl Company. The bottom hatches would have been closed and dogged shut inside the craft. Excess air would be bled out of the tanks and pipes, and a thick coat of grease applied to the valves and moving parts, as no one would want the submarine's delicate mechanisms to rust in the months that would pass before anyone's return. Logs would be placed beneath the hull to hold it steady on the sand, and mooring lines would be run out from the rings on the hull to large trees up the cliff that rimmed the cove. Finally, the "manhole," the hatch atop the conning tower, would be bolted shut, the two-inch-diameter screws turned tightly so that no water could enter, nor could any unwelcome visitors, unless they came armed with a massive wrench and a few strong men to slowly turn the bolts loose to open the hatch.

After mothballing the craft, the crew would then have rowed their small skiff through the surf to *Explorer*'s waiting steam tender. As the submarine's crew scrambled aboard, the tender's crew finished raising the anchor. The ten-der swung about, and with a thick belch of smoke and a blast of the steam whistle, headed southeast through the narrow channel. As the tender cleared the channel, she turned east and headed for Panama City, a full day's steam away. Before the tender turned past the rocks at the channel entrance, some of the men still on deck probably looked back at the iron submarine up on the beach, as it diminished in size and disappeared from view. Some of them may have suspected, or even known, that they would never see the strange little craft again.

The archaeological evidence additionally shows that the submarine sat on the beach, washed by rain and storm surges that finally knocked it off its perch of logs and snapped the rotting mooring lines. Still somewhat buoyant despite its multi-ton iron hull, *Explorer* drifted slightly off the beach into water that completely covered it at high tide, thanks to the Bay of Panama's maximum 20-foot tidal range.[1] Stuck up against a rock ledge, its bow turned out toward open water, *Explorer* settled into the sand as the waves dug a partial grave for the rusting hull.[2]

Amazingly, the rusty hull was still mostly watertight. Julius Kroehl, Ariel Patterson, and their workers had built it to withstand the pressures of depth, and the crew had laid her up well. The interior slowly rusted, a humid cave for decades, as trapped moisture and small leaks formed a crust of calcium carbon-ate and iron oxide that covered the interior. The only light that came inside was the sun's rays reflecting through the forward view port and the glass ports in the manhole, the only sound the drumming of the waves and the heavy thumps as seaborne logs hammered against the partially submerged derelict.

So it remained for years, perhaps for decades, until the thick glass dead-lights were broken either by human hands or by the many logs that wash up in the surf, and the sea at last gained complete access to *Sub Marine Explorer.* No one ventured inside, however—the hatch remained bolted shut. Isla San Telmo was well off the beaten path, miles away from the major sea lanes that ran north and south, as well as miles distant from the facilities of the Pacific Mail Steamship Company at neighboring Isla Taboga. The local pearl divers had no use for the machine, and there was a story, growing dimmer with the passing years, that it was a thing of death, and that to enter it was to die.

Sometime between 30 and 50 years after *Explorer*'s owners and crew aban-doned her, someone apparently came to pull the submarine off the beach, perhaps to scrap her. They wrapped a 1½-inch-diameter wire rope three times

around the stubby conning tower, ran it to open water to their waiting vessel—probably a powerful steamer—and started to pull. The wire rope they
used has been found, cinched tightly up against the conning tower, one loop
slipping over the others. The entire salvage boat probably vibrated, and then
would have come two loud sounds—the partial failure of the hull as the tower
bent slightly offshore, too weak to take the flooded hull with it, and then the
whining parting of the wire as it snapped, leaving *Explorer* in the surf and sand,
dented slightly but unmoved.[3]

Respite was short-lived. The salvagers came back, and with an oxy-acetylene torch, they cut off the bolt heads and the hinge of the hatch, wrenching it
free to again admit men inside *Sub Marine Explorer*. Those men dropped inside
the partially flooded hull and used tools to cut out, pull free, and strip every
accessible brass and copper pipe and valve they could find. They even beat out
the brass portholes—but for some reason left behind a few pieces, including
the brass main dive manifold. Their ransacking of *Explorer* revealed an even
greater treasure, perhaps, in the several tons of gears that had once cranked the
submarine's single propeller, which they had already hacksawed off along with
the submarine's rudder. The gears were too big to lift out of the derelict, and
its quarters were too small to dismantle or break up the gearing mechanism
inside, so they blasted. Explosive charges tore off the ballast tank plates and
punched into the submarine's offshore side at the stern. Now exposed, the
gears were pulled out of the ruptured bottom and sides, and rafted over to the
waiting ship of the scrappers.[4]

With that, they stopped, leaving a seemingly stripped out hull of rusting
iron to slowly succumb to the sea. Damage notwithstanding, *Explorer* continued to hold together until the battering of heavy hardwood logs, such as
the one observed in the surf in 2006, breached the wrought iron shell of the
upper hull, gradually opening up the compressed air chamber. Sea creatures
freely entered the hulk at high tide—fish and the occasional sea snake, and
in the forest of iron reinforcing rods of the air chamber, moray eels. Some
made their homes there, like the generations of small oysters and barnacles
that coated the interior.—Built to harvest the resources of the sea, *Explorer* like
all wrecks had been transformed by human and natural forces into a marine
habitat. That is what she was when we found her. She was also an archaeological resource, at least intriguing and most probably significant. Even in 2001–2,
with the submarine's identity not yet known, it was clear that this was an early

craft, and quite probably a lost or missing link in the history of submarines. To understand the vessel's context and significance, we framed three seasons of fieldwork around a series of research questions and themes.

RESEARCH QUESTIONS

The initial questions we sought to answer were the identity and the context of the wrecked submarine. "Pin the name on the wreck" is a game that dates back to the earliest years of nautical archaeology, because people are not content to leave something nameless, and a name is the first step in learning the story that provides the all-important context. To achieve this, archaeological technique is meticulously and comprehensively applied to collect every bit of data from the wreck and its site, and then that data is assessed against a series of questions. A scholar spends much time, usually an entire career, analyzing past societies by posing questions in a descending order and testing them through excavation and analysis.

As part of my research focus into the eighteenth- and nineteenth- century expansion of the Euro-American capitalist system into the Pacific Rim, and the role of maritime trade, commerce, and technology in that expansion, I would have selected *Sub Marine Explorer* or Julius Kroehl as a high-priority target for assessment, had I known about them. But the name of the craft and its history lay buried in a series of obscure articles and newspaper accounts not yet accessible. Archaeological "discovery" of resources from the postmedieval period almost always spurs additional and extensive archival research. Kroehl and *Explorer* would require this kind of dedicated research. As I noted in the preface, the accidental "rediscovery" of the submarine came because of a vacationing interest in Panama, especially its nineteenth- and early twentieth-century role as a highway for emerging American interests. Once the identity of the submarine and its age became apparent, it was obvious that *Sub Marine Explorer* was an ideal subject for study, not only for its significance as an early submarine but also for its part in the larger American technological effort to establish economic and political domination over the crucial isthmian highway.

We had several key questions about the submarine's design and technology. Was it representative of the craft of its time, or was it unique? Where and how did it fit into a "family tree" of submarine development? Historical accounts suggested that the submarine was used successfully, but it had been abandoned after its first season of work in Panama. Was there an inherent design flaw or another factor that led to its abandonment? Was the application of this technology appropriate to the local environment in which it was employed? Was the technology employed recklessly?

We are fortunate to have access to detailed archaeological and architectural information from three projects assessing *Explorer*'s contemporaries—a presumed Confederate craft in New Orleans, *H. L. Hunley* in Charleston, South Carolina, and *Intelligent Whale,* the other New York–built "lockout"-capable submarine dating to within a year of *Explorer.* There is also a considerable literature on the development of both diving bells and submarines, and as we have seen, both were relevant to *Explorer,* which represented a transition from bell to submarine.

Other questions revolved around the transition of *Explorer* from working craft to wreck. What were the site formation processes? When and how did the missing components leave the submarine? Was there a comprehensive salvage effort or piecemeal plundering? What had caused the damage to the submarine, and were the processes of corrosion and damage ongoing? Was *Sub Marine Explorer* at risk, and what were the options for its preservation?

As standard nautical archaeology uncovered the story of *Explorer,* by describing it and explaining how and why it was built the way it was, further questions emerged about innovation of the craft. Although Julius Kroehl had taken a speculative risk, the craft had ostensibly proven successful and safe (for its time). Yet it had somehow failed, and had even largely disappeared from the historical record. As the next chapter details, we developed a hypothesis for this—that the effects of pressure on human bodies, created by the lockout capability of the submarine, were poorly understood, and apparently there was no successful means to counteract or cure those effects. Thus, *Explorer* was a craft ahead of its time, with a fatal flaw in its operation, not in its design. That error could not be rectified until four decades after Julius Kroehl's death and the final abandonment of *Sub Marine Explorer.*

We knew at the beginning of the project that we needed to assess *Sub Marine Explorer* in its cultural, historical, and technological contexts. One factor at play was a degree of racism that merged with the Americans' sense of cultural, national, and technological superiority, resulting in a misapplication of effort in the Pearl Islands. Most of the principal actors in the Pacific Pearl

Company were involved in other technological and speculative ventures that ultimately proved a failure.

Sub Marine Explorer also needed to be assessed as part of the larger environment, namely the cove, the pearl beds, Isla San Telmo, and even the Archipiélago de las Perlas. This required the integration of the local population of fishermen and pearl divers, who continued to work the waters as their ancestors had for centuries past, into the team of oceanographers and marine biologists investigating the craft. A. J. Parker has argued that "a 'mariner's perspective' would seem to be key in understanding the world as experienced by maritime communities, both on and off the land."[5] Paul Rainbird, in assessing the archaeology of islands and the concept of maritime cultural landscapes, details how "seamarks" such as coastal features, but very particularly sea shoals and reefs, provide a "map" of the undersea world, not only physically but also in terms of how mariners, or in this case, how local pearl divers would use it.[6] As Rainbird notes, "we need to accept that people were at home with the sea."[7] In the 2008 field season, as detailed below, we used local divers' knowledge and employed breath-holding inhabitants of the neighboring village of La Esmerelda, along with remote sensing data from a state-of-the-art autonomous underwater vehicle (AUV), to better assess where *Explorer* had and had not worked in 1869.

We sent the AUV, a REMUS 100 vehicle, into the deeper waters where *Explorer* had once gone, according to the available written record. These were areas with few oysters and pearls. The breath-holding divers went into the shallows where the oysters thrived, although these areas clearly reflected the effects of centuries of overfishing—and indeed, the submarine may have attempted to collect its initial harvest in these oyster-stripped shallows. Thus, only the depths remained, a place where *Explorer* went and found wanting. Why was the nature of the oyster beds not taken into account by the Pacific Pearl Company? Did racism prevent them from asking the people who knew, the local divers? If so, the company's failure to obtain local knowledge and thus understand the physical and maritime cultural landscape into which it had dropped *Sub Marine Explorer* meant that the submarine was sent blindly into the field. The company discovered that building a craft that could go deeper than the breath-holding divers could go, who had already worked the area for centuries, did not guarantee success, but rather the opposite. This basic fact faced the Pacific Pearl Company whether or not Isla San Telmo was at the heart of the pearl diving area in the archipelago, or whether the submarine worked off Panama, Mexico, or Venezuela. Thus the beached submarine is another material example of the timeless lessons of making assumptions, faulty research, and inadequate planning. The submarine was built in an atmosphere of growth, speculation, and risk, all married to a sense that technology and a can-do attitude would win the day. They did not.

FIELD SEASONS, 2004–2008

The serendipity of the initial discovery was a double-edged sword. On the positive side, a fascinating discovery was gradually revealed to indeed be very significant. *Sub Marine Explorer* is a rare example of the earliest generation of working submarines from the pioneering developmental period of the mid-nineteenth century. While future archaeological discoveries may reveal the remains of other, earlier craft, as of 2012, only five submarines whose date of construction predates 1870 are known to have survived: Wilhelm Bauer's *Der Brandtaucher* of 1850, now a museum display in Kiel, Germany; an unnamed Confederate submarine that probably dates to 1862 and is now on display in New Orleans, Louisiana; Confederate submarine *H. L. Hunley* of 1863, archaeologically recovered and currently undergoing analysis and conservation in Charleston, South Carolina; *Intelligent Whale,* now a museum display at the National Guard and Militia Museum in Sea Girt, New Jersey; and *Sub Marine Explorer.*

   Sub Marine Explorer and *Intelligent Whale* are the only two submarines of this handful of early survivors that had a pressurized compartment which allowed divers to enter and exit the craft at depth; this compartment is one of the world's oldest "lockout" dive chambers. Although a self-propelled craft, *Sub Marine Explorer* is clearly one of the most sophisticated of all known late nineteenth-century submersibles. Built for war but used in peace, it is as yet the only Union-built submarine from the Civil War, other than *Intelligent Whale,* known to have survived. If we were to attempt a reconstruction of *Explorer* and its operation despite the lack of documentation, it was imperative to record as much data as possible. The negative edge of the sword was that news of its "discovery" might lead to potential loss, not only loss of data due to corrosion, but also from the increased human impact of expanding tourism in the Pearl Islands and from a threat in 2004 of renewed attempts to remove the craft from the beach and sell it for scrap to "iron pirates."

These concerns led to the first two seasons of work in 2004 and 2006, all conducted under archaeological permits issued by the Director Nacional del Patrimonio Histórico of the Instituto Nacional De Cultura (INAC). The 2004 fieldwork was underwritten by Eco-Nova Productions Ltd. of Halifax, Nova Scotia, producers of the National Geographic International Television series "The Sea Hunters," and by a grant from the Council of American Maritime Museums (CAMM). CAMM provided funding through their Sally Kress Tompkins Fund for documentation of the Isla San Telmo submarine to the standard currently being applied to the recently raised Confederate Civil War submarine *H. L. Hunley* and to the standard recommended in the United States for historic vessel recording projects by the Historic American Engineering Record (HAER) of the National Park Service.

A major issue in all field seasons was access to the site. The Pearl Islands are as isolated from mainland Panama in the twenty-first century as they were in the nineteenth. Boat and air service connect the mainland to the resort island of Contadora, but private boats are the only way to get to the other islands. Isla San Telmo, as the outermost island in the archipelago, is particularly remote. To work at the site, we had to hire a boat and take an all-day trip to San Telmo, and then use the hired boat, anchored in the lee of Isla Del Rey, as our home and laboratory . San Telmo, as a nature sanctuary, is not available as a place to stay. We were fortunate in boat hires, especially after 2004 when I made the acquaintance of Captain James Dertien and his vessel *Cheers,* which runs exceptional fishing charters out of Panama City. *Cheers* became our "home away from home" for all remaining seasons of work with *Sub Marine Explorer.* Each field season on site lasted approximately one week.

In 2004 we proceeded to work with the CAMM grant, which maximized the other resources we had through television show funding. This allowed us to conduct a more thorough, nondestructive documentation of the submarine through a three-dimensional laser scan of the submarine's exterior. Hand measurements of the interior were the basis for initial architectural drawings by Todd A. Croteau of the Historic American Engineering Record of the National Park Service. The laser recording was done with a Cyrax™ system, the same system employed in the ongoing documentation of the Confederate submarine *H. L. Hunley.*[8] The Cyrax 3D laser scanning system consists of a Cyrax scanner, a personal computer, and Cyclone software. Cyrax captures the three-dimensional surface geometry of complex structures and sites with a combination of completeness, speed, accuracy, and safety.

The operator orients the scanner toward the object or structure to be mapped, selects the desired measurement area and scanning density, and then the instrument autoscans. Complete surface geometry of exposed surfaces is remotely captured in minutes in the form of dense, accurate "3D point clouds," ready for immediate use. The scanner can be rotated or moved around the site to capture entire scenes. As soon as Cyrax has scanned a structure or site, its suite of Cyclone software provides the basis for a wide variety of applications, including those that require export to computer-aided design and rendering software. The Cyrax system was selected for the documentation of *Sub Marine Explorer* because of its applicability and cost-effectiveness. We retained Pacific Survey and Epic Scan Ltd. of Medford, Oregon, as the contractor to do the 3D laser scan. They had the requisite experience from their work on the *Hunley* project and were easily accessible for the data capture and documentation needed after the fieldwork. They also donated a portion of their time and cost to see the project completed. The scan of *Explorer,* completed by Doug DeVine and Carlos Velasquez, captured 1.5 million x, y, and z coordinate points and took a two-person team one day. Post-fieldwork data capture and computer modeling required 30 hours of work.

The 2004 analysis of *Explorer* resulted in hundreds of digital images, digital video, Cyrax data, and an initial written description and preliminary plans for the submarine. Among the results of the 2004 season was the realization that the processes of site formation were ongoing, and that additional damage and loss of data from the submarine was more than a threat—it was occurring.[9]

One sidelight of the 2004 season was an e-mail from the Scientific Exploration Society (SES) of England, asking if they could do anything to help, as they were planning an expedition to Panama.[10] Keen to see if any additional corrosion or damage had resulted in the loss of external structure, I provided them with images for comparative purposes, historical information and observations made to date, the submarine's coordinates, and I asked them to assess the ongoing impacts to the submarine since the 2004 season. Their survey in April 2005 confirmed observations of the extent and nature of external damage and loss of structure that we had made in 2002 and 2004, but it did not provide empirical evidence of ongoing damage or deterioration.[11]

There was a down side to this activity in that the media often distort archaeological and historical reality. Unfortunately, a press release[12] by the Scientific Exploration Society led to an article in the *Times of London* claiming that

the SES had been in the neighborhood of the wreck at the request of the author and principal investigator, identified as a "maritime museum in Canada,"
and that they had properly identified the submarine there as Julius Kroehl's
Sub Marine Explorer. The article went on to suggest, erroneously, that *Explorer*
had been the inspiration for Jules Verne's *Nautilus* in *20,000 Leagues Beneath
the Sea.*[13] The story went around the world, and to this day many readers of
Internet blogs are convinced that Col. John Blashford-Snell of the SES discovered and identified *Explorer* and that it was the inspiration for Verne's *Nautilus.*
While Colonel Blashford-Snell apologized for any misunderstanding, I note
this aspect of the story only to point out how media stories can distort archaeological and historical reality. Invariably in shipwreck discovery and archaeology
a fair amount of effort is expended, and "credit" for a discovery is often bitterly
fought over, which can be as much of a media feeding frenzy as hype.[14]

No one "discovered" *Explorer.* The submarine was never truly lost. The
locals knew it well, had their own folklore about it, but avoided it where possible. What was forgotten was its identity and its historical and technological
context. This is what we were eventually able to provide.

The 2006 field season was funded by the National Oceanic and Atmospheric
Administration (NOAA) Office of Ocean Exploration, which assembled a
multidisciplinary international team from the United States, Canada, Panama,
and Australia. The team was drawn from the ranks of three federal agencies
(NOAA, the National Park Service, and the US Navy) and from the University
of Nebraska. The project team was divided into a field team and a post-fieldwork team that conducted laboratory analysis and data processing. The field
team was selected for specific expertise, as well as for crossdisciplinary abilities,
for example, oceanographer/archaeologist, architectural drafter/photographer,
archaeologist/corrosion measurement technician, and for diverse skills in diving, engineering, equipment maintenance, and vessel operation.

The results of 2006 were many. Oceanographer Bert Ho of NOAA conducted a preliminary bathymetric survey of the cove in which *Explorer* lies.
Archaeologists Larry Murphy, Dr. Michael "Mack" McCarthy, Bert Ho, and
Todd Croteau, with help from a television crew from Germany's *Der Spiegel,*
conducted a comprehensive visual and photographic assessment of the exterior of the submarine both digitally and in large-format 8-by-10 black and
white negatives; additionally, a Total Station instrument provided electronic
measurements of exterior features. Seasonally lower tides than previous field

seasons provided clearer documentation of the lower portions of the exterior as well as a hitherto unavailable "dry" level of access to the interior for assessment, documentation, and analysis.

The exceptional level of lighting provided by *Der Spiegel* inside the sub also provided naval architectural historian and draftsman John W. McKay of Fort Langley, British Columbia, with enough detail for the completion of a set of interpretive reconstruction drawings and plans of *Explorer*. For the first time, we were able to gain a comprehensive sense of how the submarine was built, how it operated, and the incredible level of sophistication inherent in Julius Kroehl's forgotten craft

The "optimal conditions" for working inside *Explorer* were at low tide, when much of the interior was not flooded. High tide completely flooded the craft with water made murky by suspended sediment. While working at low tide introduced air and some light, it also meant that each wave brought massive amounts of water surging through the holes at bow and stern. As the tide rose, the team was confronted with being submerged, battered, and occasionally overwhelmed inside a half-buried working compartment not much larger than an average urban sewer drain. You would have to carefully brace yourself to hold tight and not snap off a weakened piece of machinery (or cut and bruise yourself), simultaneously holding your breath while also grasping a camera, dive light, measuring tape, and slate. These were arduous working conditions not suited to the claustrophobic. We also had to contend with trying to ascertain, in varying light levels, whether a mass of corrosion represented the remains of piping, an instrument's mounting plate, or rivets. It took all three field seasons, and multiple pairs of eyes, to gradually sort out what exactly the layers of rust and marine growth obscured, and every one of the team who spent hours inside *Explorer* only gradually came to understand Julius Kroehl and Ariel Patterson's amazing craft. Archaeology is often defined by the amount of patience the archaeologists have, and work on *Explorer* is yet another reminder that patience, a willingness to take physical risks, and stubbornness are essential job skills for nautical archaeologists.

The other major aspect of the 2006 fieldwork was to conduct an assessment of *Explorer*'s interaction with its environment, particularly its rate of corrosion. Dr. Donald Johnson of the University of Nebraska worked closely in the field with Jacinto Almendra, the chief conservator for Panama Viejo, Larry Murphy, and Lt. Cdr. Joshua Price, deputy supervisor of salvage for the US Navy, to take a series of mid-hull corrosion potential (Ecorr) readings from several transects from the exterior and interior. This involved the water-dredge excavation and subsequent reburial of the entire length of the offshore (port) side of the submarine to its bottom. The excavation showed how *Explorer* came to rest on a dense layer of gravel and driftwood. Dr. Johnson's analysis also included deploying a YSI 600XLM Multiparameter Sonde sensor in the working chamber and on the exterior to measure environmental parameters such as pH, dissolved oxygen, and salinity on 24-hour increments with tidal variation, and visual assessment of the submarine's corrosion and concretion.[15]

Among the observations made in 2006 was that the disappearance of wrought iron from the port side hull, which faces seaward, is probably accelerated by wave action and splash of seawater and corrosion product over the top centerline to the starboard side. This area is also the most likely to be impacted by floating logs and other debris, which, when combined with increased corrosion, accounts for the missing port side hull. One large log, for example, was seen to wash up and strike the submarine in 2006 when the team arrived. Heavy scale appearing on the starboard side suggests corrosion product buildup. An area adjacent to the ground connection was chosen to measure metal thickness. After removal of about 4.5 cm of scale from the exterior side, shiny base metal appeared. A hole was drilled there and the interior side was scraped and cleaned.

Caliper readings of 11.3, 13.9, 12.1, 11.6, and 12.1 mm were averaged to yield a metal thickness of 12.2 mm, or 0.48 inch. Five overlapping wrought-iron strakes form the upper hull. Two shells of best boiler iron ½ inch thick, with pieces overlapping 4 inches, were double riveted (6). If the hole was drilled in an overlap area, then one-half of the original wall thickness remains. This corresponds to a corrosion rate of 0.5 inch × 1,000 mils/inch ÷ 137 = 3.6 mils per year or more than twice the rate predicted. This may be reasonable considering the large cast iron cathode. Converting iron oxide thickness on the exterior, the equivalent metal thickness would be about 0.75 inch. Since 0.48 inch (direct measure of thickness) + 0.75 inch (calculated from external scale) exceeds 1.00 inch, it was Donald Johnson's conclusion that oxide corrosion product has indeed carried over from port to starboard as suggested above. Although no rivets were obtained for analysis, galvanic effects between rivet and hull was not visually evident.

Because the port side undergoes intermittent splash, high corrosion rates are primarily responsible for the disappearance of port side hull metal. Mechanical impact and abrasion are contributing factors. The carryover appears similar to flash corrosion wherein high oxygen levels yield the ferric oxyhydroxides FeO (OH). This corrosion product tends to dry out to form the reddish/orange of red ferric oxides hematite and magnetic maghemite. Evidence of these oxides in various forms depending upon degree of dryness was observed on the upper starboard hull.

Photographic documentation of *Explorer*'s condition in 2006, and the collection of metal samples drilled from the exterior and interior for laboratory analysis, concluded the submarine fieldwork, but a walking survey of the nearshore area by Mack McCarthy and Jacinto Almendra discovered what might be the beachside shore camp of the Pacific Pearl Company crew of 1869. It may also be a precontact indigenous site or a more modern scatter of oyster shells and broken glass bottles.[16]

At the conclusion of the 2006 study, in our report to INAC, we noted that the submarine is a significant cultural resource of international significance with strong connections to Panamanian and US history that unfortunately is in danger of additional damage, loss of data, and perhaps complete loss. The submarine is at risk from the processes of surf, surfborne agents of mechanical and erosional damage, and human intervention, ranging from climbing onto and into the craft, breaking fragile concretion and corroded cast iron fittings, to the possibility (conveyed to us in 2004) of illegal scrapping by "iron pirates" seeking to feed the then-lucrative scrap metal market. Despite well-intentioned response by authorities from the nearby village of La Esmeralda and security guards from ANCON, the private operators of the nature preserve encompassing Isla San Telmo, visitors can arrive by boat and be present for hours, even a day or more, without contact or intervention. We outlined various options for the Panamanian government at the end of the 2006 season and noted that a 2008 final survey was likely, given unanswered questions and the need to see what another two years would bring in terms of damage to *Explorer*. As we wrote those recommendations, we did so fearing that in 2008 we would find the craft collapsed or even gone. Fortunately, Jim Dertien and the local authorities at La Esmeralda kept an eye on *Explorer* and when plans were made for 2008, we did so knowing the submarine was still there.

The 2008 field season was funded by the Waitt Institute for Discovery, which also provided the research vessel *Plan B* and access to additional colleagues from the undersea robotics and natural sciences to continue the multidisciplinary study of the *Explorer* site. As with all other field seasons, this season was also conducted under an archaeological permit issued by INAC. Working from *Plan B*'s auxiliary craft, the team completed a detailed sidescan sonar and magnetometer survey of the cove where *Explorer* lies, as well as an autonomous underwater vehicle multibeam sonar survey of portions of the offshore zone surrounding Isla San Telmo and several dives to the pearl beds where *Explorer* likely worked in August 1869. This provided a clearer, three-dimensional look at the maritime landscape in which *Explorer* is situated. The sonar and magnetometer survey of the cove where *Explorer* rests, conducted by Steve Bilicki and Joe LaPorte, discovered a large wrought-iron beam, 10 feet long, 10 inches wide, and six inches thick, lying off the bow of *Explorer* in four feet of water (at mean low tide). The presence of this large, singular artifact cannot be explained, but it is possible that it was related to *Explorer*'s operation, perhaps serving as a more "permanent" mooring for the craft.

Another key goal was the opportunity to assess the colonization of *Sub Marine Explorer* by marine organisms; this was accomplished by Dr. Erich Horgan of Woods Hole Oceanographic Institution. Dr. Horgan's assessment found a diverse range of organisms common to both the nearby tidal rocks, as well some from deeper water that have adapted to the darker, enclosed environment inside the submarine. Finally, the ongoing assessment of *Explorer* in 2008 included a detailed reassessment of the interpretive reconstruction drawings in the field with John W. McKay, and an evaluation of ongoing mechanical damage to the submarine. For the first time since 2001, "new" damage to *Explorer* was observed. This included a partial collapse of the upper hull in the aft section, and two large "hits" by submerged logs that knocked concretion off the port hull midships and at the stern. The 2008 season also included additional documentation inside the working chamber, with detailed photography and additional filming of both the sub's mechanisms and its biological colonization by photographer Lance Milbrand, who worked with Dr. Horgan and archaeologist Fritz Hanselmann, as well as the principal investigator and John McKay, to complete documentation of every exposed aspect of *Sub Marine Explorer*. A very significant aspect of the 2008 field season was the survey of the surrounding seabed—the submerged maritime cultural landscape in which *Explorer* worked—by a REMUS 100 autonomous underwater vehicle.

That survey, conducted by Woods Hole Oceanographic Institution's Mike Purcell and Greg Packard, found that the waters immediately in front of the cove where *Explorer* lies were shallow and most likely not where the submarine had operated, despite the proximity to the cove, because none of the depths were close to those recorded in the contemporary news accounts of *Explorer's* dives. The waters to the west, however, were deeper, and it appears that dive operations would have taken *Sub Marine Explorer* offshore. Dives on the pearl beds in the area found very few oysters in depths greater than 80 feet, suggesting that *Explorer's* technological advantages took it into waters that probably were accessible to the breath-holding local divers, but were less than optimal for oysters and pearls. In doing so, the dives also exposed *Explorer's* crew to decompression sickness. This was a breakthrough observation, and a critical aspect in assessing *Explorer's* abandonment in a larger context.

9

Sub Marine Explorer's Context, Condition, and Options

All Californians in New York have big pet schemes,
each one bigger than the other—too big, which is the reason
probably why none of them fill.

—*San Francisco Chronicle,* January 1889

FTER three field seasons and seven years of research and analysis, it
is clear that *Sub Marine Explorer* is indeed an evolutionary "branch"
in the family tree of submarine development. *Explorer* is, as Baird
noted in 1903, a link between the diving bell and the submarine, borrowing
her basic systems configuration for pressurization from Van Buren Ryerson's
Explorer of 1858, but with fundamentally different aspects that make it a true
submarine, and particularly a submarine with a lockout diver chamber.[1] Different in design and form from *H. L. Hunley* and the Confederate submarine
of New Orleans, *Explorer* is most closely linked to *Intelligent Whale,* a similar
craft, and the earlier New York submarine of Alexandré in 1851.

Historical accounts and "conventional wisdom" of the nineteenth century
placed *Intelligent Whale* into the category of a "failure," even a deadly one,
but as early as 1900, submarine developer and engineer John P. Holland had
dismissed those allegations and perceptively commented that *Intelligent Whale*
had not been competently handled.[2] The archaeological, architectural, and historical assessment of *Intelligent Whale,* completed by Peter W. Hitchcock in
2002, confirms the accuracy of Holland's assertions.[3] The same is true of *Explorer.* Technologically ingenious, the craft was dangerous only if not properly
handled. The fatal flaw for both craft was the fact that technology outstripped

human ability to understand and cope with the consequences of employing it, as we will see in this chapter.

Similar to *Intelligent Whale, Explorer* does not represent the principal thrust in submarine development, which is better seen in other American-built craft like *H. L. Hunley* and Holland's own craft, the *Fenian Ram* of 1881, and his subsequent "Holland" class boats, the submarines ultimately incorporated into the US, British and other navies in the early twentieth-century. The same holds true with foreign-built submarines such as Phillip's *Marine Cigar,* de Villeroi's *Alligator,* Peral's *Peral,* or Reverend Garrett's *Resurgam.* These one-atmosphere, sealed craft (*Alligator* had a separate lockout chamber) led directly to the modern submarine.[4]

Explorer and *Intelligent Whale* represent an alternate line of evolution, in which the diving bell became a submarine, only to die out, and the basic principle devolved back to the sophisticated diving bells of today. *Explorer* was also incredibly sophisticated. One of the key observations of the ongoing excavation and analysis of *H. L. Hunley* is the discovery of key features of modern submarines that surprised the pundits. Flush-riveted construction, pumped ballast tanks, and sublimation of form to submerged operation characterize *Hunley*—and they characterize *Explorer.* Modern submariners have commented on *Explorer's* turtleback form, one reminiscent of modern nuclear submarine hulls, and the use of compressed air tanks to "blow ballast" and surface.

Some shipwrecks are artifacts that relate to an associated maritime landscape of where the land meets the sea.[5] *Sub Marine Explorer,* wrecked in close context to the site of its final operations, is such a resource. Isla San Telmo, as the 2008 autonomous underwater vehicle survey showed, rests at the edge of a formerly rich series of pearl oyster beds that were known to the pre–European contact inhabitants of the islands. After these inhabitants' demise, the beds were successively depleted by heavy "fishing" in the early Spanish colonial period and again in the eighteenth and early nineteenth-centuries. The Pearl Islands seemed the ideal location to operate the submarine and utilize its technological advantage for greater profit than the earlier, breath-holding divers could make. In the case of *Explorer,* however, its technology was in the wrong place because it was there at the wrong time. By the time *Explorer* arrived, the pearl beds had been effectively fished out. This pushed the submarine into increasingly deeper, more dangerous waters that ironically were less favorable habitat for the oysters. As previously noted, the Pacific Pearl Company doubtless realized that whether the submarine worked in Panama,

Baja California, or Venezuela, the same circumstances applied, and so they ultimately abandoned their expensive craft on Isla San Telmo as a less expensive alternative to bringing it back to New York for harbor work or trying again to sell it to the military.

Our assessment of the landscape shows that the placement of the wreck is therefore not an accident, even if it eventually drifted or was pulled ashore. An aerial perspective of the submarine shows that it lies in the cove, hemmed in by submerged rocks and reefs that make its drifting into the cove highly improbable. More than likely, the craft lies in close proximity to the site where it was laid up. *Sub Marine Explorer* is part of the landscape encompassed by the cove and inshore area that was the site of secondary activities associated with the oyster harvesting in the broader context of San Telmo and its surrounding waters and submerged oyster beds. The only known contemporary account of the submersible's operations places it at Isla San Telmo in late 1869, and at the conclusion of its last known dives, that press account reported that "it was decided, the experiment having proved a complete success, to lay the machine up in an adjacent cove."

We determined in the 2006 field season that the cove was the probable base of operations for the submarine because it lies in the lee of the island and away from the open ocean. As such it would have housed a temporary camp for the pearling operation. The most recent charts of San Telmo date to the mid-twentieth century, and these do not tell whether the immediate offshore area was of sufficient depth to accommodate *Explorer*'s 1869 dives, which reportedly reached a depth of 30 m (100 ft). The 2008 sonar survey of the waters surrounding Isla San Telmo determined that the area offshore and to the west were shallower, although some areas had depths approaching 80 feet. Dives to assess the area, including dives with local pearl divers from the neighboring village of La Esmeralda, as well as biological assessment dives by scuba conducted by Dr. Horgan, revealed rock-based clusters populated by larger numbers of immature (smaller) oysters in the shallows along the western (windward) side of San Telmo.

Investigation found that the channel between San Telmo and neighboring Isla del Rey possesses an ideal habitat for oysters (a channel lined with rocks); however, its oysters are more immature, clustered in waters that do not exceed 10 meters in depth at high tide. As noted previously, those beds would have been fished out by the native breath-holding divers in 1869, as they are today. Although *Explorer* was based at Isla San Telmo in the once-rich pearling waters of the archipelago, the submarine was not in an ideal location. The depths it is reported to have worked required a tow of the submarine away from the island, into open ocean waters on the windward side, where its dives were at depths beyond the ideal range for the oysters it sought. The pearl oyster, *Pinctada mazatlanica,* thrives on hard rocky bottoms in shallow depths up to 70 feet, but it does not live in water exceeding 110 feet in depth.[6] *Explorer* arrived too late, and its touted technological advantage was for naught as it was forced to look for oysters in deeper waters that had not been fished out.

One of the principal observations of the study of *Explorer* is that it represents another effort to employ technology to exploit a resource, but it was a technology deployed blindly, without any concepts of habitat, fisheries management, or sustainability. Oddly, Dr. Wolfred Nelson, a former resident of Panama, opined in 1889 that the pearl fisheries, "at one time of inestimable value," had been "destroyed by the reckless methods employed. Men in diving armor ruined them by taking up too many oysters, and for many years no fishing was allowed."[7] The Pacific Pearl Company was the only known company to employ "diving armor" in the Pearl Islands, after a previous effort with a diving bell failed decades earlier.[8] Another, longer-term American resident of Panama, Tracy Robinson, remarked in his memoirs that "from 1860 to 1870 pearls and pearl shells from the fisheries in Panama Bay figured to a considerable extent; but the oyster beds were overworked, and gave out, so that shipments almost entirely ceased."[9] One wonders, especially considering Nelson's observation, whether the Pacific Pearl Company, even in failure, managed to devastate the remaining oyster population, or whether it was simply blamed by the locals for doing so. This may explain the origin of the story, first heard after "rediscovery" of the submarine, that it had been the reason the pearl fishery had declined.[10]

FAILING TO ASSESS LOCAL CONDITIONS

The technology embodied by *Sub Marine Explorer* is part of a larger American story in which the submarine is an evocative artifact of a "nation whose citizens have long seen technological innovation and technical aptitude as the most readily verifiable measures of their superiority over both the 'Old World' of their ancestors and the 'exotic' non-Western cultures they encountered in North America and elsewhere."[11] Just as Mark Brumagim and his fellow investors sought to reap better results from both California and Mexican mines with steam power, modern stamp mills, and Ryerson's patented steam amalgamator, they also sought to use *Explorer*, as they repeatedly noted, to do a "better job" than breath-holding, shark-fearing naked divers.

In assessing the role of *Explorer* within the context of pearl diving, we can see the submarine within the "big picture." In world systems theory, the submarine is an artifact of an American effort to use "superior aspects" of civilization to capitalize on resources of the frontier, or in this case, what historian Aims McGuiness calls an effort to remake Panama "into a nexus of the world economy."[12] While earlier efforts had concentrated on transforming Panama into an easier-transited, globally linked hub, the Pacific Pearl Company was specifically focused on integrating pearls, a natural resource of Panama, into the expanding global market, furthering the dream of an ever-expanding American empire in the Pacific. The Panama Railroad and the steamers that met it on other side of the isthmus were already successful aspects of the use of Yankee technology to incorporate Panama into an American-dominated market system. The Pacific Pearl Company assumed that the submarine would be another such use of technology, part of the larger agenda to industrialize and consolidate control of the rich natural and mineral resources, and thus the profits to be had, in the West and the Pacific.[13]

The New York- and California-based investors had done their "market research" on the submarine, hiring Julius Kroehl and Ariel Patterson to build a craft capable of doing what the investors needed. But when it came to assessing Panama, the investors at best had only that information gained by transiting through Panama and by consulting with fellow American and British "experts." One wonders if they had consulted, in Spanish, with Panameños, especially local pearl divers. The evidence, seen in the failure of the first and last field season of 1869, is that they did not. This omission would have been in keeping with the attitudes of the day, as expressed in this dismissive assessment of the United States' newly acquired Hispanic American territories (and by extension, all of Latin America):

> The Spaniards had scarcely proceeded any way in the great work,—
> if they had not rather retarded it, when the Anglo-Saxons, the true
> and perhaps only type of modern progress, hastily stepped in, and
> unscrupulously swept away both their immediate forerunners as
> effete workers, and the aborigines of the land, all as lumberers and
> nuisances in the great western highway of civilization. This highway
> is fated to girdle the globe . . . and there need not be the slightest

doubt but that the empire, or rather the great union of peoples and nations in the Pacific will soon—perhaps in fifty years, perhaps a century—rival, if not surpass the magnificent States of the Atlantic. Indians, Spaniards of many provinces, Hawaiians, Japanese, Chinese, Malays, Tartars and Russians, must all give place to the restless flood of Anglo-Saxon or American progress.[14]

In the trial of *Sub Marine Explorer,* the few Panameños that enter into the picture are the local elite, such as "the President of the State, General Olarte" and "the Secretary of State, Mr. Bermudez," to whom Kroehl gave a ride in the craft in Panama Bay when he reassembled it. It was a demonstration, however, not a consultation.

It is unlikely that the locals were consulted, despite their exceptional knowledge of the maritime landscape, including the knowledge that they had actively fished (and fished out) the pearl beds. Among the Americans, racist attitudes prevailed. They and the "whiter" Panamanian elites of the day viewed the black divers, living simply and in what a westerner would define as poverty, as ignorant or worse. Many of the black divers were also former slaves, which relegated them to a lower social class.[15]

Most Americans of the time were contemptuous of black Panamanians.[16] These attitudes surfaced during the initial American contact with Panama during the gold rush of 1849–57. In July 1849 R. R. Taylor wrote to his wife that "it appears to be as fine a country as one would wish, but it is cursed with the most lazy indolent population that breathes."[17] Sample Flinn, writing to his father in May 1849, complained that he was "in a strange land, amongst a strange, lazy, black, good for nothing class of people."[18] Dr. James Tyson, passing through in 1849, commented on black Panamanians' "filthy habits and obscene exhibitions, their indolence and ignorance," and offered a prescription: "the influx of men from rougher climes and bleaker regions will probably exercise a salutary influence, by showing them the advantages of industry and patient toil."[19] Irish traveler William Ryan, writing in 1850, noted that "the Americans whom I had heard speak of Panama . . . informed me that it was one of the dirtiest and most disgusting places they had ever seen . . . and, to use their own phraseology, overrun with niggers."[20]

The fact that the pearl divers who lived in the *Archipiélago de las Perlas* were black, and the descendants of slaves, made it unlikely that their opinions or observations were sought by anyone associated with the Pacific Pearl Company. It was, after all, their "inefficiency" and "fear" of sharks and rays that had prevented the proper exploitation of the pearl fishery. Nothing could have been further from the truth; breath-holding divers had fished out the pearl beds through their hard labor on more than one occasion in the hundreds of years of Spanish domination of the region.

The racist, dismissive attitude of the time is clearly demonstrated in an 1855 account of a visit to a pearl-diving village in the Archipiélago de las Perlas:

> It is a straggling collection of bamboo and palm-thatched huts, and the inhabitants are of the usual mixed races of the Spanish, Indian, and Negro, where the latter darkly overshadows the others. Some canoes timidly approached the vessel as the anchor was dropped, and a few dark natives, in scant drapery, climbed aboard. The inhabitants of the town had been so much startled, as they told us, with the arrival of a steamer in their rarely-visited port, that they collected together their valuables, their pearls and money-bags, and hid themselves in the neighboring woods. One of the more knowing natives, whose experience had extended to the modern mystery of a steamboat, soon restored the people to confidence by assurances of safety, and the declaration that the United States was at peace with the Pearl Islands. The boats were soon lowered, and after a long stretch in the bay, we landed upon the reef, which extends out for half a mile or so from the white beach which borders the town. Straggling along this, some picking up stores of choice shells, some refreshing themselves with the green cocoa-nuts hurled down by nimble sailors from the tops of tall palms, which grow down to the water's edge, and others startling flocks of pelicans by their random pistol-shots, we make our way up the beach, through a fleet of stranded canoes, hollowed out of single trunks of huge trees, and go in and out among the huts of the town. Children of both sexes, and of all ages, from the toddling piccaninny to the supple youth, gather about us, and display their glossy ebony forms in natural ease, and unconscious nakedness. . . . Of the fishery we could see nothing, although we had a couple of supple divers with us who had been expressly provided to show us the modus operandi. But that part of the programme was omitted as a concession to the ladies, I believe, and much to the disappointment of Lord C, who

had already made up his betting-book, and had given odds, barring the sharks, upon the wind of the little nigger.[21]

The same attitude persisted little more than a decade later when the Pacific Pearl Company came to Panama. Their smugness notwithstanding, the Pacific Pearl Company arrived too late on the scene for their technological advantage to make a difference. If they had come earlier, *Sub Marine Explorer* might well have promoted a rapid, industrialized scale of exploitation that would have within a period of a few years cleaned out the pearl beds, for the concept of a renewable or sustainable fishery was not part of the business plan for the Pacific Pearl Company.

SPECULATION IN AN AGE OF AUDACITY

This brings up the question of the business acumen of the directors of the Pacific Pearl Company. The company, formed ostensibly by prominent men of sound judgment, was formed in New York at a time when that city and its "audacious and most driven businessmen" were transforming America's economic system, forging what historian Thomas Kessner terms a "fresh business culture of daring investment, converting a proliferation of markets . . . to a consolidated commerce in virtual property signified by stocks, bonds and assorted certificates."[22] Many of these businessmen, notes Kessner, were "ruthless in exploiting the land, the markets, the political system, and their own workers."[23]

This new economy came to the forefront during the Civil War, as the war created tremendous opportunities for profit. New York, as the nation's largest center of commerce and banking, took control, forming "the vast concentrations of capital, broad expertise, and innovative strategies that developed the mechanisms for nineteenth-century finance."[24] New York's bank profits tripled during the Civil War years, insurance policy values grew from $141 to $865 million, and individual fortunes blossomed.[25] These "immense pools" of capital were available for new investment outlets, and if a project or a product beckoned that had even a faint hope of a government contract, it was pursued. The fact that Congress was rife with corruption abetted schemes to sell something to the government, even if it did not work as advertised. It was the time of "shoddy," a term originally devised for shredded rags that were mashed into a pulp and reprocessed as "wool" for Union uniforms, only to disintegrate once on a soldier's back. In short order, "shoddy" became a well-known term "for all sorts of flimsy government issue, ranging from slipshod shoes to haphazard artillery."[26] The war economy benefited the risk-taking investor. Those who "plunged their fortunes into circumstances both treacherous and futile . . . not infrequently claimed bold rewards."[27] By the end of the war, the most dynamic sector of the US economy was financing, and one-fourth of the country's banking resources were not only in New York but within a one-mile area in Manhattan.[28]

In this climate, speculators often invested in a variety of new companies and endeavors, playing the lottery within a system that was increasingly "complex, abstract, and anonymous."[29] One such investor, New York Brahmin Moses Taylor, invested his capital in "transportation, utilities, mining, banking, and communications," for example.[30] In this fashion, it is easy to see how a diverse group of investors, loosely bound together by political, governmental, and Masonic affiliations, would come together to form the Pacific Pearl Company, in the hope of a government contract, or if not, with the idea of controlling the Pacific pearl trade. Apparently the company did not conduct detailed research into local conditions or the ultimate implications of the technology, either with regard to overfishing or, as we will see, the technology's impact on the workers in the submarine.

Who really were the investors in the Pacific Pearl Company? Other than Julius Kroehl, his friend C. A. Morris, whose stock certificate has survived in a private collection, and William Headlam Jr. of Chicago, who listed his shares in his 1878 bankruptcy,[31] we know only the names of the officers of the company, as discussed in chapter 5—William M. B. Hartley, William H. Tiffany, John Chadwick, Mark Brumagim, and Charles D. Poston. In some cases, confidential business information on some of them is available through the records of credit specialists Dun & Company. With those and other records, it is possible to gain a better understanding of the speculators who formed and ran the Pacific Pearl Company.

After Charles D. Poston lost his seat in Congress, he traveled for a time, and ultimately returned to Arizona, where he died in poverty in a Phoenix hotel room in June 1902.[32] One biographer notes that the last 30 years of his life "were filled with rash, unsuccessful schemes and a pathetic quest for a variety of jobs."[33] Poston's 12,500 shares in the Pacific Pearl Company, which he left in the care of George Wrightson, and which are now in the collections of the

Sharlot Hall Museum in Prescott, Arizona, were valued at $100 per share. It is particularly noteworthy that Poston never redeemed his shares, suggesting that he and probably all the other shareholders in the company never received any value for their investment in *Sub Marine Explorer*.[34] The failure of the company may have been one of several blows that marked the beginning of a 30-year downslide in Poston's life.

Mark Brumagim did somewhat better. In March 1869 Dun & Company's evaluation of him as the president of the Mariposa Mining Company of California noted that "he is without doubt honest in his intentions & means to make the ppy [property] a valuable one. . . . At the present time cannot be said to be worth any money except in the prospective."[35] Later that year, in September, Dun & Company noted that Brumagim had just made "a good deal of money" in selling the Mariposa Mining Company's stock, but he was in default of payments and would have to "manipulate the stock again." However, "parties were induced to buy the stock representations being made of positive value of the ppy and that they had large means for the working of the mine which as far as known has not been carried out."[36]

Van Buren Ryerson and Brumagim had a falling out over the amalgamator and its use at the Mariposa and Eureka mines. Ryerson won, and in 1877 the courts awarded Ryerson his claim against Brumagim. Clearly the partnership was over. The fact that the press called it as a "long-standing" suit indicates that these two partners in the Pacific Pearl Company had been out of sorts with each for some time.[37] In 1881 Dun & Company reported that Brumagim was still working to make the Mariposa mining property pay a dividend. The mining company stock, "which he placed upon the mkt & which for a time was thot [*sic*] to be good, but it appeared to fizzle out suddenly & B. received a great deal of adverse criticism at the time from those who lost money in the speculation."[38] However, while there had been "some valuable discoveries made & recently proved," Brumagim was embroiled in lawsuits, and in 1882 lost a key case. This, Dun & Company noted, "will make it necessary to make an assessment on the stock, which will be done very shortly in order to save the property."[39] Brumagim eventually lost control of the Mariposa Mining Company but retained an interest in the Candelaria Mine in Mexico, albeit one he also effectively lost control of because he was tied up in litigation to regain control until his death in 1914.

In 1889 a San Francisco newspaper column suggested that Brumagim had a weakness similar to Poston's—endless and often fruitless speculation:

New York, Jan. 5. Another Electric Scheme. Passing along Broadway one day last week might have seen . . . an old-time Californian
who in his day played many parts and is not through yet . . . I refer,
of course, to Mark Brummagim [*sic*]. . . . Mark came on to New
York . . . many years ago, and has since been seeking fickle fortune
in the highways of Broadway and the by-ways of Wall Street. Mr.
Brummagim has waxed gray somewhat, but beneath the rim of his
sealskin cap a couple of eyes twinkled with good humor. . . . He
has a big scheme on hand. All Californians in New York have big
pet schemes, each one bigger than the other—too big, which is the
reason probably why none of them fill. Brummagim's scheme will
make him a millionaire when he gets it to working OK. It is an
electric invention that is to revolutionize mining, for he can take
all kinds of rebellious ores and at a cost of 25 cents, or two bits,
per ton, California vernacular, make them free milling up to 99
per cent of the assay value. That is the scheme in a nutshell, and it
works lovely—on a small scale. The idea is to be practically illustrated on a large scale presently.[40]

It was a scheme not dissimilar to *Sub Marine Explorer* and the Pacific Pearl
Company, with technology again seen as the expedient means of extracting riches. The problem was, as before, making it pay out on the big scale.
Brumagim's electric scheme went nowhere. Twenty years after *Explorer*'s last
dive off Isla San Telmo, Mark Brumagim demonstrated that he had learned
nothing from that failure. Ever optimistic, ever speculative, he remained a be-
liever in technology conquering all. As previously noted, the last decades of his
life were spent in a protracted legal battle over the Candelaria silver mine in
Mexico that remained unresolved at the time of his death. His struggles with
the mine "revealed the hazards American capitalists faced when investing in
Mexican silver mines" because they "frequently underestimated the expenses
necessary to rehabilitate them and make them profitable."[41]

Like Brumagim, William H. Tiffany had gone to California during the
gold rush and stayed until the Civil War, returning to New York in 1863. Formerly a patent agent and an attorney, Tiffany on his return was associated
with his brother Charles' firm, Tiffany & Co., in addition to the Pacific Pearl
Company. Thanks to political connections, Tiffany secured an appointment as
assessor of internal revenue for the Ninth District of New York, but in January

1869 President Andrew Johnson removed him from office.[42] In July 1869 he served as president of the National Arms Company.[43] Dun & Company noted, "We can get very little information about him but the little that we do get confirms the impression that has little or no respons[ibility]."[44] A month later, the Dun & Company agent added, "Think him of very doubtful respons[ibility] said to have done a party in Cala [California] out of 150 [thousand dollars]."[45]

William M. B. Hartley published a small booklet entitled *Money and Usury* in 1869. The subject and timing of the publication are most revealing. The post–Civil War economy of the United States was shrinking, and banks, under pressure to restrict their lending, were doing so and charging high interest rates for what they lent. Without sufficient capital, business opportunities could not be pursued. "People look each other in the face and ask . . . why men who are fearless, industrious, liberal and working for success, should not succeed?"[46] Left unsaid in Hartley's book was his probable conviction that lack of capital is what had doomed the Pacific Pearl Company. More banks, more money, and more lending at lower interest rates would benefit the economy, as money would flow into all sorts of ventures, Hartley argued. While a contracting postwar economy was one of several factors in the demise of the Pacific Pearl Company, bad investments made in ignorance of local conditions and a blind belief that technology could conquer any obstacle played the dominant role in the demise of *Sub Marine Explorer.* Audacious speculation is an oft-repeated mistake made by investors, and a timeless lesson at the dawn of the twenty-first century. Hartley did not long outlive the Pacific Pearl Company. Following the tragic death of his son Edward in 1871, Hartley returned to Canada, where he died, a prominent lawyer, in Montreal on February 1, 1875.[47]

Not much detail is known of the later years of company investors Chadwick or Wrightson.[48] In the end, the backers of the Pacific Pearl Company would have seen better returns investing in the Panama Railroad or the Pacific Mail Steamship Company. Instead, the endeavor they chose employed the combined genius and creation of Van Buren Ryerson and Julius Kroehl, but it still failed because of the company's lack of due diligence in regard to the status of the pearl fishery in Panama, as previously noted, and because of a flaw in the adoption of *Sub Marine Explorer*'s lockout diving technology. The ultimate failure of the Pacific Pearl Company and the abandonment of *Sub Marine Explorer* is not all that surprising, given the character of the times, one that encouraged enthusiastic and at times reckless speculation, and the character of

Brumagim, Poston, Chadwick, and Tiffany. These company officers probably shrugged off the loss and went on to the next endeavor that caught their eye.

A Technological "Flaw"

One of the great ironies in the story of *Sub Marine Explorer* is that the adoption of the latest technology had little to no effect on the success of the endeavor. But even more ironic is that the use of this latest technology had a fatal flaw that manifested itself in repeated dives to depth, and for which there was no known cure in the nineteenth century.

The 1869 *New York Times* account of *Explorer*'s dives describes how the submarine operated by the release of compressed air into the working chamber

> until it has gained sufficient volume and force as to counter-balance the tremendous pressure of the water from without, [and] when this is done the hatches in the bottom of the machine are opened, and the men proceed to take in the oysters, the air within the working chamber completely checking the ingress of the water. When the men have been down a sufficient length of time, and have collected all the shell within reach, air from the compressed-air chamber is let into the ballast or water-chamber, and as the air slowly forces out the water, the machine slowly and surely rises to the surface.[49]

Thus the crew working inside the craft labored at the same ambient pressure of the submarine's maximum depth. The same *New York Times* article references 12 days of diving to a depth equal to 46 pounds per square inch, with the submarine "remaining under water four hours" before ascending. Because we know that saltwater exerts one atmosphere of pressure (14.7 psi) for every 33 feet of depth, we can determine from 46 psi pressure that *Explorer* was working at a depth of 103 feet.[50]

Using the US Navy's standard air decompression table, the men inside *Explorer* at 100 feet deep would have exceeded their limit for being underwater without decompression in 25 minutes.[51] At two hours, they would have to decompress with stops at 30 feet for 12 minutes, 20 feet for 41 minutes, and 10 feet for 78 minutes—for a total of 1 hour, 32 minutes, 40 seconds. They stayed, however, for four hours, and according to the newspaper accounts of their dives, they did not decompress. After their first four-hour dive, *Explorer*'s crew "made one downward trip each day for eleven days." Repetitive, no-decompression diving to 103 feet for 12 days can bring only one result: decompression sickness. Not one in 100 individuals could avoid decompression sickness in such a circumstance, which probably explains the reference in the article to their condition after the last dive on the 12th day: "All the men were again down with fever; and, it being impossible to continue working with the same men for some time," the dives were terminated and *Explorer* was laid up.

The idea that illness had played a role in laying up the submarine is reflected in a reference from the previously mentioned Wolfred Nelson, which I believe, despite some inaccuracy, refers to the end of *Explorer* and its crew: "While on the subject of pearl fishing I wish to recall the fate of an expedition fitted out in this city (New York) to visit the same islands. The party went to the Isthmus, taking with them a small steamer in sections, which was put together on the Panama side of the Isthmus. It was in the year 1858, while there was an epidemic on the Isthmus. The sailors, engineers and officers contracted the disease. That expedition never left the shores of Panama, for all died except one, who returned to this city."[52] If you substitute "submarine" for "steamer," 1858 for 1869, and accept that decompression sickness or fever killed off the crew, leaving only one, presumably Henry Dingee, to survive, Nelson's story could very well reflect the contemporary public "story" of the end of *Sub Marine Explorer.*

In 1869, particularly in a tropical environment such as Panama where outbreaks of yellow fever and malaria were common, the symptoms of decompression sickness would have appeared close to those of fever; for example, pain in the joints, loss of feeling, paralysis, blindness, dizziness, convulsions, unconsciousness, choking, asphyxia, rashes, and itching.[53] The crew of *Explorer* were quite possibly no strangers to these symptoms, hence the reference to "again down with fever," to which they mistakenly attributed them. It is likely that the crew's sickness was one of the factors that doomed the Pacific Pearl Company's plans to shift from Panama to Mexico's Baja Peninsula, despite initial plans to do so.

Decompression sickness was little known to physicians in 1869, let alone the public. The "modern age's first disease," writes Dr. John L. Phillips in *The Bends,* was the direct result of the Industrial Revolution and the power of steam-driven machinery to compress air for technical applications.[54] Knowledge of the deleterious effects of pressurized air began to emerge after the technology for both pumps and compressors improved in the 1840s. It was Charles-Jean Triger of France, developer of the first modern caisson in 1840 to work the coal mines of the Loire Valley, which lay beneath the water level under layers of silt, mud, and sand, who first noted the effects of pressure. Triger called this manifestation of breathing problems and pains *mal de caisson;* within a few decades it was termed "caisson disease." Triger hired two local physicians, B. Pol and T. J. J. Watelle, to treat his crews and determine what was causing the malady. These pioneers were the first to study decompression sickness, including exposing themselves to the caissons and suffering the results. Their work concluded with a recommendation that a second airlock be added to the caissons to allow workers to decompress before returning to the surface. Their basic observation was correct, but it took decades before the procedure was adopted and a more sophisticated understanding of how to regulate the decompression emerged.[55]

Throughout the 1850s, workers who emerged from mines and caissons suffering from decompression sickness, in increasing numbers as the technology spread, were treated with cold water "ablutions," lineaments, oils, and scarification (bloodletting). As caissons and compressed air technology spread rapidly to the United States in the 1860s, and as a result, cases of decompression sickness rose dramatically.[56]

This was certainly the case with two major bridge-building projects, the St. Louis (Eads) Bridge over the Mississippi River and the Brooklyn Bridge over the East River. In St. Louis, as the project began in the summer of 1868 under the direction of James B. Eads, a caisson sunk 60 feet down allowed men to work shifts of four to six hours. Decompression sickness began to appear, and men emerging stooped over from pain or paralysis were said by unsympathetic coworkers to be adopting the "Grecian bend," then a popular style of walking adopted by women wearing hoop skirts. In time, the disease took on a shortened nickname, "the bends."[57]

The bends were no laughing matter. As the caisson sank deeper, the number of cases of the bends increased, and on March 19, 1869, a worker died after emerging from the depths. He was followed by six other victims in the next 10 days. What mystified physicians was the realization that not all men responded to the caisson in the same way. Some men emerged with no symptoms at all, which now is seen as the fact that some of them had become acclimated to the pressure. Dr. Alphonse Jaminet at St. Louis studied the stricken and autopsied the dead, and called for rest, a ban on alcohol and other stimulants, and a decompression schedule that would now be seen as inadequate but was a step in the right direction.[58]

In Brooklyn, the construction of the bridge across the East River, beginning in May 1870, called for two caissons. By February 1871, as the first caisson sank deeper, workers in New York began to feel the effects, and the first cases of the bends appeared. Anxious to avoid the problems of St. Louis, engineer Washington Augustus Roebling asked his physician, Andrew H. Smith, to become the bridge company's official physician and tackle the problem. Better trained than Jaminet, Smith learned more than his peer, particularly spurred along when his employer, Roebling, was also stricken with the bends and permanently paralyzed and weakened. Smith proposed the use of a variety of therapies, and picking up again on the ideas of Pol and Watelle, he designed but did not build a decompression chamber. It would take a few more decades for the practice of decompression to begin, especially as Jaminet's and Smith's results were published.[59]

Later tunneling projects, especially those under New York's Hudson River between 1879 and 1881, saw an increasing number of cases of the bends and escalating fatalities. Engineer Ernest William Moir developed a recompression chamber to treat the tunnelers stricken with the bends in 1889, and while his treatments were too fast by modern standards, Moir paved the way for what ultimately would be the satisfactory treatment of decompression sickness. The next step forward was the work of French physiologist Paul Bert, who discovered that nitrogen buildup in the body under pressure was causing the bends. Following Bert's death in 1886, a new generation of researchers turned to the problem. Fifty years after decompression sickness was first experienced, the work of John Scott Haldane, building on that of Bert, resulted in a more sophisticated understanding of the bends.[60]

Between 1903 and 1906 Haldane built a more sophisticated chamber and tested and developed a process of carefully staged decompression. Confident of the laboratory results, Royal Navy divers in 1906 tested Haldane's method and found it to work in open water. Forty years after Julius Kroehl launched *Sub Marine Explorer,* and 37 years after the submarine's last, injurious (and perhaps fatal) dives off Isla San Telmo, human knowledge had at last caught up with technology and provided the means for safe operation of *Sub Marine Explorer.* It was, of course, far too late for either the submarine or the Pacific Pearl Company. The "flaw" in the submarine was that its technology outstripped human knowledge of how to use it effectively. This flaw was not unique, as we have seen, in that "the ultimate limits of technological progress will be determined by the physiologic limits of the humans who use them."[61]

EXPLORER'S CONDITION AND OPTIONS

Capitalist systems are Darwinian and so too is the ocean environment. Like the Pacific Pearl Company, *Explorer* is succumbing to the environment in which it worked. The submarine is embedded in sand and gravel to a depth of approximately 1 meter, but it is not concreted to or rusted onto the seabed. It rests on a substrate of shingle, cobble, and driftwood buried beneath the sand. A thicker layer of concretion on the lower hull in the buried portions suggests that the submarine's bow and offshore hull have been buried to this approximate depth for quite some time. Visual observation, measurement, and comparison of photographic and light detection and ranging (lidar) documentation observed no discernable difference in mechanical damage (i.e., holes) in the upper and inshore areas until 2008, when a portion of the upper shell collapsed.

However, additional damage to the offshore (port) exterior hull was noted at the edges of the holes, especially at the bow and at the stern. A substantial gap in the outer (pressure) hull of the compressed air chamber as well as the lower portions of the port quarter suggests that wave energy is channeled and attenuated at the stern. Surf-borne transport of gravel, rocks, and driftwood along the exposed lower stern is actively eroding the cast iron there as well as at the bow. In February 2008, during the course of the survey, a visit to the submarine after a high tide period revealed two large impacts, one to the stern post, and the other midships on the port (offshore) ballast tanks that knocked off concretion and exposed bare metal.

Surf-transported cobble and gravel, as well as sand, are directly deposited into the interior of the submarine through an eroded hole in the bow and then channeled through the interior to exit at the eroded bottom of the hull at the stern. Excavation of the interior and onsite observation demonstrated as much as 30 cm (1 foot) of tidal variation of the sand and gravel level in the interior, and observations between 2001 and 2008 also point toward more substantial seasonal variation, with decayed organic material suggesting as much as 1 meter of change in the sand level inside *Explorer* each seasonal cycle of littoral erosion and accretion. Driftwood, including substantial logs deposited on the beach, and a larger hardwood log drifting in the surf and battering against the submarine at the time of the team's arrival in 2006, as noted previously, suggests that surf-transported logs may be responsible for some of the damage, especially at the junction of the lower and upper hulls—the area of the greatest damage. This area is exposed to the greatest surf activity at intermediate tidal levels. As well, logs rolling over the upper portions of the submarine appear to be responsible for active deconcretion of the upper hull—the only area not covered in concretion.

High levels of corrosion at the intertidal level are separating *Explorer's* upper hull from the lower hull. In 2006 approximately one-half of *Explorer's* iron hull's thickness had been lost to corrosion, and the submarine had reached a critical stage. It may have in fact passed the point of no return. In time, *Explorer* will lose her upper shell within a few years, and then gradually breach, exposing the operating chamber. Further damage from corrosion and logs, combined with the impact of well-meaning visitors and ongoing ravages of surf and gravel will break apart Julius Kroehl's abandoned craft.

The options for *Explorer's* future are

- No action, allowing the submarine to continue its process of decay, erosion, and possible loss to metal "pirates;"
- Preservation through documentation, with a more extensive process of field documentation including possible *in situ* dismantling of portions of the craft to better understand its construction and characteristics;
- Construction of an elevated cofferdam or seawall to protect the submarine from damage from drifting logs and heavy surf; sealing the interior from unauthorized access to protect the more fragile cast-iron fittings inside the craft;
- Removal of the submarine from its shallow, inshore environment and sinking it in deeper water to stop the cycle of wet-dry exposure and deterioration, mechanical damage, and visitor intrusion and damage;
- Recovery of the craft, transportation to the mainland, and a program of conservation, further assessment, and museum display.

As of 2011, there is no official decision on *Explorer's* future. The various options, if any are chosen, will be a decision influenced by political and funding considerations. The cost and effort required to move the submarine to deeper water is the same as recovery; the only difference is the cost of conservation, which could be offset by public interest and sponsorship generated by its display. The costs of *in situ* protection through a cofferdam and sealing may not be less than conservation and introduce environmental change and impact in a nature preserve. Preservation through documentation, unless the craft is completely destructively dismantled on the beach, will not yield the same details or data as laboratory work during conservation. The costs of doing such work, especially when the nearest village, La Esmeralda, lacks medical facilities or a sewage system, have to be assessed, however. As ingenious an invention that *Explorer* is, 140 years after it was abandoned the question remains one of balancing the needs of people against an investment in an artifact of a flawed business venture.

And so there are no easy answers to the questions posed here about *Explorer's* future. Initially viewed as a craft of death or a Japanese submarine by the inhabitants of the surrounding islands, *Explorer's* historical context is now well known to them as a result of the archaeological project and especially the power of the media. Numerous news stories, and in particular the National Geographic International Television series "The Sea Hunters," have conveyed a new sense of the submarine to Panamanians and particularly to the people of La Esmeralda.

In 2006, as we worked on the submarine, a small boat approached with an armed soldier and the *cabildo,* or police chief, of La Esmeralda. They were concerned about reports of people being on the submarine. As we explained that we were archaeologists working under permit from the national government, I thought I recognized the *cabildo* from a visit we had made to his town in 2004 while filming the submarine for the "Sea Hunters." I was not only the archaeologist in charge of the project but also the host of the series for its five-year run on international television. The *cabildo* did not recognize me, because I had been clean shaven in 2004 but was wearing a full beard in 2006.

After we established that we were working with permission and had no bad intentions toward the submarine, I asked the *cabildo* in Spanish if he knew the story of the craft, and specifically asked if it was Japanese. No, he answered, I was obviously not a local, but in Panama they had a television show, *Los Cazadores del Mar* (The Sea Hunters) and they had visited his town, dived on the submarine, and learned its story. Now everyone in Panama knew that this was an American vessel from that country's Civil War, and that it had been abandoned here after a flaw in it had made its crew sick. Just the other evening, thanks to La Esmeralda's satellite, they had watched the *Cazadores.* I smiled, and asked if he remembered the archaeologist from the show who had visited his town. He stopped, looked at me, and broke into a grin. "It was you! It was you!" We hugged each other and shared reminiscences of that visit. We met again in 2008, and he told me that life is changing for his town as new resorts are planned and how as a result the old days are ending. There are no fortunes to be made diving for pearls or in commercial fishing. He is training to become a guide, so he can take visitors to the islands to explore and to go sport fishing. I asked what he and his town wanted us to do with the submarine.

The submarine was no longer feared, and was now a warmly welcomed part of their patrimony. The answer, we both realized, was for *Explorer* to remain where it has rested for nearly a century and a half. It will gradually melt into the sea and sand, visited often by the inquisitive who will pay the locals for access to the strange craft. It will occasionally be documented by archaeologists who monitor the submarine's ongoing disassembly by nature and document details revealed by the inexorable processes of time and the sea. It is not a bad fate for *Sub Marine Explorer.* It seems fitting. Its once forgotten inventor is now famous in both the city and country of his birth and in his adopted land. A once lost and forgotten craft has been restored to its proper place in the history of the submarine, and its details have been documented, thanks to archaeology. And that formerly abandoned craft still lies on a beach, now celebrated and gradually becoming one with the only home it has ever known.

Anatomy of *Sub Marine Explorer*

The hull is of peculiar shape, constructed
partly of wrought and partly of cast iron, and
is divided into three chambers.

—*New York Times,* May 1866

Between 2001 and 2008, documentation and analysis of *Sub Marine Explorer* slowly yielded a detailed sense of the construction and characteristics of this early American submarine. In 2007 a full set of interpretive reconstruction drawings were completed with John W. McKay. The study of the submarine had reached the stage where the drawings were necessary to formulate additional research questions and to document then current state of research into the craft.

Reconstructing the submarine proved to be a difficult task. Years on the beach of Isla San Telmo have brought on the destruction of some parts of *Sub Marine Explorer.* The corrosive effects of seawater, cycles of exposure to the sea and then the hot Panamanian sun, impacts from drifting logs, the abrasion of rocks and gravel in the surf, and the partial stripping of the tiny craft for salvage have removed portions of *Explorer* that can never be replaced. The loss of material also means the loss of information.

Because of the loss of original material, conjectural reconstruction of approximately 10 percent was necessary when reconstructing *Explorer* on paper. In most cases, where conjectural assumptions were made, they were based on the fragmentary information at hand, as well as information from other primary and secondary sources. What emerged from the process of preparing the reconstruction drawings is, however, a submarine that makes "sense" from the standpoint of its technology in the context of its times. We also better understand how the craft reflects both the adaptive genius of Van Buren Ryerson and Julius Kroehl.

Some questions are likely not to be resolved unless excavation of the site recovers missing portions of the craft or additional archival details become available. As the "reconstruction" of *Explorer* continued, another area of consideration was the terminology to be applied to the various parts of the submarine. While naming some parts might seem simple enough—for example, "conning tower" and "ballast tank"—some of these terms were not in use in 1864–66, when submarine engineering was in its infancy. The primary source ultimately used in the reconstruction drawings was the February 2, 1865, report of W. W. W. Wood, which contains some two dozen technical terms. Other technical terms, drawn from contemporary sources, were also employed in the drawings.

SOURCES USED TO RECONSTRUCT SUB MARINE EXPLORER

In addition to the detailed archaeological and architectural assessments undertaken in the field between 2001 and 2006, three primary sources are worthy of note. These are the only known surviving construction drawings, now in the National Archives, W. W. W. Wood's report, and the provisional patent issued in Great Britain in August 1867.[1] The drawing, signed by Julius Kroehl, was rendered in ink on linen. It is appended to Wood's report and was likely prepared by Kroehl and given to Wood as the naval officer wrote his report on the then incomplete submarine in February 1865. As a result, not every feature of *Explorer* as launched and sent to Panama is represented in the drawing, and some features, planned at the time and represented in the plans, were not ultimately built—as the archaeological and architectural assessment of the submarine ultimately revealed.

John McKay describes the plan—drawn on the scale of ¾ inch to the foot, the document stretches out for 12 feet—as what would today be called a general arrangement plan, with a longitudinal section, half plan, and partial cross section. It is the only contemporary drawing of *Explorer* known to have survived, and considering the secrecy in which *Explorer* was designed and built, its survival is amazing. Kroehl and the other principals in the Pacific Pearl Company wished to sell their submarine design to the US Navy. When naval officer W. W. W. Wood came to examine *Explorer*, he was handed a drawing that otherwise would have been filed away in the company records. Instead, the plan ended up in the National Archives. The drawing is a comprehensive plan that lays out the aspects of the craft's construction, and along with Wood's explanation, it offers the only detailed look at *Explorer* outside archaeological documentation.

When dealing with "modern" archaeological sites such as a nineteenth-century submarine, historic documents such as Kroehl's drawing and Wood's report are often available. However, the presence of such documents should never be mistaken as *comprehensive documentation*. Indeed, the ongoing study of *Explorer*'s remains in the surf of Isla San Telmo has revealed a considerable amount of additional information, answered questions about vague or misunderstood aspects of the drawing and report, and made it very apparent that both the drawing and report describe a submarine as Kroehl intended to build it—not as he built it.

Likewise, documentation of the submarine's remains provide a clearer sense of aspects of *Explorer* that reflect the likely contributions of Ariel Patterson and his workers in the old shipyard, the most obvious being the internal braces in the compressed air chamber. Essentially modified boiler stays, these hand-forged braces, made from iron bars, appear more the work of a shipyard craftsman with boiler-making experience than the work of a "submarine engineer."

GENERAL ARRANGEMENT

All measurements of the submarine are reported in the English system rather than the metric system. Among archaeologists this is an accepted stratagem where a conversion factor is provided. *Explorer* was engineered and built to the English system of feet and inches, and use of the metric system imposes a confusing mathematical conversion to *Explorer,* especially when certain features of the submarine were designed and described in the English system, such as the "four foot line" that separates the craft's cast and wrought iron sections. In the course of completing the reconstruction drawings of the submarine, this description of *Explorer* was initially drafted by John W. McKay in cooperation with the principal investigator. This appendix incorporates and expands upon that original draft (see McKay's drawings at the end of this appendix).

Kroehl divided *Sub Marine Explorer* into three distinct spaces. These are (1) the water ballast chambers, (2) the compressed-air chamber, and (3) the working chamber with its central dome. *Explorer* is 36'0" long, 10'0" in breadth, and 10'6½" in overall height. For the most part the lower section (to a line 4'0" above the underside of the bottom plate) is of cast iron that is bolted or screwed together. In form it resembles a bateau, a double-ended, flat-bottomed craft with raking bow and stern and flaring sides. Above the four-foot line, riveted wrought iron (which Kroehl described as "boiler iron"[2]) is mostly employed. This top can be considered to be "turtle-backed" in form. The 1867 patent references future versions should be "preferably of cylindrical shape with a flattened dome top."[3] The dome and the top lining of the working chamber are also wrought iron.

CONSTRUCTION

Kroehl's drawing shows that he assigned station lines to his vessel at 2' intervals, beginning with "0" at the foremost tip of the bow, what would be termed the fore perpendicular, and ending at the stern with "36," the aft perpendicular.

The lower, cast iron section of the vessel is defined by the bottom plate. It is a large and complex casting that is 34'4" long and 8'0"wide. It is 1¾" thick (this and the following framing dimension cited are taken from Wood's report) and it tapers fore and aft. There are a number of openings cast into it to accommodate trap doors, access holes, and holes for valves. There are six large openings that are roughly 3'6" wide × 3'4" long, their length being defined by athwart ship integral frames that are located at 4' intervals beginning 10' in from the bow and ending 10' in from the stern. A web, 1" wide × 4" high, is cast with each frame that ends at the ballast tanks and therefore does not run across the whole width of the bottom plate. These webs would strengthen the beams and would also serve as wash plates if any water got into the submarine.

Water ballast chambers are ranged along both sides of the vessel, and their walls are supported by frames that align with the frames of the bottom plate. "Every second frame is solid" (from Wood's report, i.e., webbed), so four tanks on each side are formed. The frame dimensions are 7" wide × 4" deep with webs and flanges that are 1" thick.

The ballast tanks tops are 1¼" thick cast iron. They are 4' long, taper at the bow and stern, and are flanged on their underside inboard and outboard edges to carry the tank plating. The flanges are 1¾" thick and 3¾" high. The outside and inside plates are 1" thick cast iron, and there is site evidence that the outside plates were fastened to the frames with 1" diameter screws that are countersunk and flush. (Wood refers to the screws as "bolts.") It is logical to assume that the bottom plate, top plates, and inside plates are also fixed to the frames with such screws.

Explorer was not built with a stern or stem post per se. Instead, "vee"-shaped outer plates were installed fore and aft. At the stern the point of the "vee" is flattened off for 6" to accommodate the propeller boss. The lower half of this stern section is missing and it is not known if a web was cast with the plate to reinforce the propeller shaft tube. Small frames were installed athwart ship here that, along with the other framing elements, form a small sealed air buoyancy tank that was likely to counter the weight of the propulsion machinery. Forward, it is not clear if there was a longitudinal web on the center line in the ballast tanks, but there more than likely was. For trim control, it was important that these tanks be separate.

Three cast iron recesses were installed in the inner plate on either side of the working chamber. They are semicircular in plan and were installed to accommodate the water ballast intake/blowoff valves. The fore and aft valves service their respective tanks, and the middle valve is common to the two middle tanks. The valves sit on an integral iron plinth that is 6" high. The plinths facilitate the movement of the valves' plugs, and the alcove recesses were planned so that the valves were not in the way of the crew in the working chamber. Interestingly, Kroehl's drawing shows the bases of the valves as being cast monolithically with the alcove's walls and bases. This would have made for a very complex and expensive casting, and while we believe that they were probably cast separately for ease of maintenance, we have followed Kroehl's original design as shown in the drawing. Excavation and analysis of the bottom of the submersible will provide the final answer to this question.

Each ballast tank has an 18" diameter access hole and cover plate in its inside plate. These were for inspection and maintenance and for the removal of scale.

In the working chamber, six large openings in the bottom plate are closed with ribbed cast iron plates. Kroehl's drawings are vague here, as they show that all six plates were hinged on the port side of *Explorer*. The hinges show on the longitudinal section, and it is likely that all were shown because their arrangement had not been finalized. However, it would have been difficult to hinge the fore and aft plates due to their irregular shapes, and as Wood's report calls for four wrought-iron trap doors, we have shown the center four to be hinged. Because there seems to be a hinged hold-open clip adjacent to the foremost trap door on the port side of the vessel, and another clip on the starboard side adjacent to the aftermost trap door, we have shown the aft three doors to hinge alternately to starboard and port, as this technique would assist in trimming the vessel when these heavy doors were open. These clips are similar to those on *Intelligent Whale*.[4] All six plates were secured by lugs and hexagonal bolts, and a rubber seal ensured the vessel's waterproof integrity.

In the bottom plate, two openings aft and one forward are also closed by lugs, nuts, and rubber seals. As they are rather small, their cover plates are simpler than the large trap doors in design. Wood refers to them as "man hole plates." The aft-most one is irregular in shape, and as it sat directly under the propulsion gearing, we may consider it as an access port to accommodate installation and repair of the gearing. The other two are 18" in diameter, and it is likely that they were used as viewing ports when the vessel's working chamber was pressurized and it was maneuvering over the seabed.

An anchor cable stuffing box and windlass are shown in the working chamber of the vessel's bow on Kroehl's drawings. Again, these are rather vague in detail, so some assumptions must be made when considering their operation. An anchor or anchors to secure the craft to the bottom would have been essential in any type of current. *Intelligent Whale* employed two ball-shaped, 350-lb. anchors, deployed by cable from two 17" diameter, 10" deep recessed sockets at the bow and stern.[5] Only one windlass and what appears to be a box or recess for a bow anchor is shown on Kroehl's drawing. The anchor may have been a ball or mushroom style. The windlass is no longer *in situ* and was either removed or has fallen. The lower bow area of *Explorer* is filled with sand and sediment and remains unexcavated at this time, and so these features have not been observed archaeologically. Most probably, like *Intelligent Whale,* the windlass deployed a cable-supported anchor, the cable passing through a stuffing box.[6]

The Kroehl drawing shows *Explorer*'s windlass as a 12" long concave barrel that is supported by bosses that are cast in the inner plates. There is little room in the working chamber here, so it would have been operated by only one man who would have used an iron bar for leverage. It is likely that a ratchet regulated the windlass. It is speculated that when the anchor was hove to the hull, the cable simply remained wrapped around the capstan barrel.

Generally speaking, the bottom section of *Explorer* seems very sound and almost overdesigned. This is due to natural uncertainties over design requirements in a fledgling field of engineering. Archaeologists and architectural historians note that "overbuilding" is a design feature in many mid nineteenth-century iron structures.[7] The overdesigned nature of *Explorer* also would also have made it expensive to build. Many of the castings are very complex, and even though the vessel is symmetrical, only a few of the mold patterns could have been used for more than two applications. Further, waterproof integrity relied on rust joints, and this technique demanded extremely tight-fitting surfaces, so much hand-fitting and grinding would have been necessary. This may help account for the reported cost, in 1865, of $40,000 for *Explorer,* which today would be slightly more than $500,000.

At the center of the vessel, a funnel-shaped dome sits on the ballast tanks.

It is of half-inch wrought iron (Wood refers to it as "best boiler iron, ½ inch thick") and is well riveted. This is clearly the conning station of the submarine, as valves, gauges, and the steering apparatus are located here. An oval-shaped sleeve extends the funnel some 20" above the top of the compressed air chamber. Kroehl's drawing shows a rather narrow sleeve here that does not flair out at the bottom. When the fittings were installed, it must have been decided that this sleeve was too small for a man to work in. The drawing also shows that a very heavy cast iron sleeve with a thick cast iron hatch (manhole plate) was planned. Two 1½" diameter bolts were used to secure the hatch; it would have been slow to unbolt and difficult for one man to open. Based on site observations (the manhole plate is missing, but there are two bolt clips and the remnants of a hinge on the existing sleeve), we have patterned the manhole plate on the small bottom plates, as this would have been a much more manageable design. A rubber seal would have made the plate watertight. Four 4" diameter holes are cut into the sleeve plate to accommodate glass "side lights." Wood mentions these but the glass and fittings for them are missing. He also mentions two "lights" in the manhole plate.

The working chamber is located along the center line of the vessel. At the dome, the chamber is roughly 5'9" high × 3'8" wide, and it narrows dramatically at the bow and stern in both directions. We estimate that this chamber could carry a maximum of seven men, and the weight of the crew would have to be considered when water was let into the ballast tanks. Forward and aft of the dome, the chamber top is ½" boiler iron, and there are connection plates at the center of these iron arches. The plates are supported by eight 3½" × 3" × ½" wrought-iron "tee" arches or "ribs" that are fitted at roughly 18" apart—the spacing varies from 14" to 20"—fore and aft of the dome. They are located on the outside of the boiler plate, and Wood refers to them as "angle iron."

At the bow and stern, the chamber top widens in both directions to form bulb-shaped enlargements. The small aft chamber was to facilitate work on the steering rod stuffing boxes and the forward chamber allowed a man to see through a small deadlight in the top shell of the compressed air chamber. Again, this light is missing. There is a large hole in the vessel where it was fitted, and Kroehl's drawing shows it, but it would have been similar to those in the dome sleeve.

Kroehl had planned to fit partitions on *Explorer* at the extreme ends of the working chamber. These seem to be watertight bulkheads with small doors (1'9" wide × 3'0" high) in them. They are shown on his drawing 1'6" inboard of the windlass and 1'4" inboard of the propulsion wheel. It is impossible to guess what the purpose of these bulkheads might be, given the extreme lack of space where they are depicted, but in all events, the idea was abandoned, as no trace of them can be found in the submersible.

Along with the dome, the vessel's compressed air chamber was not constructed as planned. Kroehl's drawing shows that the top shell of the air chamber was planned to be just under 4' above the water ballast tanks, but it was built almost 5' above them. The flared dome design would have taken up more air space than the cylindrical one, and Kroehl may have calculated that more compressed air was required generally.

The top shell of the air chamber is ½" boiler iron in five strakes that are lapped 4" and double riveted. The plates are riveted to interior frames that coincide with the spacing of the working chamber top ribs and are "tee" sections of the same dimension. A system of braces provides mutual support to the chamber top ribs and the shell frames. These are 1" square iron bolts that are arranged in alternating radial and a combined radial and vertical pattern that is best understood when seen on the current drawings. At their bottoms, the vertical bolts are connected to "tee" sections that are fixed to the ballast tank top plates. There is much concretion and erosion in this area of the hull and some of the tee sections are missing, so it is not clear whether the tees were in short lengths or ran the whole length of the top plate. Because the tees would act as stiffeners for the tank tops, we have drawn them as continuous.

There is evidence that bolt braces were also used to connect the dome to the shell; there are six socketlike connections on each side of the dome. Because the braces are missing and their arrangement is unknown, they have been shown with broken lines on the current drawings.

Four 6" diameter iron rings are fitted to the outside of the top shell. These are bolted to the shell using brackets with double straps. No reinforcing was found for the rings. They cannot be considered as lifting rings, as they are too weak to carry the weight of the hull, so they are thought to be mooring rings. They would have served not only to moor the submarine to a dock but also to allow the steam tender to moor alongside it, or perhaps the rings might have assisted in rigging the submarine for towing by the tender.

DIVING IN EXPLORER

Sub Marine Explorer utilized its heavy cast iron bottom and its buoyant compressed air chamber to achieve equilibrium, or neutral buoyancy. The heavy cast iron, which at 57,100 pounds, weighed 26,039 pounds more than the upper hull, helped to maintain balance, assisted by the flaring, air-filled ends of the working chamber at the bow and stern. To dive and submerge, the submarine introduced seawater into its other ballast chambers and then expelled it using compressed air. In 1865 W. W. W. Wood described how the submarine had "ease of descent and ascent." To dive, the operator opened the blowoff cocks in the ballast or water chambers "to admit water." As the tanks flooded, "the specific gravity of the boat is thus increased at will, and the descent may be made rapid or slow as desired by the operator, it is thus perfectly competent to descend to final limit or remain suspended at intermediate depth required."[8]

To ascend, Wood's report continued,

> the blow off cocks would be closed, the exhaust valve of the water chamber opened and air from the compressed air chamber admitted; this being at greater pressure than the water forces it out; and thus reducing the specific gravity causes the boat to rise at the will of the operator governed by the force with which the air is admitted into, and the water forced out of, the water chambers. These two chambers (compressed air and water chambers) thus perform for the boat the same office that the air bladder does for the fish, and at once does away with all necessity for suspended ballast or any other extraneous methods of sinking the vessel. The division of the water chambers into fore, aft, and amid-ship chambers, allows the perfect equilibrium of the boat to be maintained without the necessity of shifting ballast.[9]

The three chambers enclosed a total area of 1,770 cubic feet, according to Wood's report. They were divided as follows: (1) compressed air chamber, 560 cubic feet (15.8 cubic meters); (2) ballast chambers, 550 cubic feet (15.5 cubic m); and (3) working chamber, 660 cubic feet (18.6 cubic meters). According to a published account of an 1869 dive in the submarine, the compressed air chamber was pressurized to 60 pounds per square inch. The vessel was then sealed and began its dive by flooding the ballast chambers. Since each cubic foot of seawater weighs 64 pounds, completely flooding the ballast tanks would have added 35,200 pounds of weight (or 4,241 gallons of seawater) to overcome the buoyant force of the 1,220 cubic feet of the air-filled chambers. To submerge, *Explorer* needed to displace 116,745 pounds. The submarine's weight was 88,161 pounds, so it needed to add approximately 28,584 pounds, or 3,443.8 gallons, of seawater to submerge.

PROPULSION AND STEERING

It appears that Kroehl considered two steering techniques before deciding on the one he finally employed on *Explorer*. The first appears in the Pacific Pearl Company pamphlet; with this system there was no rudder proper.[10] Instead, the propeller sat in an iron frame that was hung on hinges at the vessel's stern. Just outboard of the stern a universal joint connected the propeller to the shaft. Wood refers to this as "Cathcart's plan." He was referring to the system of yoking a rudder and propeller together with a universal joint, as patented by James L. Cathcart of Washington, D.C., in 1854 and subsequently refined through the 1860s.[11] In 1869 the system was described in the *Buffalo (New York) Commercial Advertiser* :

> The CATHCART was built in Washington, D.C., in 1869, and has been running for a length of time on the Schuylkill Canal, where she is said to have been quite successful. . . . The propelling power is a common screw wheel in her stern. The most interesting feature of the CATHCART's machinery is the steering apparatus, which worked admirably. The improvement consists of a moveable joint on the shaft of the propeller, outside of the sternpost of the boat, by which the propeller can be moved laterally by a standard coming up like the rudder head to the deck of the boat. On this is fitted a semi-circular yoke about five feet long, to each end of which is a chain fastened, the bugles passing round a wheel about a foot in diameter, which is fastened to the rudder head, and fitted with cogs to catch the links of the chain. Thus the direction of the rudder and propeller are changed simultaneously, at the will of the helmsman. When going straight ahead, the direction of the rudder and wheel are on a line with the keel. But as the rudder is moved, the pressure of the wheel is shifted to the quarter, making the propeller power an aid to the rudder in steering the boat. With this arrangement a very slight deflection of the rudder produces a considerable change in the direction of the boat. It is claimed that the CATHCART steers easily in water only a few inches deeper than her draught. On leaving one of our elevators, loaded, she turned around in a space a little more than her own length, which is sufficient evidence of her good steering qualities.[12]

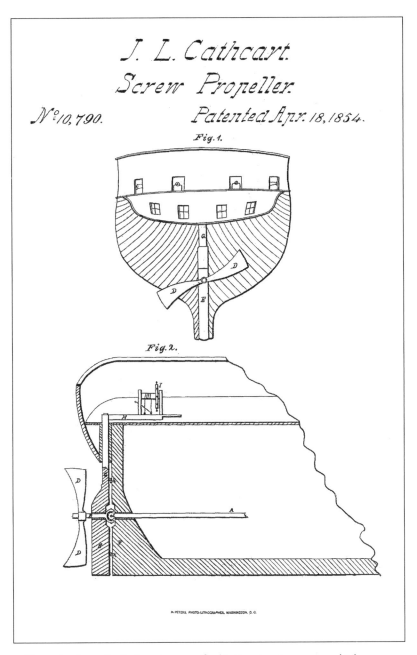

Figure A1. James L. Cathcart's patent for his Steering Apparatus, which was adopted for use on *Sub Marine Explorer*. (Courtesy United States Patent Office)

The *New York World* of July 22, 1871, had earlier commented on the Cathcart system:

> Mr. J. S. Cathcart, which has been tried on the propeller CATH-
> CART, and which is claimed to be an entire success. The improve-
> ment is a moveable joint on the shaft of the propeller, outside of
> the stern-post of the boat, by which the propeller can be moved lat-
> erally by a standard coming up like the rudder-head to the deck of
> the boat. On this is fitted a semi-circular yoke about five feet long,
> to each end of which is a chain fastened, the bugles passing round a
> wheel about a foot in diameter, which chain. Thus each motion of
> the rudder alters the direction of the propeller with the helm amid-
> ships; the pressure of the propeller is in the line of the keel of the
> boat, or directly aft as in ordinary boats, but as the rudder is moved
> the pressure is shifted to the quarter, thus making the propeller
> an aid to the rudder in steering the boat, and requiring so slight
> a deflection of the rudder that little or no swell is caused thereby.
> And this is the advantage claimed, that the boat will run without
> any wash to injure the banks of the canal, and will steer easily even
> when there is little more water in the canal than the boat draws.[13]

Presumably Kroehl's use of the Cathcart system, which is illustrated in the re-
drawn plan in the 1865 pamphlet of the Pacific Pearl Company, was abandoned
because it was impractical. Due to the universal joint a good deal of power
would have to be exerted on the propeller as its angle became more acute, and
with a hand-powered device operated presumably by one man inside a sealed
compartment, this would not have provided the same power as a steam engine.
Furthermore, the cramped internal area of the submersible did not provide adequate room for both the Cathcart apparatus and the propulsion system's machinery. The second method appears on Kroehl's drawing. With it, the rudder
is held aft of the propeller by carriers at the top and bottom. The forward ends
of the carriers were to be hinged within the vessel; we assume that this method
was dropped as the connections would have been difficult to waterproof.

Explorer's rudder, propeller, propulsion and steering machinery, and a large
section of the lower part of her stern are missing as a result of explosive demolition to salvage the machinery. However, there is an iron plate bolted to the top
of the aft ballast tank and what seems to be a carrier—it is broken off—pierces
the top shell. From this it has been determined that a more conventional rud-

der was installed with carriers top and bottom. (The rudder on the current drawings is based on Kroehl's drawing.) The rudder was controlled by a cable system; a yoke was fixed to the top of the rudder and cable linkages were attached to both of the yoke's ends. At the inboard ends of the linkages were two steering rods that passed through cast iron tubes that were set into the top shell. Stuffing boxes were fitted here, and the inner ends of the rods connected to inboard cables. The cable was likely a flexible wire of about ¼" diameter. There are pulley-like fixed guide blocks at the sides of the working chamber that lead to the vessel's dome. This is similar to the system employed on *Intelligent Whale*.[14] No evidence was found of controlling devices for the cables, but we have assumed that lockable levers or slide blocks were employed. *Intelligent Whale* was steered by a wheel at the control station, but such a system would have proved cumbersome in *Explorer* because the crew needed to freely pass and work in the cramped quarters of the submarine.

Kroehl's drawing shows a 3′6″ diameter propeller, which is confirmed in Wood's report. From the drawings it seems to be four-bladed, although at the time two- or three-bladed propellers were more common. It also seems that the propeller would turn in a counterclockwise direction, when seen from aft, to move the vessel forward. The shaft and gear mechanism is best understood by looking at the drawings, but it is not complicated; three shafts with four gears were carried on bridges with pillow blocks that could be lubricated. The machinery was operated by a heavy iron turning wheel that, due to the cramped space in the working chamber, could have been operated by only one man. The gears are of about 10″ in diameter (31.43″ in circumference) for the small ones and 18½″ for the large one (58.14″ circumference). This gives a speed advantage of about 185 percent per gearing, and there are three gearings. Thus, if the turning wheel was spun at 30 revolutions per minute, the propeller would turn at 190 revolutions per minute. While not shown on the drawings, a detachable iron crank may have been part of the mechanism to facilitate the rotation of the wheel by an operator.

When we look at the propulsion machinery, it is difficult to imagine how one man could push such a heavy weight as *Explorer* through water. However, once set into motion, the heavy turning wheel would act at least as a minimal flywheel. While Wood says in his report that the apparatus had not been tested and therefore he could not provide an opinion, he also states "the means provided for locomotion would seem ample to secure a rate of speed sufficient to overcome local currents."[15]

PIPING

Unfortunately, most of *Explorer*'s piping systems are missing. According to Wood, the pipes do not show on Kroehl's drawing because "their position will be decided when the boat is nearly finished."[16] Wood notes what was intended for the vessel but from archaeological observations, it seems that some changes were made. Much of the piping appears to have been copper or brass, and was stripped from the submersible at some stage after abandonment. Fragments and indications of differential corrosion on the interior of the submersible indicate probable placement of some piping, but some of the piping shown on the current drawings is conjectural, and not all piping installed in *Explorer* may be indicated.

Air was pumped into the compressed air chamber using a 30 hp air pump "of 7½ in[ch] diameter driven by a direct acting engine of 14 in[ch] diameter, both air pump and steam cylinder having an 18 in[ch] stroke."[17] This machinery was carried by a tender, and Wood notes that the air pressure chamber was tested at 200 pounds per square inch (psi). Just ahead of the dome there is a 1" diameter threaded hole in the top shell that is assumed to be compressed air supply. This would connect to the air pump with a hose. In the lower dome there is a crescent-shaped pipe that has a valve at its bottom end and a flanged tee in its middle that we assume to be for a pressure gauge. Both ends of this pipe discharge into the compressed air chamber. The assumption is that a pipe was connected to the hole in the shell with a valve and it led to the top of the crescent pipe. The lower end of the crescent simply discharged air into the chamber and it was controlled by the vessel's operator by the valve while using the gauge.

There are a number of similar flanges in four key positions on *Explorer*. They are located where the middle tanks join the fore and aft tanks and can be considered as control positions. At each location two flanges are fit to the top of the ballast tanks. They are about 25" apart, centered on the tank's joint, and the pipe size seems to be 1½" inside diameter. Two similar flanges are fitted directly above them and connect to the air pressure chamber. Thus, a pipe with a control valve connected the air pressure chamber to the water ballast chamber. Wood notes that a ¾" valve admitted air into the working chamber, and while no evidence of this has been found we can assume that the working chamber drew air from the compressed air chamber.

After both air spaces had been pressurized, the vessel was submerged by opening the six ballast fill and blowoff valves, probably in a prescribed sequence, until it began to sink. The valves would then be closed. To surface the valves connecting the ballast tanks to the compressed air chamber were opened, again probably in a sequence, and their corresponding blowoff valves would be opened. In the top of the center blowoff valve alcoves there is what seems to be a pipe valve that connects the two central tanks. Its design and function are not known, and even though the center blowoff valves serviced both middle tanks, it is thought that it is a water and air transfer valve.

A 2" outside diameter pipe connects to the atmosphere at the aft end of the dome sleeve and leads down into the dome. At its bottom end is a valve and a cluster of flanges for 1¼" outside diameter pipe. At the top of the ballast tanks, between the four sets of compressed air transfer valves, ¾" pipes lead to a connection tube that leads upward (the only surviving example in the submarine is heavily concreted). In the reconstruction drawing, the decision was made to connect the dome valves to the upstand pipe with 1¼" outside diameter pipe in what appears to be a logical manner. It is believed that this system forms a compressed air exhaust system to expel air from the ballast tanks. Air exhaust is mentioned by Wood, but his report is ambiguous; the provisional patent notes "a pipe is also disposed at the top of the casing passing through the roof for discharging air at any time from the working chamber when it is desired to reduce the buoyant power of the apparatus."[18]

Connected to the bottom plate in the dome area, there is a brass sleeve with a glass tube in it. It has been broken off at about 12" and it still contains mercury, so it is assumed to be the remains of a barometer used as the depth gauge. Scientific knowledge of how to assess depth through a mercury barometer was extensive in the 1860s and early 1870s:

Determining the depth below the level of the sea by means of a barometer carried down in a diving bell:

If D is the depth of the surface of the water in the diving bell below the surface of the sea, and if σ is the pressure of the atmosphere on the surface of the sea, then the pressure of the air in the diving bell must exceed that on the surface of the sea by due to a column of water of depth D. If σ is the density of sea-water, then the pressure due to a column of depth D is $g \, \sigma \, D$.

Let the height of the barometer at the surface of the sea be observed, and let us suppose that in the diving bell it is found that to be higher than a height h, then the additional pressure indicated by this rise is $g \rho h$, then σ is the density of mercury. Hence,

$$g \sigma D = g \rho h,$$

or,

$$D = \rho h = s h,$$
$$h$$

Where $s = \rho$ = density of mercury = specific gravity of mercury.
σ density of water

The depth below the surface of the sea is therefore equal to the product of the rise of the barometer multiplied by the specific gravity of mercury. If the water is salt we must divide this result by the specific gravity of the salt water at the place of observation.

The calculation of depths under water by this method is comparatively easy, because the density of the water is not very different at different depths.[19]

It must be noted that on this submersible there was no means of regulating depth (depth in a more modern submarine is controlled by propulsion and planes). In *Explorer,* you either sat on the surface, sat on the bottom, went up or went down. Further, operating the valves was a delicate matter. A very small quantity of air or water, rather like "the last straw" near the end of blowing off or flooding, made the vessel sink or rise.

Having an indication of depth and water pressure was also critical to the lockout function of the submarine. Knowing the ambient pressure at the bottom enabled the operator to allow an equal amount of compressed air into the working chamber to the point that the internal pressure was the same as the external. A sea cock used as a "test cock" would be opened to allow water to flow into the chamber at a minimal volume, and as the pressure built up, the flow would stop, indicating equalization.

AIR REPLENISHMENT AND INTERNAL ILLUMINATION

Other than ambient light introduced to the submarine through the dome and bow deadlights, Kroehl lit the interior with candles, one account noting that spermaceti candles were employed. Spermaceti, a solid, waxy product taken from a cavity in the head of a sperm whale, was one of the by-products of the whaling industry. Like sperm oil, also in the head cavity, spermaceti burned clear and bright, and because of this it became a valuable commodity.[20] Candle makers mixed the spermaceti with 5 to 10 percent paraffin to make spermaceti candles, which at the time of *Explorer*'s dives were considered the best candles, as they were brighter and lasted longer than a pure wax candle.[21] The standard measurement of light at the time, one candle power (cp), was measured as the light given off by a two-ounce pure spermaceti candle that burned 120 grains per hour.

Maintaining an adequate oxygen level in a submerged craft was and remains a critical factor in determining a submarine or diving bell's success. *Sub Marine Explorer* had the means to replenish the air in the working chamber by introducing air stored in the compressed air tanks. However, the principal means was through spraying seawater in a fine mist throughout the chamber. The idea was to force the "carbonic acid gas" that accumulated inside the sub to be absorbed into seawater, which would then release oxygen:

> Water is a powerful absorbent, having a great affinity for different gasses and combining with them in greater or less quantities according to its affinity for them; if it absorbs a certain amount of any gas at the common pressure, it will absorb double the amount at double the pressure, triple at triple the pressure and so on. Thus at ordinary pressure and temperature it will absorb of:
>
> Carbonic Acid Gas its own volume.
> Oxygen Gas $\frac{1}{27}$ of its volume.
> Nitrogen $\frac{1}{64}$ of its volume
>
> It will therefore be seen that water in its natural state contains about 4 percent of oxygen, which we can obtain from it by substituting therefore some other gas, for which it has greater affinity, for instance carbonic acid gas.

If this carbonic acid gas is placed in contact with water at rest, it will be absorbed slowly, but if the water and gas be agitated together, it will be absorbed almost instantaneous. These principals are ingeniously applied to the renovation of air in this boat by means of a force pump, furnished with a hose with a perforated nozzle or rosette. By this means when the air becomes saturated by the accumulation of carbonic gas, as shown by the burning dimly of a candle, water is thrown in the form of a fine spray or mist through the whole extent of the working chamber, the carbonic acid gas is at once absorbed and oxygen set free, rendering the air even richer (about 5%) in this important element than before.[22]

Seawater for the air purification system was admitted through an "induction pipe extending down to the water and provided with a discharge pipe with a rose head."[23] The only archaeological evidence of this system discovered at the site was a handle and rod assembly, with a plunger valve at the proximal end. Looking much like the central portion of a bicycle pump, this may be the remains of a portable "hand force" pump used to distribute seawater inside the working compartment, where water was drawn up to be discharged through a hose.

CONCLUSION

Neither the surviving plan, contemporary accounts, or the material record in the form of the remains of *Sub Marine Explorer* would be sufficient by themselves to reconstruct this unique, individual craft. However, the combination of all the evidence, as well as a "best guess" based on an understanding of the technology and materials of the time, as well as comparison with the contemporary and more intact *Intelligent Whale,* has allowed this fairly detailed and sophisticated theoretical reconstruction of *Sub Marine Explorer.* The submarine was, and remains, even as a ruin, an amazing technological and engineering achievement of the mid nineteenth-century.

SUB MARINE EXPLORER (1865)

Interpretive Reconstruction Drawings

John W. McKay September, 2007

Sheet No. 1 of 8

Figures A2–A10. Plans of *Sub Marine Explorer,* 2008. (Drawings by John W. McKay, *Sub Marine Explorer* Project)

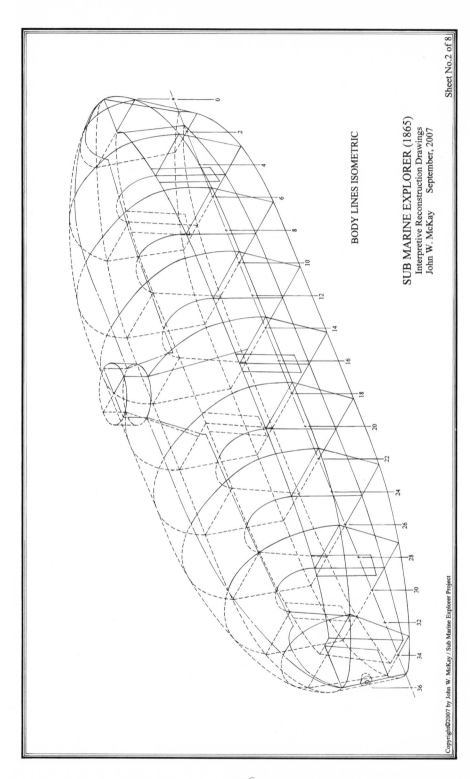

BODY LINES ISOMETRIC

SUB MARINE EXPLORER (1865)
Interpretive Reconstruction Drawings
John W. McKay   September, 2007

0
2
4
6
8
10
12
14
16
18
20
22
24
26
28
30
32
34
36

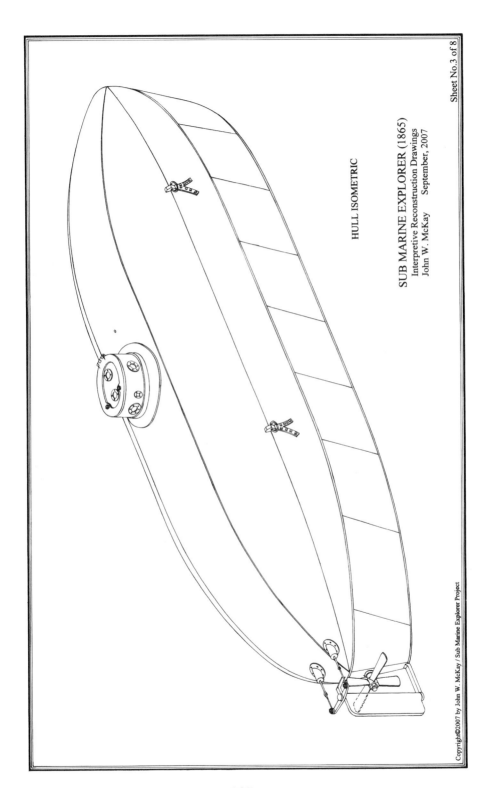

HULL ISOMETRIC

SUB MARINE EXPLORER (1865)
Interpretive Reconstruction Drawings
John W. McKay   September, 2007

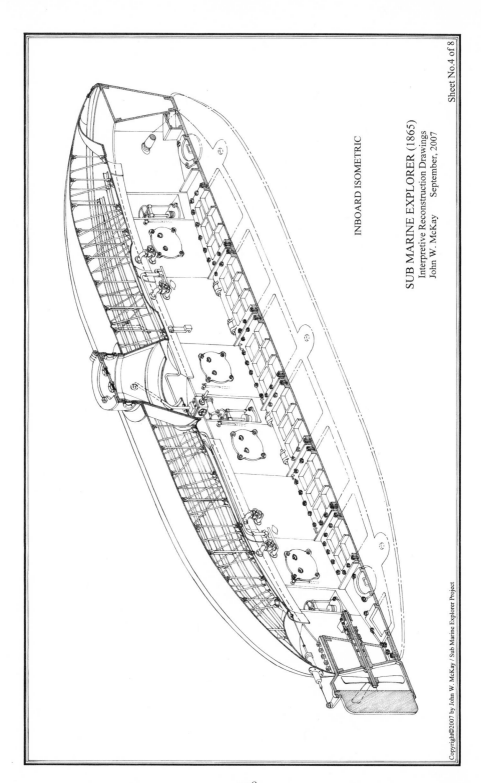

INBOARD ISOMETRIC

SUB MARINE EXPLORER (1865)
Interpretive Reconstruction Drawings
John W. McKay   September, 2007

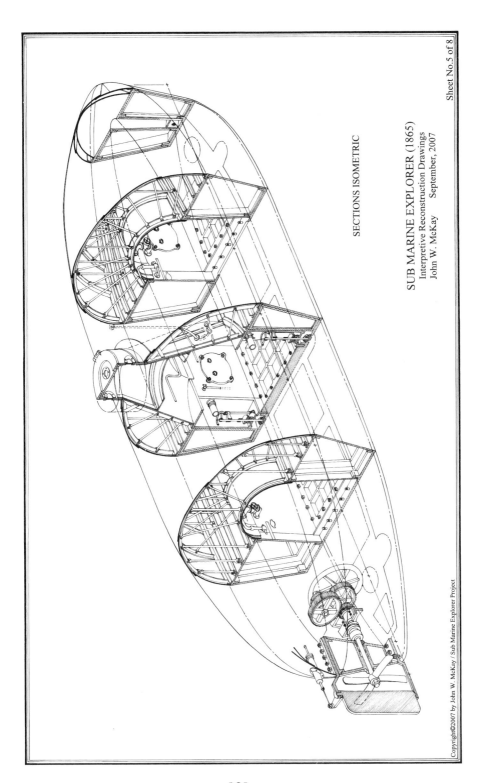

SECTIONS ISOMETRIC

SUB MARINE EXPLORER (1865)
Interpretive Reconstruction Drawings
John W. McKay   September, 2007

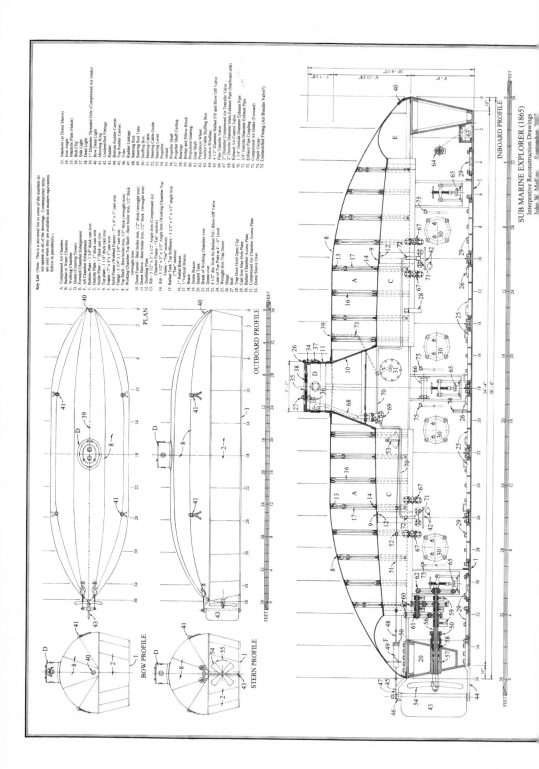

Key List (Note: This is a universal list so some of the numbers do not appear on all of the drawings. Contemporary terms are used when they are available and modern equivalents follow in parentheses.)

A. Compressed Air Chamber
B. Ballast or Water Chamber
C. Working Chamber
D. Dome (Conning Tower)
E. Forward Chamber Enlargement
   Aft Chamber Enlargement
1. Bottom Plate - 3 1/4" thick cast iron
2. Outside Plate - 1" thick cast iron
3. Inside Plate - 1" thick cast iron
4. Top plate - 1 1/4" thick cast iron
5. Frame - 7" x 4" x 1" cast iron
6. Solid Frame (Webbed Frame) - 7" x 4" x 1" cast iron
7. Flange - 3 1/4" x 1 1/4" cast iron
8. Top Shell - Best boiler iron, 1/2" thick (wrought iron)
9. Working Chamber Top Shell - Best boiler iron, 1/2" thick
   (wrought iron)
10. Dome Funnel - Best boiler iron, 1/2" thick (wrought iron)
11. Dome Sleeve - Best boiler iron, 1/2" thick (wrought iron)
12. Doubling Plate
13. Rib - 3 1/2" x 3" x 1/2" Angle iron (Compressed Air
    Chamber Frame - "Tee" section)
14. Rib - 3 1/2" x 3" x 1/2" Angle Iron (Working Chamber Top
    Frame - "Tee" section)
15. Ballast Tank Top Stiffeners - 3 1/2" x 3" x 1/2" angle iron
    ("Tee" section)
16. 1" Radial Braces
17. 1" Vertical Braces
18. Brace
19. Dome Braces
20. Sealed Tank
21. Bend of Working Chamber over
22. Dome over
23. 4 1/2" dia. Hole for Ballast Fill / Blow Off Valve
24. Line of Top Plate at 4' - 0" Level
25. Wrought Iron Top Doors
26. Hinge
27. Bed
28. Trap Door Hold Open Clip
29. Cast Iron Man Hole Plate
30. Ballast Chamber Access Plate
31. Compressed Air Chamber Access Plate
32. Dome Sleeve Over

33. Manhole (at Dome Sleeve)
34. Iron Angle
35. Manhole Plate (Hatch)
36. Bolt Clip
37. Side Light
38. Dead Light
39. 1" Diameter Threaded Hole (Compressed Air Intake)
40. Bow Dead Light
41. Mooring Ring
42. Unidentified Fittings
43. Rudder
44. Bottom Rudder Carrier
45. Top Rudder Carrier
46. Yoke
47. Rudder Linkage
48. Steering Box
49. Steering Rod Tube
50. Stuffing Box
51. Steering Cable
52. Steering Cable Guide
53. Steering Lever
54. Propeller
55. Aft End
56. Propeller Shaft
57. Propeller Shaft Casting
58. Bearings
59. Bridge and Pillow Block
60. Propulsion Gearing
61. Gear Shaft
62. Propulsion Wheel
63. Anchor Cable Stuffing Box
64. Anchor Windlass
65. 4 1/2" Diameter Ballast Fill and Blow Off Valve
66. Pipe Transfer Valve
67. 2" Diameter Compressed Air Transfer Valve
68. 2" Outside Diameter Main Exhaust Pipe (Starboard side)
69. Exhaust Air Control Valve
70. 1 1/4" Outside Diameter Exhaust Pipe
71. 3/4" Outside Diameter Exhaust Pipe
72. Exhaust Pipe Coupling
73. Compressed Air Intake (Forward)
74. Depth Gauge
75. Unidentified Fitting (Air Bleeder Valve?)

PLAN

OUTBOARD PROFILE

BOW PROFILE

STERN PROFILE

INBOARD PROFILE

SUB MARINE EXPLORER (1865)
Interpretive Reconstruction Drawings
John W. McKay, September 2007

240

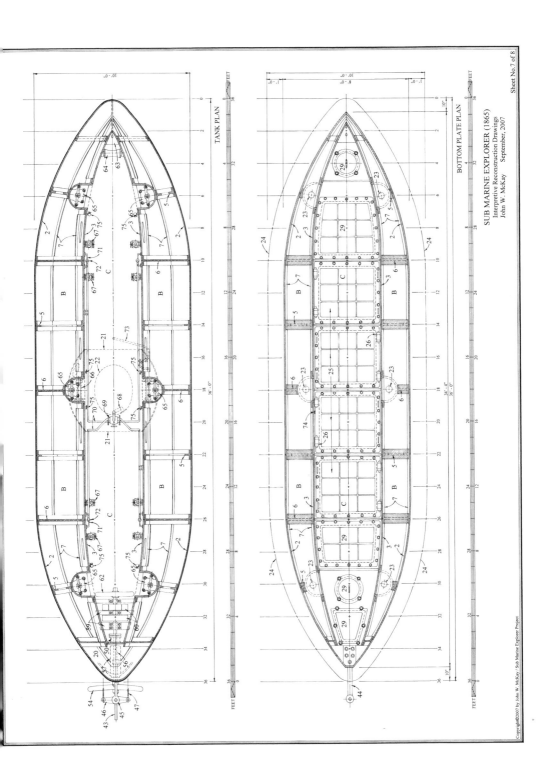

TANK PLAN

BOTTOM PLATE PLAN

SUB MARINE EXPLORER (1865)
Interpretive Reconstruction Drawings
John W. McKay   September, 2007

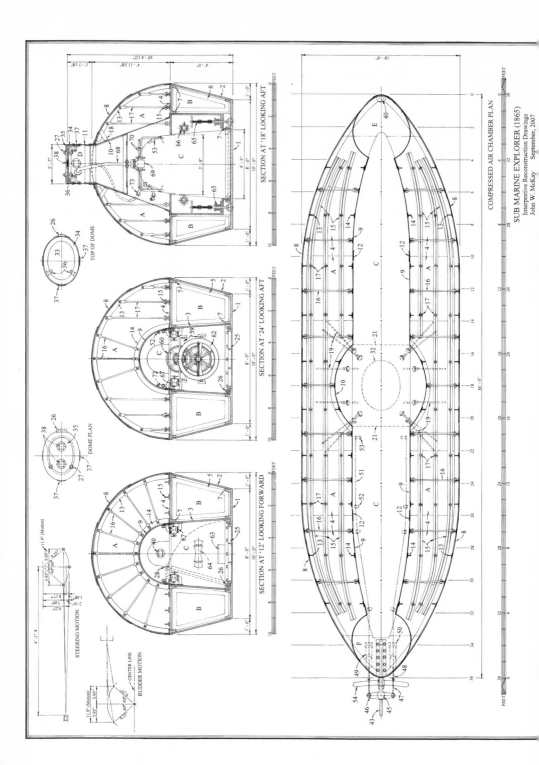

SUB MARINE EXPLORER (1865)
Interpretive Reconstruction Drawings
John W. McKay   September, 2007

COMPRESSED AIR CHAMBER PLAN

SECTION AT '18' LOOKING AFT

SECTION AT '24' LOOKING AFT

SECTION AT '12' LOOKING FORWARD

TOP OF DOME

DOME PLAN

STEERING MOTION

RUDDER MOTION

CENTER LINE

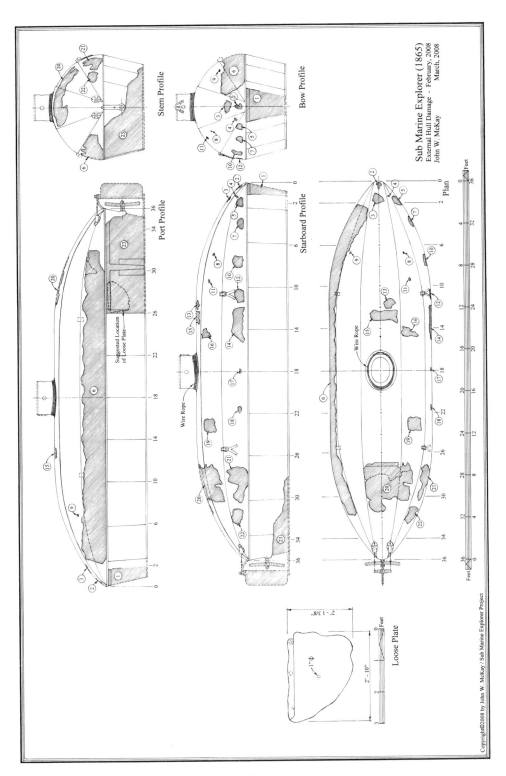

Stern Profile

Bow Profile

Port Profile

Suggested Location
of Loose Plate

Wire Rope

Starboard Profile

Wire Rope

Plan

Sub Marine Explorer (1865)
External Hull Damage - February, 2008
John W. McKay   March, 2008

Loose Plate

2' - 13/8"

2' - 10"

1" Φ

Feet

Feet

Feet

W. W. W. Wood's Report on
Sub Marine Explorer

Office of General Inspector Steam Machinery, USN
No. 256 Canal Street New York
February 2, 1865
The Honorable Gideon Wells, Secretary of the Navy, Washington, D.C.

Sir:

Under date of June 17th 1864 I had the honor to receive a communication from the Department authorizing me to examine a Submarine Boat in process of construction by Julius H. Kroehl, Esq. 32 Pine Street, New York, and report to the Department. Under date of June 20th 1864 a letter from a Mr. G. Wrightson to the Hon. Secretary of the Navy under date of June 14th 1864 was referred by the Chief of the Bureau of Construction to Rear Admiral Gregory relating to a Submarine Boat, with instructions that I should examine the apparatus if the Admiral thought proper, as proposed in Mr. Wrightson's letter, and further directing Mr. Wrightson's letter be returned to the Bureau.

The Admiral has referred the above letter to me, and at the earliest solicitation of Mr. Julius H Kroehl, the Engineer in charge of the construction of the Submarine Boat referred to, I have examined the structure which is still incomplete and submit the following report.

The letters of Mr. Wrightson and Mr. Kroehl refer to the same Submarine Apparatus. This submarine explorer is being constructed partly of wrought, and partly of cast iron, the top and sides consisting of a double shell, thereby forming compartments, which are classified as follows.

Fig. 1. The compressed air chamber on the accompanying tracing are marked A.A.

Fig. 2. The Ballast or Water Chambers marked B.B.
Fig. 3. The Working Chamber marked C.C.

The interior dimensions are: At the bottom line, length 34 feet 4 inches, breadth amid ship 8 feet. At the four foot line, length 36 feet, breadth amid ship 10 feet. Its height is 8 feet, exclusive of the man hole, which is one foot high. The interior dimensions are: At the bottom line length 32 feet 10 inches; breadth amid ship 5 feet. At the four foot line length 31 feet 2 inches. Breadth amid ship 3 feet 6 inches. The interior height is 6 feet except in the center, where it is 7 feet 11½ inches.

The lower part of the boat, up to the four foot line, is built entirely of cast iron, and forms the water or ballast chambers. These are enclosed by a bottom plate 1¾ inch thick, a top plate 1¼ inch thick to which by means of flanges 3¾ inches high by 1½ inch thick and 1 inch countersunk bolts are secured [to] the outside and inside plates of 1 inch thickness; 10 frames of 7" × 4" × 1" crosswise strengthen this part of the boat, and four solid frames of the same cross section divide the space into four water or ballast chambers.

The compressed air chamber forms the upper part of the boat above the four foot line. It has a semi-elliptic form and is built of two shells of best boiler iron ½ inch thick, the different pieces lapping 4 inches are double riveted with ¾ inch countersink rivets, and braced with ribs of 3½" × 3" × ½" angle iron and 1 inch braces. It will be tested with a pressure of 200 lbs., to the square inch.

The working chamber is enclosed by the compressed air and ballast chambers; its floor is formed of wrought iron frames 4 inches wide and 1¼ inch thick, properly fastened and secured to the ballast chambers. The floor is closed perfectly air and water tight by four wrought iron trap doors and three cast iron man hole plates. The working chamber has in the center of the boat an oval manhole "D," of 3 feet largest, and 2 feet smallest diameter; it is one foot high and has four side lights for the purpose of observing objects floating around the boat; it will be closed by the wrought iron manhole plate and two 2 inch bolts.

The manhole plate is provided with two dead lights. The two compressed air chambers are connected with each other by a 1½ inch brass pipe, and air supplied with a 1½ inch valve, over which a cap can be screwed; a ¾ inch valve will admit compressed air into the working chamber, and six ¾ inch valves and pipes connect the compressed air with the ballast chambers.

The ballast chambers have in their bottoms six 4½ inch valves F.F., which communicate with the surrounding sea water, and are provided with each a blow-off pipe, closed by a ¾ inch valve discharging into the water the air below the manhole plates. The working chamber has a 1 inch blow-off valve also discharging below the manhole plate. All these pipes are not marked in the annexed tracing, as their position will be decided when the boat is nearly finished.

To admit light into the boat, and allow objects to be observed above and around, eight lights (thick glass) are fitted at the top and sides, and four in the floor to observe objects below. The boat is provided with a 3½ foot propeller, worked by hand; the propeller forms the rudder, which is constructed after Cathcart's plan with a universal joint.

The calculated weight of the boat is:

Wrought Iron	31,061 pounds
Cast Iron	57,100 pounds
Total	88,161 pounds

The contents of the Boat are:

Compressed Air Chambers	560 Cubic Feet
Ballast Chambers	550 Cubic Feet
Working Chamber	660 Cubic Feet
Total	1,770 Cubic Feet

and will displace 56¾ tons of sea water of 2,000 lbs., per ton.

The air is forced into the compressed air chamber by an air pump of 7½ inch diameter driven by a direct acting engine of 14 inches diameter, both air pump and steam cylinder having 18 inch stroke. If constructed entirely of wrought iron, the difference between it and cast iron will have to be supplied with cast iron or lead ballast to sink it. The shape of the boat is given for the purpose of facilitating the operations within, and enabling work to be performed at nearly the extreme ends.

This Submarine Boat or Explorer is now nearly completed at the works of the Pacific Pearl Company, for whom it is being constructed. The important consideration in a submarine apparatus are:

1st The supply of air, which is all important.

2nd The ease of descent and ascent.

3rd The ability to move from place to place with sufficient power and velocity to overcome local currents.

4th Security from interruption while operating beneath the surface of the water.

It is claimed that these points are all attained in the Submarine Explorer, although the apparatus, submitted to my inspection is not yet completed and experimental evidence was therefore impracticable. I am able to present to the Department evidence on most points quite conclusive and satisfactory.

On the first and most important point, the supply of air, no doubt can exist, for both chemical science and the experience of practice prove, that an all sufficient supply can readily and certainly be obtained, without resort to the atmosphere above the surface when the boat is submerged. It is a well known fact that all natural waters contain air and a surplus of oxygen gas, were it not for this, fishes could not live. Its presence too is demonstrated by the air pump.

It is equally known that water is a powerful absorbent, having a great affinity for different gasses and combining with them in greater or less quantities according to its affinity for them; if it absorbs a certain amount of any gas at the common pressure, it will absorb double the amount at double the pressure, triple at triple the pressure and so on. Thus at ordinary pressure and temperature it will absorb of:

Carbonic Acid Gas its own volume.

Oxygen Gas $\frac{1}{27}$ of its volume.

Nitrogen $\frac{1}{64}$ of its volume

(See Beck's Chemistry pages 128 and 182; Henry volume 1 page 276; Annals of Philosophy Vol. 6 page 340, Vol. 7 page 215; Gray's Chemistry pages 159 and 185; Gray's Natural Philosophy page 176; Parker's Natural Philosophy page 161; Youmen's Chemistry page 65.)

It will therefore be seen that water in its natural state contains about 4 percent of oxygen, which we can obtain from it by substituting therefore some other gas, for which it has greater affinity, for instance carbonic acid gas.

If this carbonic acid gas is placed in contact with water at rest, it will be absorbed slowly, but if the water and gas be agitated together, it will be absorbed almost instantaneously (See Beck's Chemistry page 182). These principles are ingeniously applied to the renovation of air in this boat by means of a force pump, furnished with a hose with a perforated nozzle or rosette. By this means when the air becomes saturated by the accumulation of carbonic gas, as shown by the burning dimly of a candle, water is thrown in the form of a fine spray or mist through the whole extent of the working chamber; the carbonic acid gas is at once absorbed and oxygen set free, rendering the air even richer (about 5 percent) in this important element than before.

The operation may be repeated, whenever the air becomes impure and is limited of course only to the amount of water surrounding the apparatus. Nor is this theory only. This apparatus, though in a different shape, was used in blasting and removing Diamond Reef in New York Harbor from 1868 to 1862 and to the efficiency of the arrangement for purifying the air, the annexed certificates bear testimony.

It will be seen that by the means here used, the object is accomplished perfectly, the noxious gases are removed and virtually restored to the atmosphere. In this respect the Submarine Explorer has a vast superiority over all other vessels designed for such purposes, of which I have any knowledge.

The means employed in the boat of the American Submarine Company [*Intelligent Whale*], a tube extending from the boat to the surface of the water and sustained by a copper float, is liable to interruption from objects drifting against it, or carried under, if the current be strong and cutting off the supply of air from the surface.   While in Alexander's [Lambert Alexandré's copy of Payerne's boat], Villeroi's [designer of *Alligator*, a Union submarine lost off the coast of North Carolina while in tow to Charleston in 1863], and other similar boats, reservoirs of condensed oxygen are carried down to supply, what exists in limitless quantities on every side, and the cumbrous paraphernalia of endless revolving cloths passing through reservoirs of lime-water, blowers, cogwheels, and attachments are used, to do the work of a simple force pump. These contrivances, compressed oxygen and lime-water, are very injurious in their effects to the operations within by causing irritation to the throat and lungs. In this first and most important point therefore the Submarine Explorer will in my opinion prove successful for the means above stated, and for the reasons set forth.

2nd. The ease of descent and ascent. In the Submarine Explorer the descent is accomplished by opening the blow-off cocks in the ballast or water chambers, and admitting water through the water-valves. The specific gravity of the boat is thus increased at will, and the descent may be made rapid or slow as desired by the operator; it is thus perfectly competent to descend to final limit or remain suspended at intermediate depth required.

Should it be desired to ascend, the blow-off cocks would be closed, the exhaust valve of the water chamber opened and air from the compressed air chamber admitted; this being at greater pressure than the water forces it out; and thus reducing the specific gravity causes the boat to rise at the will of the operator governed by the force with which the air is admitted into, and water forced out of, the water chambers. These two chambers (compressed air and water chambers) thus perform for the boat the same office, that the air bladder does for the fish, and at once does away with all necessity for suspended ballast or any other extraneous methods of sinking the vessel. The division of the water chambers into fore, aft, and amid-ship chambers, allows the perfect equilibrium of the boat to be maintained without the necessity of shifting ballast.

3rd. The ability to move from place to place with sufficient power, and velocity to overcome local currents; on this point I can not express a decided opinion from any experiment shown or evidence adduced. The means provided for locomotion would seem ample to secure a rate of speed sufficient to overcome local currents.

4th Security from interruptions while operating beneath the surface of the water. In this respect from the construction and means devised for the different operations required in a vessel of this kind, I consider the means provided sufficient security while submerged.

The uses to which a boat, such as is above described can be applied, in Naval Warfare, would be the removal of submerged obstructions in the channels of rivers and harbors. Approaching hostile fleets at anchor and destroying them by attaching torpedoes to their bottoms and exploding such localities as are commanded and covered by the guns of an enemy. The importance of a successful application of the principles involved in such a vessel for such purposes are of much importance and can not be too highly estimated. The means and appliances for the successful prosecution of which are secondary to the vessel itself and involve other means in their accomplishment.

In conclusion I would respectfully suggest that practical tests of the Submarine Explorer be made on its final completion, that a correct report may be made conclusive of the merits and value for the purposes proposed. The letter of Mr. G. Wrightson is herewith returned as directed.

> I am very respectfully,
> Your Obedient Servant
> W. W. W. Wood,
> General Inspector of Steam Machinery for the Navy.

Inventory of the Personal Effects
of Julius Kroehl, 1867

AFTER Julius Kroehl's death in Panama, the US consul there forwarded an inventory of the effects taken from Kroehl's hotel room after his death. It is a rare and tantalizing look at Kroehl. Some of the items listed are both exciting and frustrating in what they must have represented, primarily the "trunk containing papers." Conant and Rostrop were consular officers sent to inventory, pack, and transport Kroehl's effects to the US consulate.

The inventory reflects Kroehl's professional interests and activities—tools, books, drafting instruments, surveying equipment, and the chemicals that an engineer, surveyor, and photographer would use, as well as the accoutrements of a traveler of his time who intended to stay for a while in Panama, and a veteran of military service who realized the need for niceties as well as necessities, as evidenced by his silverware.

Inventory of the Personal Effects of
Julius H. Kroehl, taken by M. Rostrop and
John C. Conant, September 10, 1867

1 Leather trunk containing papers &c. . . . . N/A
9 shirts $5.00
3 pair white pants $3.00
1 white vest $1.00
2 pairs drawers . . . .$.50
3 bundles Cigars $3.00
1 glass cutter $5.00
7 pair socks & 12 collars $1.00

9 plated forks & 2 spoons...$4.00

1 lock...$2.00

1 cigar box..$50.00

1 gold pen silver handle.. $1.50

11 N.G. stamps[1] $1.10

US Gold coin... $60.00

New Granada money $4.30

1 cigar box of envelopes $2.00

1 box patent dryer[2] $1.00

1 trunk books (has no key) $5.00

3 cloth coats..$46.00

1 pair pants..$2.00

1 vest $1.00

2 linen vests $1.50

1 pair white pants $1.00

1 Chinese hat[3]...$.50

Nitrate of silver[4] $8.00

Photographic bath[5]..$.50

1 Hammock $8.00

1 lot books $2.00

1 Dictionary $5.00

1 letter scale $5.00

3 trusses[6]..$3.00

1 waiter...$3.00

1 tin box of private papers.. N/A

1 gold pen with engraving..$5.00

Lead pencils...$.20

1 carving knife & steel $2.00

2 doz. Knives $5.00

3 forks $1.00

1 doz. Large spoons...$4.00

1¼ doz. Small spoons $2.50

Stationery..$2.00

2 blank books..$2.00

1 bundle cigars $1.00

1 box for cigars ....$.20

1 box of drafting utensils..$2.00

1 knife $1.00
1 silver plated tea pot . . . . N/A
1 silver plated cream pitcher in box. $25.00
1 silver plated sugar bowl . . . . N/A
A silver plated coffee pot . . . . N/A
2 carpet bags. $2.00
Inkstand, shears, pipe brushes &c. $4.00
1 field glass[7] $3.00
1 surveying instrument $10.00
1 steel rule. $2.00
1 box books $5.00
1 box tools $3.00
1 umbrella. $2.00
1 letter press $2.00
1 gold watch & chain . . . . N/A
1 shirt stud . . . . N/A

The valuations attached to the above were by the parties who made the inventory. I have had the things carefully stored until his friends could be heard from. His wife, Sophia Rosa Kroehl, lives in Georgetown, D.C. I find from his papers that he has left a will somewhere.

Thos. Kilby Smith
US Consul

Notes

PREFACE

1. Personal communication (e-mail) from Leif Blackmon of Medfield, Mass., February 17, 2006.

2. As described in the Web site www.panama-isla-contadora.com/ubootd.html, accessed on March 3, 2002.

CHAPTER 1

1. Kiaupa et al., *History of the Baltic Countries,* 60–62.

2. The timber trade depended on the huge forests that covered the Eurasian plain from the Baltic coast into Siberia. The northern forests of Scotch pine (*Pinus sylvestris*) and spruce (*Picea excelsa*) yielded massive amounts of timber. The Baltic countries that provided the timber for the trade included Sweden (which at that time included what is now Norway and Finland), Russia, Prussia, and Poland. The initial timber trade, first dominated by the Dutch in the seventeenth century, passed into British hands in the late eighteenth-century as Britain's merchant marine and navy grew into prominence.

3. Albion, *Forests and Sea Power,* 141.

4. Oddy and Playfair, *European Commerce,* 223–24.

5. Milner, *The Baltic,* 137.

6. Albion, *Forests and Sea Power,* 147.

7. Fischer and Fischer, *Scots in Eastern and Western Prussia,* 55–57, 201. The American Kroehl family of the twenty-first century pronounces their name as "Crail." In answering Krehl's petition, the Duke of Stettin admonished local officials on Krehl's behalf: "John Krehl, a merchant in the Castle Liberties, has approached us and informed us how he had lived in Königsberg almost from his boyhood up, and how after having attained ripe years, he had for more than sixteen years carried on his business there. He also complains that he has not been able, in spite of all his efforts, to obtain the rights of a burgess, on account of his being of Scottish extraction. He begs of us to intercede on his behalf. Now we are fully aware of the decrees issued by our diets in this matter, and we have no intention to annoy you, but you will easily see for yourselves how ungracious a thing it would be on your part to let Krehl, a man who has dwelt among you so long and has been carrying on a large trade, the benefits of which in taxes and duties you also reap, come under the common rule of the exclusion of Scotsmen, and to put him on a level with a stranger who only recently put foot in your town and as to whose intentions you are utterly

ignorant. Such harsh treatment would be a discredit and a detriment to you and yours. It would be a disgrace in the eyes of the strangers and above all of the English nation, between which and the Scottish there is such excellent understanding and with which you carry on so much commerce. We do not doubt, therefore, that you will take everything into due consideration, and that you will not refuse to admit Krehl as a burgess; especially since this case shall not establish any precedent. Given in the camp before Stettin, July 10th, 1677."

8. Johanna Philippine Dorothea Heanes, age 57 years and a native of Germany, arrived at New York from Hamburg on the bark *Sir Isaac Newton* on November 16, 1848. Her husband, John Heanes, is listed as a 56-year-old merchant from England. *Registers of Vessels Arriving at the Port of New York from Foreign Ports, 1789–1919.* National Archives, Washington, D.C., microfilm publication, M237, Roll 76.

9. Albion, *Forests and Sea Power,* 337.

10. Ibid., 338.

11. Clark, *Iron Kingdom,* 391–94.

12. Ibid., 284–376, passim.

13. Ibid., 415–19.

14. Ibid., 420–22.

15. As cited in Clark, *Iron Kingdom,* 430.

16. Nelson, *New Jersey Coast,* 370, entry for George Frederick Kroehl.

17. Passenger list for ship *Fairfield,* July 29, 1844, Passenger Lists of Vessels Arriving at New York, New York, 1820–1897, Records of the US Customs Service, Record Group (RG) 36, National Archives (NA), Microfilm Roll M237–55, List #609, line 23.

18. Frederick E. Prime to Brig. Gen. J. G. Lauman, Headquarters Department of the Tennessee, June 8, 1863, in Scott, *War of the Rebellion,* ser. 1, vol. 24, pt. 3, p. 391.

19. Homberger, *Historical Atlas of New York City,* 70.

20. As cited in Homberger, *Historical Atlas,* 70.

21. Ibid.

22. Ibid.

23. Nadel, "Germans," in the *Encyclopedia of New York,* 403.

24. Faust, *German Element,* 582. Also see Nadel, *Little Germany,* 16–22.

25. The *New York City Directory* lists Julius as an "engineer" at 4 (and occasionally 6) Broadway from 1855 until 1862. In 1858–59 Julius lived at 311 West 19th, close to his brother, Henry (who was at 269 West 19th). In 1862 Julius was living at 8 St. Mark's Place in the heart of Kleindeutschland (now the East Village). Trow, *New York City Directory,* 1858, 456; 1859, 452; 1860, 481; 1861, 482; 1862, 479. Julius was not listed in the directories of 1863 and 1864 while he was serving with the US Navy.

26. Record of Naturalization for Julius Kroehl, New York City Court of Common Pleas, Bundle 91, Record 57.

27. Kirsch, Harris, and Nolte, *Encyclopedia of Ethnicity and Sports,* 180.

28. Nadel, *Little Germany,* 97–98.

29. General Membership Minutes, July 20, 1850, as transcribed in Probst, "New York Turn Verein," 15.

30. Nadel, *Little Germany,* 120–21.

31. Newhall, *Daguerreotype in America,* 55, citing the *Daguerreian Journal* 1 (1850): 49.

32. *Scientific American,* November 1, 1851, 50.

33. "Premiums, Awarded by the Managers of the Twenty-Fourth Annual Fair of the American Institute, October 1851," in State of New York, *Documents of the Assembly . . . Seventy-Fifth Session, 1852,* vol. 7, no. 129, p. 619.

34. *Scientific American,* November 1, 1851, 50.

35. Trow, *New York City Directory,* 1855–1856, 456.

36. *Scientific American,* March 25, 1854, 220, and January 13, 1855, 418.

37. Gayle and Gayle, *Cast-Iron Architecture in America,* 19.

38. Ibid., 21–22.

39. Fisher, *Epic of Steel,* 97.

40. Swank, *History of Iron Manufacture,* 142.

41. Ibid., 98.

42. Ibid., 99.

43. Burrows and Wallace, *Gotham,* 659.

44. *Civil Engineer and Architect's Journal* (London) 17 (1854): 347.

45. Carstensen and Gildemeister, *New York Crystal Palace,* 42.

46. *Scientific American,* March 25, 1854, 220.

47. Ibid.

48. *New York Times,* October 23, 1853.

49. *Scientific American,* March 25, 1854, 220.

50. Ibid.

51. City of New York, *Proceedings of the Board of Assistant Aldermen* 61 (January 14, 1856): 101.

52. City of New York, *Proceedings . . . Approved by the Mayor* 24 (April 14, 1856): 114.

53. Kahn, "Bogardus, Fire, and the Iron Tower," 201.

54. Gayle and Gayle, in *Cast-Iron Architecture,* 187, summarize the trial. The filings and proceedings are in "James Bogardus v. the Mayor and Aldermen of the City of New York," Records of the District Courts of the United States. The judgment is noted in the *New York Times* of April 10, 1858. In time, the city had 11 fire watchtowers built in New York, but after the introduction of street alarm boxes, and impaired visibility thanks to new, high-rise buildings, the towers fell out of use and were retired. Only Kroehl's fire watchtower in Mount Morris Park (renamed Marcus Garvey Park in 1973) survives in the twenty-first century. It is a New York City landmark and is also listed on the National Register of Historic Places.

CHAPTER 2

1. Ripley and Dana, *New American Cyclopaedia,* 520.

2. Ibid., 521.

3. Bacharach, "History of the Diving Bell," 18.

4. Davis, *Deep Diving and Submarine Operations,* 610; Bacharach, "History of the Diving Bell," 18.

5. The bell is displayed in a park and has a plaque on it noting its history.

6. Davis, *Deep Diving and Submarine Operations,* 567–68.

7. "Diving Operations at Portsmouth," *Journal of the Franklin Institute,* 265.

8. Now known as the "standard" diving suit and helmet.

9. For example, there is a glowing discussion of Pasley's work in the *Army and Navy Chronicle* (Washington) of June 13, 1839, p. 374, and in "Explosion of Gunpowder by the Voltaic Battery," in Timbs, *Year-Book of Facts in Science and Art,* 142. "Submarine armour" was known as "submarine armor" in the United States and is the spelling used in this book.

10. "Description of a Diving Dress, invented and used by Charles Condert," *Journal of the Franklin Institute,* 147–49.

11. "Report on Mr. L. Norcross's Diving Apparatus," *Journal of the Franklin Institute,* 25–26.

12. "Gossip with Readers and Correspondents," *Knickerbocker,* 208–9.

13. Stadden, "Hannis Taylor."

14. Taylor, *New and Alluring Sources of Enterprise,* as cited in Lundeberg, "Marine Salvage and Sea Mine Technology," 107.

15. Lundeberg, "Marine Salvage and Sea Mine Technology," 109.

16. Patent No. 578, "Submarine Armor," June 20, 1838, US Patent Office, Washington, D.C.

17. Ibid.

18. Ibid.

19. As cited in Lundeberg, "Marine Salvage and Sea Mine Technology," 109.

20. "The Marine Armor," *Knickerbocker,* 374.

21. Ibid.

22. Lundeberg, "Marine Salvage," 110.

23. Lundeberg, "Marine Salvage," 111.

24. William Taylor's only child, Sarah T. Ingall, provided a biographical sketch of her father when she related her autobiography. "Her parents were Capt. Geo. W. and Rebecca (Hawkes) Taylor, the former a native of New Jersey and the latter of Lynn, Massachusetts. . . . She is the only daughter of her parents. Her father, Captain Taylor, was a man of wonderful inventive genius, improving the diving-bell of his day by several valuable inventions, and later invented the Taylor Submarine Armor, the first submarine apparatus after the diving-bell that was practically successful. He was an intimate friend of Professor Morse, inventor of the telegraph, and of Goodyear, whose inventions have made India rubber and its combinations so valuable. These three were mutual confidantes in their various inventions, all equally struggling to accomplish great results with limited means. Finally, Captain Taylor took Goodyear along on a submarine diving expedition on the coast of Florida, which gave both a financial start. After devoting himself for years to the use and improvement of diving apparatus, he engaged in raising sunken ships containing valuable cargoes. Mrs. Ingall has now in her possession a small wooden toy horse taken by Captain Taylor from the cabin of the British frigate *Hussar,* which was sunk in Long Island Sound after striking on the rocks at Hellgate during the Revolutionary War,

and which contained treasure intended to be paid to the troops then stationed in the neighborhood of New York. Captain Taylor was a practical business man as well as an inventor. He took contracts for raising sunken ships and their cargoes, or such parts as were considered valuable, and had amassed a fortune of $100,000 at the time of his death. His last contract was to raise a large American ship, the Mississippi, sunk in the Straits of Gibraltar. The United States Government paid him $5,000 to make the trip and see what could be done. On making an exploration he agreed to do the work for $25,000, pending the accomplishment of which work he died, in April, 1851. Among Captain Taylor's inventions might be mentioned a floating bomb-proof battery with means of revolving heavy guns, practically an iron-clad Monitor except that it did not contain motive power. Also, a submarine boat for attacking an enemy's ship, very similar to our torpedo-boats. Doubtless, had Captain Taylor lived during the late Civil War, his inventions and his capacity for their practical application would have immediately revolutionized the methods of naval warfare then existing. " Foote, *Pen Pictures from the Garden of the World,* 585–86.

25. As cited in Lundberg, "Marine Salvage and Sea Mine Technology," 111–12.

26. Bauer, *Surfboats and Horse Marines,* 118.

27. Obituary of George W. Taylor, *Washington National Intelligencer,* June 14, 1850.

28. *Gleason's Pictorial Drawing Room Companion,* 1854, 400.

29. Whipple, *Circular of James A. Whipple.*

30. Dickman, "Captain James A. Whipple," 94–101.

31. *New York Times,* January 20, 1853.

32. Driver and Martins, "Shipwreck and Salvage in the Tropics," 554.

33. "Gossip with Readers and Correspondents," *Knickerbocker,* 208–9.

34. Patent 6,250, "Diving Bell," April 3, 1849, US Patent Office, Washington, D.C.

35. Ibid.

36. Gardner, *Dictionary of All Officers,* 400.

37. *New York Times,* December 30, 1854.

38. Ibid.

39. *New York Times,* December 27, 1854.

40. "Gossip with Readers and Correspondents," *Knickerbocker,* 209.

41. *New York Times,* December 27, 1854.

42. *New York Daily Tribune,* February 6, 1856.

43. Mosk, "Capitalistic Development in the Lower California Pearl Fisheries," 465.

44. *New York Times,* April 21, 1856.

45. Sears, "On Appliances for Facilitating Submarine Engineering and Exploration," 243–45.

46. The lawsuit is detailed in the Rowland G. Hazard and Caroline (Newbold) Hazard Papers in the Rhode Island Historical Society Library.

47. In 1864, while leaving his home in Kansas City, Missouri, Hallett was shot and killed by an assailant in a dispute over the railroad. His widow returned to New York.

48. Bourne, *Inventions or Devices,* 1.

49. Compton-Hall, *Submarine Pioneers,* 15–16.

50. As cited in Abbot, *Beginnings of Submarine Warfare,* 14–15.

51. Compton-Hall, *Submarine Pioneers,* 33–36.

52. See, for example, Barber's 1875 account and Abbot's 1881 account, as well as the 1963 work by Wagner, *Submarine Fighter of the American Revolution.* An excellent study is found in Roland, *Underwater Warfare in the Age of Sail.* A full-scale "replica" of *Turtle* (there are no known plans, but Barber in 1875 offered a reconstruction based on the 1775 description) was built as a bicentennial project, and is now in the collections of the Connecticut River Museum in Essex, Connecticut. In 2003 the Handshouse Studio of Massachusetts built another replica in cooperation with the US Naval Academy and the Massachusetts College of Art. The story of another modern, working replica is found in the excellent work by Manstan and Frese, *Turtle: David Bushnell's Revolutionary Vessel.*

53. Dickinson, *Robert Fulton, Engineer and Artist,* 73. 82–123 passim. Also see Compton-Hall, *Submarine Pioneers,* 41–49, passim, and Parsons, *Robert Fulton and the Submarine.* "The electric shock which a large torpedo gives when seized is so severe, that no one who has experienced it desires to experience it again." *Library of Universal Knowledge,* 1881, 482.

54. Seven of Fulton's drawings of *Nautilus* are in the Manuscripts and Archives Division of the New York Public Library.

55. Friedman, *US Submarines through 1945,* 11–12.

56. Compton-Hall, *Submarine Pioneers,* 56–58, and Ragan, *Submarine Warfare in the Civil War,* 15.

57. Ragan, *Submarine Warfare in the Civil War,* gives an excellent and thorough account of *Alligator's* career.

58. See Compton-Hall, *Submarine Pioneers,* 59.

59. Field, *Story of the Submarine,* 224.

60. Corbin, *Romance of Submarine Engineering,* 105–7.

61. Perrin-Gouron, "Le Docteur Prosper PAYERNE Sa Vie, son oeuvre."

62. See Bethge, *Der Brandtaucher.* Rediscovered in 1887 and raised from Kiel Harbor, *Brandtaucher* was displayed in various locations before being moved to the Militärhistorisches Museum der Bundeswehr in Dresden, where it is now on display. Also see Compton-Hall, *Submarine Pioneers,* 60–63.

63. See Harrie, *Great Lakes' First Submarine.* On November 9, 1852, Phillips received Patent 9,389 for improvements in steering submarine vessels. Ragan, in *Submarine Warfare in the Civil War,* 215–16, also does a remarkable job of placing Phillips in a proper context, drawing on his own knowledge of submarines and from Phillips's correspondence with the US Navy.

64. See, for example, Corbin, *Romance of Submarine Engineering,* 87–88, and Compton-Hall, *Submarine Pioneers,* 63–64.

65. *Scientific American* 7, no. 11, November 29, 1851. Pease & Murphy operated New York's Fulton Iron Works, which specialized in marine engines and machinery.

66. Ibid.

67. *Scientific American* 8, no. 12, December 4, 1852.

68. *Scientific American,* November 29, 1851.

69. *New York Times,* March 8, 1852.

70. This is an English description of a dive in Payerne's craft in France. See Field, *Story of the Submarine,* 224. An article on test dives with the submarine appeared in *Chambers' Edinburgh Journal,* on August 8, 1846, 96.

CHAPTER 3

1. Irving, "Tales of a Traveller," 410.

2. Kornblum, *At Sea in the City,* 187–88.

3. "Hurl Gate Rocks," *Hunt's Merchants' Magazine and Commercial Review* 21, no. 12 (December 1849): 664.

4. "Submarine Blasting," *Hunt's Merchants' Magazine and Commercial Review* 30, no. 11 (February 1854): 191.

5. Ibid., 194.

6. Wells, *Annual of Scientific Discovery,* 89.

7. Ibid., 195.

8. "The Blasting of Rocks Under Water Without Drilling," *Hunt's Merchants' Magazine and Commercial Review,* 27, no. 3 (September 1852): 325.

9. Wells, *Annual of Scientific Discovery,* 89.

10. *New York Times,* March 27, 1852.

11. *New York Times,* March 31, 1852; Francis Metallic Lifeboat Company, *Francis' Metallic Life-Boat Company,* 69–72.

12. See Blunt and Blunt, *American Coast Pilot* (1854), 264, for a description of Diamond Reef.

13. *New York Times,* August 11, 1853.

14. Patent 8,776, "Blasting Rocks Under Water," March 2, 1852, US Patent Office, Washington, D.C.

15. The office was Husted's—he had advertised from it in January 1854 offering real estate loans from "Van Ness, Husted & Co., dealers in real estate." *New York Times,* January 27, 1854. Peter V. Husted's middle name was Van Ness, and the senior partner was therefore probably a relative.

16. New York City directories, 1854–1864; also see Husted's US passport application, August 25, 1879, Microfilm Publication M1372, 694 rolls, General Records of the US Department of State.

17. *New York Times,* November 13, 1851, and September 17, 1852. General Scott lost the election of Democratic candidate Franklin Pierce. The Whig Party subsequently dissolved.

18. Patents 398,259 (1889) and 398,260 (1889), US Patent Office, Washington, D.C.

19. City of New York, *Annual Report of the Comptroller . . . 1852,* 73.

20. Port of New York, *Centennial Hand-Book of the Naval Office of Customs,* 4–5.

21. Ibid., 8.

22. Ibid., 29, and R. G. Dun entry for Peter V. Husted, vol. 266, p. 358, June 29, 1855, R. G. Dun & Company Collection. Baker Library Historical Collections, Harvard Business School.

23. R. G. Dun entry for Husted.

24. Philip Hone, in his diary, on April 17, 1849, noted that "the official patronage of the naval officer is confined to the clerks who are employed about his person." Tuckerman, *Diary of Philip Hone,* 2:358. Also see Holt, *Rise and Fall of the American Whig Party,* 432, 651. Bokee remained loyal to Husted and vice versa. In 1854 Husted advertised real estate and mortgage loans from his office at 4 Broad Street and listed Bokee as a reference. *New York Times,* January 27, 1854.

25. Ibid.

26. R. G. Dun entry for Peter V. Husted, vol. 266, p. 358, April 11, 1860. A later entry, in 1866, notes that Husted "does good bus [*sic*] but is always in some trouble gets in deeply in speculation & is troubled how to extricate himself. R. G. Dun entry for Peter V. Husted, vol. 266, p. 400, subpage 5, December 30, 1867. In the later 1860s and early 1870s, Husted was a principal in the lumber firm of Husted Dunbar & Co. and president of the New York Match Company. He owned three homes and was considered "strictly honest" at first, although later "speculative and sanguine" and not worthy of credit. R. G. Dun entry for Peter V. Husted, vol. 266, p. 400, subpage 5, entries of December 16, 1867, October 1868, May 7, 1870, June 9, 1874.

27. Petition of Husted & Kroehl. The *Journal of the House of Representatives* notes on January 25, 1855, that Representative John Wheeler of New York's 6th Congressional District submitted the "memorial of Husted and Kroehl, submarine engineers, submitting a proposition to remove, without expense to the government, all the rocks obstructing the navigation in 'Hell Gate,' East river, making the same a clear river passage to a depth of twenty-two feet at mean low water," which was referred to the House Committee on Commerce. *Journal of the House of Representatives,* 33rd Cong. 2nd sess., p. 241.

28. Hearn, *Circuits in the Sea,* 23–29. The project was successful and messages were exchanged in 1858 before the cable failed after three weeks of operation. It took several years and much effort and expenditure before a new cable was laid in 1866 and remained in operation.

29. The *Charlottetown (Prince Edward Island) Examiner* of April 16, 1855, reported that "Mr. Huested" was a passenger on a ship on April 12 traveling from Cape Tormentine to Cape Traverse.

30. Taylor, *At Home and Abroad,* 278–79.

31. MacLeod, *Biography of Fernando Wood,* 327. In the federal census of 1880, Husted was listed, at age 61, as a hotel keeper, living with his 38-year-old wife, Sabina, three boarders and a servant. He died in February 1899 and was interred at Brooklyn's Green-Wood Cemetery on February 15, 1899.

32. *New York Times,* July 11, 1855.

33. *New York Times,* April 11, 1855. Maillefert had a longstanding interest in Diamond Reef, and in October 1851 had fired a few 125-pound charges on it in a demonstration of his work. *New York Times,* October 18, 1851.

34. *New York Times,* July 11, 1855.

35. *New York Times,* July 20, 1855.

36. Ibid.

37. *New York Times,* July 25, 1855.

38. Ibid.

39. *New York Times,* July 28, 1855.

40. *New York Times,* August 8, 1855.

41. *New York Times,* September 13, 1855.

42. *New York Times,* June 20, 1856.

43. *New York Times,* July 11, 1856.

44. *Scientific American,* August 16, 1856, 386.

45. Ibid.

46. *New York Times,* April 11, 1855.

47. *New York Times,* December 6, 1856.

48. Ibid.

49. *Boston Post,* December 15, 1856.

50. The marriage certificate, signed by the Rev. Joseph Aschwardeu, is included in Sophia R. Kroehl, "Widow's Naval Pension Application File," Records of the Department of Veterans Affairs, National Archives.

51. I am deeply indebted to John McKee, who conducted significant genealogical research on the Luebers, discovering family records at St. John Evangelist Roman Catholic Church in Frederick, as well as Holy Trinity Catholic Church and St. Stephen Martyr Catholic Church in Washington, D.C. John shared his research with me in an extensive e-mail on January 5, 2008.

52. Sackersdorff, born in Prussia in 1820, was the same age as Julius. He was working with the city in 1858 and had worked previously on assignment for the US Army Corps of Engineers. In November 1853 he applied for a passport for a professional trip to the West Indies, with Samuel Hein accompanying him as his traveling companion. Sackersdorff listed his cousin Henry Kroehl's business (Kroehl & Dill) as his address. I am indebted to Bruce Kroehl, who shared this information in an e-mail on March 26, 2009. Hein joined the Coast Survey as a clerk in 1836 and served as disbursing officer between 1847 and 1877. See Letters Sent, 1851–57, and Received, 1847–65, by Disbursing Agent Samuel Hein, Records of the US Coast and Geodetic Survey, National Archives. On the Coast Survey at this time, see Slotten, *Patronage, Practice, and the Culture of American Science.*

53. The office was described in *Bohn's Handbook of Washington* in 1852: "The buildings occupied for the uses of the United States Coast Survey are situated on the W. side of New Jersey Avenue, about a sixth of a mile from the Capitol. They consist of four old houses, in a block, presenting a decidedly rusty exterior, and in no way looking like public buildings. The room of the Superintendent, Prof. A. D. Bache, is at the North end, and that of the Assistant in charge of the Office is at the South end. At present this place is filled by brevet Major J. J. Stevens, U. S. corps of Engineers. The office of Mr. Samuel Hein, Disbursing officer of the Survey is in the South middle building. Most of the rooms in the upper stories is appropriated to computers, draughtsmen and engravers. The fire proof building South of the office, contains the Archives, or Records of Observations, the Library, the Standard Weights, Balances and Measures, the Instruments not in use, and the engraved copper plates" (71).

54. See Cloud, "Smart Germans in the Survey and in Washington."

55. Throughout this period, Husted was "doing well & making money" and also was working in partnership with Daniel Moss in the operation of a hotel and saloon at 30 Bowery Street in New York. In 1858 Husted was "deemed reliable," as he and Moss "pay promptly and are said to be making money." Husted was the silent partner, with Moss running the day-to-day business in his own name, which led to troubles when Moss's former partner, a Mr. Reed, sued for payment of monies for a building he and Moss had once owned. Moss lost, and transferred his interest in the business to Husted to avoid it being attached by Reed. By then, the "house was not doing very well," and in 1860 Husted mortgaged the property and its contents to Jesse W. Benedict of New York. As of 1862, the business failed, and Moss left the hotel and saloon, but Husted worked out terms with Benedict and continued operating the hotel. R. G. Dun entries for Peter V. Husted, vol. 266, p. 358, July 14, 1858, June 23, 1859, April 4, 1860, April 11, 1860, January 26, 1861, May 30, 1861, January 8, 1862, March 1, 1865. Husted died in New York in 1881.

56. Ryerson, *Ryerson Family Genealogy,* 175–76.

57. *Trow's New York City Directory,* 1850.

58. *Brief Account of Submarine Machines,* 6.

59. Ibid., 7.

60. Patent 1,852, October 19, 1858, US Patent Office, Washington, D.C.

61. *New-York Submarine Engineering Company.*

62. *Brief Account of Submarine Machines,* 9.

63. *New York Times,* October 28, 1859.

64. Corporation of the City of New York, *Annual Report of the Comptroller . . . 1859,* 75, and also City of New York, *Documents of the Board of Aldermen . . . 1859,* 232.

65. *Scientific American,* November 21, 1859, 332.

66. An excellent account of the *Water Witch* episode can be found in Smith and Bartlett, "A Most Unprovoked, Unwarrantable, and Dastardly Attack."

67. *Brooklyn Daily Eagle,* December 15, 1858.

68. According to his family, "this patent was destined to make his fortune, but he died while negotiations were in progress. The idea was carried out by others." Ryerson, *Ryerson Family Genealogy,* 176.

69. *Brief Account of Submarine Machines,* 8.

70. Ibid.

CHAPTER 4

1. Von Steinwehr (1822–77), born in Blankenburg in the Duchy of Brunswick (Germany), immigrated to the United States in 1847 and served in the US Coast Survey. He returned to Germany in 1849 and in 1854 came back to the United States with his American wife. Promoted to brigadier general in October 1861 after the First Battle of Bull Run, von Steinwehr also served with distinction through the war, including a trying ordeal in which his command was hard hit at Gettysburg.

2. *New York Herald,* June 8, 1861.

3. Asboth joined the Union Army in July 1861 as chief of staff to Gen. John Charles Frémont and was promoted to brigadier general in September. He served with distinction

during the war and was twice wounded. Kornél (Cornelius) Fornet (1818–94) was a highly decorated veteran of the failed 1848–49 Hungarian war of independence who emigrated to the United States in 1849. He served as a major with Frémont and was badly wounded in the shoulder in September 1861, which ended his active military career.

4. *Philadelphia Inquirer,* June 20, 1861. I am indebted to John McKee and Bruce Kroehl for tracking down this information.

5. *Philadelphia Inquirer,* July 9, 1861. Also see the *New York Herald,* July 17, 1861. The *Herald* article noted that the job was done to the "entire satisfaction of the superintendent of the military [rail]road, who speaks highly of their skill."

6. Secretary of the Navy, "Report of the Secretary of the Navy," in *Message from the President,* 3:519.

7. These pontoons, which were prefabricated and bolted together at flanged angle iron joints, were the invention of fellow Prussian Hermann Grundt of Berlin.

8. US Patent 34,329, dated February 4, 1862, was assigned to Hess, Kassel & Company. The firm appears in *Trow's New York City Directory* for 1862 as importers at 24 Park Place, p. 389.

9. Letter, Gideon Welles to Julius Kroehl, Washington, D.C., January 16, 1862, Records of the Office of the Secretary of the Navy, National Archives.

10. Baird, "Submarine Torpedo Boats," 852.

11. Letter, Welles to Kroehl, Washington, D.C., February 27, 1862, Records of the Office of the Secretary of the Navy.

12. Bauer, *Surfboats and Horse Marines,* 118.

13. "Report of Julius H. Kroehl" as cited in Stewart, *Official Records of the Union and Confederate Navies,* ser. 1, 18:427.

14. Hearn, *Capture of New Orleans,* provides an excellent overview and analysis of the campaign.

15. Hearn also has published the definitive Farragut biography, *Admiral David Glasgow Farragut.*

16. Hearn, *Capture of New Orleans,* 179–83.

17. "Report of Julius H. Kroehl" in Stewart, *Official Records.*

18. Ibid.

19. Hearn, *Capture of New Orleans,* 180.

20. "Report of Julius H. Kroehl" in Stewart, *Official Records,* 18:428.

21. Hearn, *Admiral David Glasgow Farragut,* 57–58.

22. "Report of Julius H. Kroehl" in Stewart, *Official Records,* 18:429.

23. Bell, private diary entry, April 20, 1862, as cited in Stewart, *Official Records,* 18:695.

24. Bacon, "One Night's Work, April 20, 1862," 306.

25. "Report of Julius H. Kroehl" in Stewart, *Official Records,* 18:429; Bell, private diary entry, April 20, 1862, in Stewart, *Official Records,* 18:695; and Bacon, "One Night's Work," 306. Hearn also summarizes the night on the river in *The Capture of New Orleans,* 201–3.

26. Ibid.

27. Bell, private diary entry, April 20, 1862, in Stewart, *Official Records,* 18:696.

28. "Report of Julius H. Kroehl" in Stewart, *Official Records,* 18:429.

29. "Report of Julius H. Kroehl"; Bell, private diary entry; and Bacon, "One Night's Work."

30. "Report of Julius H. Kroehl," 18:430.

31. Porter, *Naval History of the Civil War,* 180; Hearn, *Capture of New Orleans.*

32. "Report of Julius H. Kroehl," 18:430.

33. *New York Times,* June 2, 1862.

34. Letter, David D. Porter to J. H. Kroehl, May 20, 1862, as cited in Stewart, *Official Records,* 18:431.

35. David D. Porter to Gustavus V. Fox, US Steamer *Octorara,* Ship Island, May 24, 1862, in Thompson and Wainwright, *Confidential Correspondence of Gustavus Vasa Fox,* 2:105, 108.

36. *New York Times,* June 1, 1862.

37. "Report of Julius H. Kroehl," in Stewart, *Official Records,* 18:426–30.

38. Ibid., 430.

39. Pass for Julius H. Kroehl, signed by Gideon Welles, Navy Department, July 19, 1862, countersigned by Charles Wilkes, Commanding James River Flotilla, July 24, 1862. Original on file in Sophia R. Kroehl, "Widow's Naval Pension Application File," Record 2412, Certificate 5096, National Archives.

40. An excellent summary of the struggle for the James can be found in Browning, *From Cape Charles to Cape Fear.*

41. Ragan, *Submarine Warfare in the Civil War,* 66.

42. Ibid., 14–16, 18, 68–70.

43. Ibid., 79.

44. Ragan, *Submarine Warfare in the Civil War,* 84–92, passim.

45. I have relied on Weddle, *Lincoln's Tragic Admiral,* 55–58, 102–5.

46. "Memorandum of Acting Master Rogers, US Navy, telegraphic engineer, for Acting Rear-Admiral Lee, US Navy, regarding magneto-electric machines for use in the James Rover," On Board Flagship Minnesota, September 16, 1862, in Rawson and Stewart, *Official Records of the Union and Confederate Navies in the War of the Rebellion,* ser. 1, 8:72.

47. "Report of Acting Rear-Admiral Lee, US Navy, regarding obstructions in the James River," in Rawson and Stewart, *Official Records,* 8:73–74.

48. Gustavus V. Fox to Julius H. Kroehl, Navy Department, December 1, 1862. Original on file in Sophia R. Kroehl, "Widow's Naval Pension Application File," National Archives.

49. Kroehl's appointment certificate, signed by Gideon Welles, Navy Department, December 4, 1862. Original on file in Sophia R. Kroehl, "Widow's Naval Pension Application File."

50. S. P. Lee to Julius Kroehl, USN., US Flag Steamer *Philadelphia,* Hampton Roads, Va., December 5, 1862. Original on file in Sophia R. Kroehl, "Widow's Naval Pension Application File."

51. Gideon Welles to Julius H. Kroehl, Navy Department, December 10, 1862, Letters Sent by the Secretary of the Navy to Officers, Records of the Secretary of the Navy, National Archives.

52. Julius H. Kroehl to Gideon Welles, New York, December 10, 1862.

53. Gustavus V. Fox to Julius H. Kroehl, Navy Department, December 11, 1862, Letters Sent by the Secretary of the Navy to Officers, National Archives.

54. Gustavus V. Fox to Julius H. Kroehl, Navy Department, December 13, 1862, Letters Sent by the Secretary of the Navy to Officers, National Archives.

55. Julius H. Kroehl to Gustavus V. Fox, New York, December 15, 1862, Letters Sent by the Secretary of the Navy to Officers, National Archives.

56. Rear Admiral David D. Porter to Gideon Welles, USS *Black Hawk,* December 17, 1862, in Stewart, *Official Records of the Union and Confederate Navies in the War of the Rebellion,* ser. 1, 23:635.

57. Gideon Welles to Rear Admiral David D. Porter, December 24, 1862, Stewart, *Official Records,* 23:647.

58. Report of Acting Volunteer Lieutenant Kroehl, U. S. Navy, suggesting means for destroying torpedoes, December 23, 1862, Stewart, *Official Records,* 23:646.

59. Rear Admiral Lee to Captain B. F. Sands, USS *Dacotah,* US Flag Steamer *Philadelphia,* Hampton Roads, December 29, 1862, in Rawson and Stewart, *Official Records of the Union and Confederate Navies,* 8:331.

60. Ibid.

61. Lieutenant Commander D. L. Braine to Rear Admiral S. P. Lee, USS *Monticello,* January 7, 1863, in Rawson and Stewart, *Official Records,* 8:409.

62. Lt. Cdr. Braine to Rear Adm. Lee, USS *Monticello,* January 19, 1863, in Rawson and Stewart, *Official Records,* 8:451.

63. Gideon Welles to Julius H. Kroehl, Navy Department, January 10, 1863. Original on file in Sophia R. Kroehl, "Widow's Naval Pension Application File."

64. B. F. Sands to Julius H. Kroehl, US steamer *Dacotah,* Off Cape Fear River, N.C., January 23, 1863. Original on file in Sophia R. Kroehl, "Widow's Naval Pension Application File."

65. The passage is referenced in a note on the bottom of Sands's letter of January 23rd to Kroehl, from Lt. Cdr. D. L. Braine to Captain Denker, Str. *Baltimore,* and is dated January 26, 1863.

66. D. L. Braine to Julius H. Kroehl, US Steamer *Monticello,* Beaufort, N.C., January 29, 1863. Original on file in Sophia R. Kroehl, "Widow's Naval Pension Application File."

67. See Milligan, *Gunboats Down the Mississippi,* 3, 79, 93–94.

68. Julius H. Kroehl to Rear Admiral D. D. Porter, Hampton Roads, Va., December 23, 1862, in Stewart, *Official Records,* 23:646. USS *Cairo* was sunk by a Confederate "torpedo" on December 12, 1862. See Milligan, *Gunboats Down the Mississippi,* 104.

69. I am indebted to John McKee for finding the reference to Kroehl's training with the Coast Survey. See US Coast Survey, *Report of the Superintendent . . . 1863,* 53.

70. Ibid.

71. David D. Porter to Julius H. Kroehl, US Mississippi Squadron, Yazoo River, March 5, 1863. Original on file in Sophia R. Kroehl, "Widow's Naval Pension Application File."

72. Milligan, *Gunboats Down the Mississippi,* 136–37.

73. "Abstract Log of the USS *Carondelet* . . . March 4 to May 17, 1863," in Stewart, *Official Records of the Union and Confederate Navies,* ser. 1, 24:687–88.

74. Milligan, *Gunboats Down the Mississippi,* 138.

75. Ibid., 139.

76. Ibid., 139–40.

77. "Abstract Log of the USS *Carondelet,*" in Stewart, *Official Records,* 24:688.

78. Acting Rear Admiral D. D. Porter to Rear Admiral D. G. Farragut, US Mississippi Squadron, March 26, 1863, in Stewart, *Official Records of the Union and Confederate Navies,* ser. 1, 20:28.

79. Rear Admiral D. G. Farragut to Acting Rear Admiral D. D. Porter, US Flagship *Hartford,* March 27, 1863, Stewart, *Official Records,* 20:33.

80. Clarence Fendall to Ferdinand H. Gerdes, as cited by Theberge, *The Coast Survey,* n. 59. Fendall, a talented but difficult member of the Coast Survey, was a protégé of Gerdes. See Theberge, *The Coast Survey,* 481–535, for an excellent discussion of the Coast Survey's work with Porter and Grant.

81. "The Iron-Clad Cincinnati," *Harper's Weekly* 7, no. 338 (June 20, 1863): 1.

82. Milligan, *Gunboats Down the Mississippi,* 122.

83. Clarence Fendall to Ferdinand H. Gerdes, May 1, 1863, Fendall Letters to F. H. Gerdes, Records of the US Coast and Geodetic Survey, National Archives.

84. David D. Porter to Julius H. Kroehl, US Mississippi Squadron, flagship *Black Hawk,* June 6, 1864. Original on file in Sophia R. Kroehl, "Widow's Naval Pension Application File."

85. Shea and Winschel, *Vicksburg Is the Key,* 153.

86. Frederick E. Prime to Brig. Gen. J. G. Lauman, Headquarters Department of the Tennessee, June 8, 1863, in Scott, *War of the Rebellion,* ser. 1, vol. 24, pt. 3, p. 391.

87. The letter, dated June 13, 1863, is reproduced in Simon, *Papers of Ulysses S. Grant,* 8:383.

88. Clarence Fendall to F. H. Gerdes, USS *Blackhawk,* off Vicksburg, June 16, 1863, Records of Assistant F. H. Gerdes, Records of the US Coast Survey, National Archives.

89. Bell, *Mosquito Soldiers,* 129.

90. Ibid., 10–11.

91. Ibid., 10.

92. Sophia R. Kroehl, General Affidavit, December 9, 1889. Original on file in Sophia R. Kroehl, "Widow's Naval Pension Application File."

93. Gideon Welles to Julius H. Kroehl, Navy Department, August 8, 1863. Original on file in Sophia R. Kroehl, "Widow's Naval Pension Application File."

94. Acting Rear Admiral David D. Porter to A. D. Bache, Superintendent, US Coast Survey, off New Orleans, August 5, 1863, in Stewart, *Official Records of the Union and Confederate Navies,* ser. 1, 25:341.

95. Report of Acting Rear Admiral Lee, August 25, 1863, in Rawson and Stewart, *Official Records of the Union and Confederate Navies,* ser. 1, 9:181.

CHAPTER 5

1. Affidavit of Henry Kroehl, and affidavit of Alexander Clinton, MD, originals in Sophia R. Kroehl, "Widow's Naval Pension Application File," National Archives. Dr. Al-

exander Clinton was a member of a prominent family that included Revolutionary War leaders, governors, and mayors. In 1865 Dr. Clinton resided and practiced at 230 West 14th in Manhattan. See *Trow's New York City Directory,* 1865, 167.

2. The *San Bernardino Guardian* of March 9, 1867, notes Ryerson's role in the Greenleaf Mining Company. Ryerson Hill is a valley landmark to this day.

3. Patent 32,448 for Ryerson's amalgamator was issued on June 4, 1861. See US Patent Office, *Annual Report of the Commissioner of Patents for the Year 1861,* 1:367. On May 1, 1866, Ryerson received another patent, 54,412, for an "Improved Method of Extracting Precious Metals From Ores," which further refined his steam process for amalgamation.

4. Browne, *Resources of the Pacific Slope,* 30, and Raymond, *Mineral Resources,* 14.

5. Cross, *Financing an Empire,* 1:86, 89.

6. Brumagim's papers are held by the Meriam Library at California State University, Chico. A brief biography is appended to the guide to the papers, available at the Online Archive of California, http://www.oac.cdlib.org/findaid/ark:/13030/tf0489n3jd. Brumagim resided in Marysville, moving to San Francisco in 1860 and remaining there until 1881, when he returned to New York.

7. *San Francisco Daily Alta California,* February 1, 1868.

8. *Pacific Pearl Company of New York,* 1863, title page. The New York Division of Corporations confirmed in an e-mail to me on January 10, 2005, that the company had filed a certificate of incorporation on November 18, 1863, with its principal location in New York.

9. North, *Samuel Peter Heintzelman,* 19.

10. Ibid., 19–20.

11. Colt had an interest in submarines and was also involved, in 1842, in the development of "torpedoes," or underwater mines, but after failing to win government contracts, lost interest. See Houze, Cooper, and Kornhauser, *Samuel Colt,* 66–67.

12. Houze, Cooper, and Kornhauser, *Samuel Colt,* 30–32. Also see Thompson, *Civil War to the Bloody End,* 319.

13. Hartley went to what would become the Yale Law School, graduating in 1841. In 1843 the law school merged with Yale. I am indebted to John McKee, who forwarded to me a May 18, 2009, communication on this subject from Nancy F. Lyon, archivist, Yale University Library. Hartley was an adventurous soul who had joined Italian patriot Garibaldi "in the trenches" in Italy in 1855, the same year he also patented a device for manufacturing hollow, explosive-filled shells (Patent 12,574, granted to Hartley on March 21, 1855, for an "Improved Press for Making Cylindro-Conical Hollow Projectiles by Pressure," *Annual Report of the Commissioner of Patents . . . 1855,* 257). Known as "Major Hartley" for his overseas service, Hartley doubtless ensured Colt's delivery of arms to Garibaldi in 1860. While working with Colt, Hartley maintained a residence in Hartford, Conn., where he was placed in command of "Colt's Regiment" at the time of its formation at the beginning of the Civil War. Hartley was mechanically inclined, and with an eye for invention, he invested in and advertised a locomotive whistle through a pamphlet he published (Hartley, *Harrison's Automatic Whistle for Locomotives,* 1857). Hartley was also a shareholder and officer of the Sterling Mountain Railway Company of New York,

which incorporated in 1864, and a charter member of the British North America Mining Company in 1855. He was also a member of the New York Yacht Club, and in 1866 owned the steam sloop *Wave* (Peverelly, *Book of American Pastimes,* 30). That same year, Hartley was described by commercial reporter Dun & Company as president of the Santa Rita Mining Company as well as the Ashburton Coal Mining Company, owning "a large tract of land in Arizona which is as yet undeveloped neither is the Santa Rita Mine developed" (entry for Wm. M. B. Hartley, May 18, 1866, Dun & Company Records, vol. 412, p. 130). Hartley was also a member of the International Order of Odd Fellows (a brief biography can be found in *The Official History of Odd Fellowship,* 435). Hartley edited and published a number of works, including a history of Hartford, genealogies, and catalogues of private libraries. Hartley died in Montreal, Canada, on February 1, 1875, and his obituary appeared in the *Central Law Journal* of February 12, 1875, p. 116. The obituary provided a brief account of his career, including the time with Garibaldi, and also noted he had been a "successful stock operator on Wall Street" as well as one-time US vice consul in Liverpool. Hartley maintained a lifelong interest in iron manufacturing, steam technology, and ordnance. His interests are characterized by correspondence on the subject, including letters to the editor, such as one to the editors of the *Mechanic's Magazine* of January 10, 1857, which stretched over three pages in length on the subject of rifled ordnance (pp. 33–35).

14. North, *Samuel Peter Heintzelman,* 19–20.

15. In Poston's papers at the Sharlot Hall Museum and Archives, Prescott, Ariz., is an undated "list of stocks left with George Wrightson Attorney for Charles D. Poston." It lists 500 shares of Pacific Pearl Company stock. The list illustrates the diversity of mineral interests Poston had, and his portfolio, such as it is, most probably indicates the type of investments made by speculators eager to control the rich mineral resources of the West and the Pacific and other regions. Among the 18 companies listed (seven of them oil companies) are the Arizona Mining Company, (5,976 stocks), American Chrome Company, (1,600 stocks), Gaspé Lead Company (1,000 stocks), Vermont Quartz Mill Gold Company (1,000 stocks), Maricopa Copper Mining Company (200 stocks), and Prescott Consolidated Mining Company (1,383 stocks).

16. The four brothers were the sons of Thomas Wrightson, who emigrated from England with his family, arriving in New York in May 1832. They settled in Albany. Three of the sons joined the Sonora Exploration and Mining Company, two as directors and one, John, as an employee. John Wrightson (1815–1859) was killed in Arizona. His brother William (1827–1865) died six years later, but brother Thomas (1822–1897) survived to old age. See North, *Samuel Peter Heintzelman,* 19–20, 194. Born on August 30, 1834, in Albany, New York, George Wrightson is listed in the 1850 and 1860 US census at his parents' home in Albany, and in 1880 he was living in Chicago. He maintained his contacts in Arizona and died in Mexico City on April 7, 1895.

17. *Trow's New York City Directory* for 1865–66 lists the company offices at 30 Pine, which is between Broad and William Streets, approximately two blocks from the New York Stock Exchange. The directory also lists Tiffany, Chadwick (whose home is listed as Albemarle), Wrightson (whose home is listed as Albany), and Hartley (whose residence is listed as 25 9th Avenue). See pp. 166, 417, 752, 969, and 1067.

18. Hollister, *Historical Record of the Class of 1840,* 52. Also see *Obituary Record for the Undergraduates of Yale University,* 28.

19. LeCount and Strong, *San Francisco Directory,* 1854, 133, and Langley, *San Francisco Directory,* 1859, 281; 1860, 319; 1861, 346; and 1862, 399. In a letter from San Francisco, dated September 7, 1851, Hiram Grimes wrote to Louis Adler, noting that if he wished to purchase "about thirty lots in Sonoma, please call upon Mr. Wm. H. Tiffany, cor[ner] Sacramento and Stockton Sts. here in this city." Hiram Grimes Papers, MSS C-B 103, Bancroft Library, University of California, Berkeley.

20. William H. Tiffany was born on February 10, 1819, in Killingly, Conn., seven years after his brother Charles. He never married. Tiffany died in Stamford, Conn., on December 21, 1880. He is buried in the family plot next to his brother in Brooklyn's historic Green-Wood Cemetery. See Drexler, *Addresses of the Living Graduates of Yale College,* 25, and Hollister, *Historical Record of the Class of 1840,* 52. Tiffany was a member of Yale's famous Order of Skull and Bones.

21. Shaw, *History of Essex and Hudson Counties,* 454. The Chadwick Patent-Leather Company was one of several patent leather manufacturers in the city (ibid., 639). It was described in November 1867 as handling 200,000 hides a year in its operation ("More About Newark," 17–18). Chadwick was listed in the 1851 Newark city directory as "patent leather," along with the company, at 34 Front Street, with his residence at 21 Washington. Pierson, *Directory of the City of Newark,* 86.

22. See Urquhart, *History of the City of Newark,* 771, 941.

23. American Institute of the City of New York, *Annual Report,* 1847, 49.

24. I am indebted to John McKee for discovering this fact.

25. *Pacific Pearl Company,* 1865, 3.

26. Letter, Van Buren Ryerson to his attorney, San Bernardino County, Calif., Greenleaf, January 8, 1864, Ralf Mulhern Collection, San Diego, Calif. Butterworth was president of the Quicksilver Mining Company, which had gained control of the New Almaden mercury mines of Santa Clara County (near San Jose and some 50 miles south of San Francisco) with the support of President Lincoln. In 1864 Butterworth resigned his presidency to become the general manager of the New Almaden mines and remained in the job until 1870. He died in San Francisco in 1875.

27. *Brooklyn Eagle,* December 13, 1865.

28. Silka, "Williamsburg, Brooklyn: The Home of the First Successful Commercial Submarine," 75–76.

29. Lain, *Brooklyn City Directory,* 1864, 368; 1865, 96.

30. Chase, *Art of Pattern Making,* 236.

31. I would like to thank the late Hank Silka for suggesting this to me.

32. Overman and Fesquet, *Moulder's and Founder's Pocket Guide,* 18–19.

33. Ibid., 208.

34. Abbott, "Novelty Iron Works," 728–29.

35. Overman and Fesquet, *Moulder's and Founder's Pocket Guide,* 219.

36. Julius H. Kroehl to Gustavus V. Fox, New York, June 14, 1864, Records of the Office of the Secretary of the Navy, "Officer's Letters," National Archives.

37. Julius H. Kroehl to Joseph Smith, New York, June 14, 1864, Records of the Office of the Secretary of the Navy, Miscellaneous Letters Received, National Archives.

38. George Wrightson to Gideon Welles, New York, June 14, 1864, Records of the Office of the Secretary of the Navy, "Miscellaneous Letters Received," National Archives.

39. Gideon Welles to George Wrightson, Navy Department, and Gideon Welles to W. W. W. Wood, Navy Department, June 17, 1864, Records of the Office of the Secretary of the Navy, Miscellaneous Letters Sent, National Archives.

40. Gideon Welles to Julius H. Kroehl, Navy Department, June 17, 1864, Records of the Office of the Secretary of the Navy, Miscellaneous Letters Sent, National Archives.

41. Julius H. Kroehl to Gideon Welles, New York, June 18, 1864, Records of the Office of the Secretary of the Navy, Miscellaneous Letters Received, National Archives.

42. Gideon Welles to Julius Kroehl, Navy Department, June 16, 1864, Records of the Office of the Secretary of the Navy, Miscellaneous Letters Sent, National Archives.

43. Gideon Welles to Julius H. Kroehl, Navy Department, June 23, 1864, Records of the Office of the Secretary of the Navy, Miscellaneous Letters Sent, National Archives; Gideon Welles to Rear Admirals Dahlgren, Farragut, Lee and Bailey, Navy Department, June 23, 1864, Records of the Office of the Secretary of the Navy, Letters to Officers Commanding Squadrons or Vessels, 1861–1886, National Archives.

44. Kroehl to Smith, June 14, 1864, National Archives.

45. In this aspect of the submarine's construction I am convinced that Kroehl was influenced by Grundt's patent for iron pontoons.

46. Kroehl to Smith, June 14, 1864, National Archives.

47. Bourne, *Treatise on the Steam-Engine,* 292.

48. Letter and report, W. W. W. Wood to Gideon Welles, New York, February 2, 1865, Records of the Office of the Secretary of the Navy, Miscellaneous Letters Received, National Archives.

49. Gustavus V. Fox to Julius H. Kroehl, Navy Department, February 15, 1865, Records of the Office of the Secretary of the Navy, Miscellaneous Letters Sent, National Archives.

50. Julius H. Kroehl to Gustavus V. Fox, New York, February 25, 1865, Records of the Office of the Secretary of the Navy, Miscellaneous Letters Sent, National Archives.

51. Gustavus V. Fox to Julius H. Kroehl, Navy Department, March 2, 1865, Records of the Office of the Secretary of the Navy, Miscellaneous Letters Sent, National Archives.

52. The note is appended to the end of Wood's report and letter to Welles, February 2, 1865.

53. Buhl, in "Mariners and Machines," notes that technology "becomes for some men the basis of their livelihood and future prospects and for others a threat," 727.

54. *Brooklyn Daily Eagle,* November 12, 1865.

55. *Brooklyn Daily Eagle,* December 13, 1865.

56. *Pacific Pearl Company,* 1866, title page.

57. *New York Times,* May 31, 1866.

58. W. W. W. Wood to Julius H. Kroehl, June 11, 1866, as cited in *Pacific Pearl Company,* 1866, 10.

59. *The Pacific Pearl Company,* 1866, 7–8.

60. Ibid., 16.

61. Ibid.

62. Morris's stock certificate appears online at http://en.wikipedia.org/wiki/index. html?curid=14080546.

63. Lytle and Holdcamper, *Merchant Steam Vessels of the United States,* 68.

64. "Passengers Sailed," *New York Times,* December 12, 1866. *Henry Chauncey* was built by William H. Webb for the Pacific Mail Steamship Company and completed in 1865. She was 319 feet long, with a 43-foot beam, a 28-foot depth of hold, and was registered at 2,656 tons. See Ridgely-Nevitt, *American Steamships on the Atlantic,* 364.

65. Julius Kroehl, Last Will and Testament, December 7, 1866, Surrogate's Court, New York County, New York, Index of Wills Probated in Kings County from January 1, 1850, to December 31, 1890, liber 35, p. 39.

CHAPTER 6

1. Scarlett, *South America and the Pacific,* 2:285.

2. Ibid., 2:289.

3. Duncan, "*Chile* and *Peru,*" 272.

4. Fletcher Webster, Acting Secretary of State of the United States, to William M. Blackford, US Chargé d'Affaires at Bogotá, Washington, D.C., May 20, 1842. Document 1814 in Manning, *Diplomatic Correspondence of the United States,* 5:354.

5. James Buchanan, Secretary of State of the United States, to Benjamin A. Bidlack, US Chargé d'Affaires at Bogotá, Washington, D.C., June 23, 1845. Document 1818 in Manning, *Diplomatic Correspondence of the United States,* 5:357.

6. Letter, John M. Clayton, Secretary of State of the United States, to Thomas M. Foote, United States Chargé d'Affaires at Bogotá, Washington, D.C., July 19, 1849. Document 1822 in Manning, *Diplomatic Correspondence of the United States,* 5:363.

7. Crackbon, entry for April 14, 1849, "Narrative of a Voyage from New York to California Via . . . Panama," California State Library.

8. Borthwick, *Three Years in California,* 17–18.

9. Letter, Albert Wells to "My Dear Sir," Panama, December 5, 1849, New York Historical Society.

10. Marryat, *Mountains and Molehills,* 26.

11. Meyer, *Bound for Sacramento,* 21–22.

12. Taylor, *Eldorado,* 22.

13. Ten Broeck, Diary, entry of April 17, 1853, Huntington Library.

14. Marryat, *Mountains and Molehills,* 27–28.

15. Parks, *Colombia and the United States,* 273.

16. Kemble's *Panama Route* is the classic and standard reference. McGuiness's *Path of Empire* offers an excellent synthesis and analysis of the United States' impact on Panama not only during the gold rush years of 1849–50 but well into the twentieth century.

17. Linne and Leijer, *Darien in the Past,* 68, 70.

18. Bancroft, *History of Central America,* 1:109. Also see Donkin, *Beyond Price,* 313.

19. Bancroft, *History of Central America*, 1:111–13; Donkin, *Beyond Price*, 314.

20. As cited in Richman, *Spanish Conquerors*, 73–74.

21. Bancroft, *History of Central America*, 1:375.

22. Mackenzie, "History of the Pearl Oyster Fishery in the Archipielago de las Perlas," 58–65.

23. Mosk, "Capitalistic Development in the Lower California Pearl Fisheries," 461–68.

24. Belcher, *Narrative of a Voyage Round the World*, 222–23.

25. Meyer, *Bound for Sacramento*, 41.

26. *San Francisco Daily Alta California*, July 19, 1852.

27. Ibid.

28. *Scientific American*, August 2, 1862.

29. "Mother of Pearl and Its Uses," *The Technologist*, 222.

30. An article about Kroehl in the *Panama Star and Herald*, on September 12, 1867, noted that the "pearl diving machine now lying in our harbor was brought by him to Panama 12 months ago," i.e., September 1866. That may have been an error, as it first mentioned the submarine as a new arrival in December—or it took Kroehl two months to ship *Explorer* across the isthmus. An article in the *Georgia Weekly Telegraph* of April 25, 1871, reminisced about how the "sub-marine monster of boiler iron" had been "forwarded to its destination across the Isthmus, in sections, then reconstructed."

31. *Panama Star and Herald*, December 8, 1866.

32. *Daily Cleveland Herald*, January 9, 1867. Spurred by this report, journalist and author J. Ross Browne, an old friend of Charles D. Poston's, wrote in his encyclopedic *Resources of the Pacific Slope* (p. 63) that the pearl fisheries would benefit from submarine operations, and he noted that a "New York company is now in operation in the pearl islands of the bay of Panama, with a diving apparatus, specially adapted to this business, which is stated, in January 1867, to be in successful working."

33. *New York Daily Tribune*, January 21, 1867.

34. *New York Times*, March 14, 1867.

35. *Brooklyn Daily Eagle*, March 4 and March 11, 1867.

36. *Panama Star and Herald*, April 4, 1867.

37. *Panama Star and Herald*, May 30, 1867.

38. This was the small steamer *Panama*. On February 15, 1865, the *New York Times* had reported that "the Panama Railroad Company launched their beautiful side-wheel steamer *Panama*, on the 28th ult. The *Panama* was shipped out from New York in pieces, and put up anew in Panama. She is to be used to carry passengers backward and forward between the shore and the ships."

39. *Panama Star and Herald*, June 22, 1867.

40. *Panama Star and Herald*, June 25, 1867.

41. *New York Times*, July 5, 1867.

42. Thomas Kilby Smith to his daughter, August 21, 1867, in W. G. Smith, *Life and Letters of Thomas Kilby Smith*, 429.

43. "Apparatus for Submarine Exploration," Provisional Patent No. 2466, August 29, 1867, was granted on the basis of a "communication from abroad by George Wrightson,

of New York City." Woodcroft, *Alphabetical Index of Patentees and Applicants for Patents of Invention,* 51. The patent was never fully completed and hence was not granted. It may have been done as a result of the work of a rival group, headed by William R. Taylor, John Adam Weisse, and William Mont Storm, who had built in New York a "Submarine Explorer" based on the Ryerson patent, and receiving a patent of their own on May 1, 1866. Why the patent for Kroehl's Explorer was never completed is so far a mystery. It may be that the final critical drawings needed for the patent were in Kroehl's hands or were not yet finished when he died in Panama.

44. *Panama Star and Herald,* September 12, 1867.

45. Thomas Kilby Smith to the Hon. William M. Evarts, Secretary of State, United States Consulate, Panama, September 12, 1867, General Records of the Department of State, "Despatches, 1789–1906," Records Group 59, National Archives, College Park, Md.

46. Ibid.

47. *San Francisco Daily Alta California,* February 1, 1868.

48. *Panama Star and Herald,* February 29, 1868.

49. *Philadelphia Inquirer,* August 24, 1868.

50. *Georgia Weekly Telegraph,* April 25, 1871.

51. *San Francisco Daily Alta California,* August 29, 1869.

52. *Boston Journal,* August 28, 1869.

53. Ibid.

54. *Georgia Weekly Telegraph,* April 25, 1871.

55. *The New York State Business Directory,* 1870, 801.

56. The company was dissolved by process on April 2, 1924. E-mail communication from the Division of Corporations, State of New York, January 10, 2005.

57. Lytle and Holdcamper, *Merchant Steam Vessels,* 68.

58. *Chicago Inter Ocean,* September 2, 1878.

CHAPTER 7

1. "Inventory of the Personal Effects of Julius H. Kroehl taken by U. Rostrop and John C. Conant," September 10, 1867. The inventory was attached to the dispatch of the US consul reporting Kroehl's death, Records of the Department of State, "Despatches," Record Group 59, National Archives. In 1870 the office of the Fifth Auditor of the US Treasury reported it had paid the estate of Julius Kroehl $65.00 in cash the consulate had collected from Kroehl's room at the time of his death. Secretary of the Treasury, *Annual Report . . . 1870,* 145.

2. Thomas Kilby Smith to Secretary of State, Panama City, September 21, 1867, Records of the Department of State, "Despatches," Record Group 59, National Archives.

3. *New Yorker Staats Zeitung,* September 26, 1867.

4. The inventory is included in this book as Appendix 3.

5. Julius Kroehl, Last Will and Testament, December 7, 1866, Surrogate's Court, New York County, New York.

6. The Lueber household is enumerated in the 1880 Federal Census on p. 4, Enumeration District No. 45, Washington, D.C., at 817 Eighteenth Street N.W.—mother Helen M.

Lueber, age 73, Sophia Kroehl, age 48, Helen M. Rolle, then a widow, age 41, brother Francis, age 43, and sister Mary, age 25. US Census Bureau, Records, National Archives.

7. Letter of David Dixon Porter, US Naval Academy, Annapolis, Md., December 28, 1867, in Sophia R. Kroehl, "Widow's Naval Pension Application File," National Archives.

8. Letter of David Dixon Porter, US Naval Academy, Annapolis, Md., February 8, 1868, in Sophia R. Kroehl, "Widow's Naval Pension Application File."

9. Affidavit of Alexander Clinton, M.D., New York, April 10, 1868, in Sophia R. Kroehl, "Widow's Naval Pension Application File."

10. Affidavit of Henry Kroehl, Asbury Park, New Jersey, September 22, 1879, in Sophia R. Kroehl, "Widow's Naval Pension Application File."

11. "Widow's Brief" [Application] No. 2142, in Sophia R. Kroehl, "Widow's Naval Pension Application File."

12. Affidavit of Sophia R. Kroehl, Washington, D.C. December 9, 1889, in "Widow's Naval Pension Application File."

13. Letter of Alexander Strausz, Palatka, Florida, March 28, 1890, in Sophia R. Kroehl, "Widow's Naval Pension Application File."

14. Declaration for Widow's Pension, July 10, 1890, Certificate 5096, in Sophia R. Kroehl, "Widow's Naval Pension Application File."

15. *New York Times,* December 6, 1890.

16. Ibid.

17. The *New York Times* for September 30, 1883, lists the death of Mrs. P. Kroehl Heanes, mother of Henry Kroehl. Mrs. Heanes apparently went by the name Philippine in life. She and her husband, John, are buried in Henry's family plot at Green-Wood Cemetery in Brooklyn.

18. Letter, Jewell & Nicholson to the Secretary of the Interior, Washington, D.C., December 29, 1892, in Sophia R. Kroehl, "Widow's Naval Pension Application File."

19. Letter, Sophia Kroehl to the Hon. Assistant Secretary [of the Interior], Washington, D.C., January 3, 1893, in Sophia R. Kroehl, "Widow's Naval Pension Application File."

20. Appeal, Docket No. 16,626, Sophia Kroehl, Washington, D.C., January 18, 1893, in "Widow's Naval Pension Application File."

21. Ibid.

22. Supplemental Application form, September 20, 1916, in Sophia R. Kroehl, "Widow's Naval Pension Application File."

23. Letter, Mary Lueber to the Commissioners of Pensions, Washington, D.C., October 1, 1916, in Sophia R. Kroehl, "Widow's Naval Pension Application File."

24. Letter, Mary Lueber to US Pension Agency, Washington, D.C., December 10, 1916, in Sophia R. Kroehl, "Widow's Naval Pension Application File."

25. Letter, Commissioner to the Hon. Tracy L. Jeffords, Washington, D.C., December 28, 1916, in Sophia R. Kroehl, "Widow's Naval Pension Application File."

26. These observations come from conversations with Bruce Kroehl.

27. I am indebted to Tomas Mendizabal of the Instituto Nacional de Cultura, who tracked down the reference and took us to the cemetery.

28. A detailed walking reconnaissance of the entire cemetery by the author and colleagues in 2004 resulted in these observations.

29. During the visit to the cemetery, and despite the presence of an armed police guard (recommended by the government), we were approached by several locals who shared these stories but who did not wish to leave their names. One man insisted that a US microwave weapon had been tested during the battle and that his mother, caught in the fighting, was "melted." For official accounts see Cole, *Operation Just Cause: Panama,* and Yates, "Operation JUST CAUSE in Panama City." For a Panamanian perspective, see Figueroa et al., *El Chorillo: Situación y Alternativas.*

30. Thanks to John McKee, who researched this and many other facts about Julius and Sophia. A recent account of Holy Rood Cemetery and its condition is found at http://en.wikipedia.org/wiki/Holy_Rood_Cemetery.

31. I stood in front of the vandalized and empty Lueber family crypt on a gray, rainy day in December 2010. Barred by a steel gate, it is open to the elements, set against the hillside in the graveyard overlooking the busy traffic of Wisconsin Avenue.

32. Those copies of the Pacific Pearl Company pamphlet are found at the Autry National Center, Los Angeles; at the Henry E. Huntington Library and Archives, San Marino, Calif.; the US Naval Historical Center Library at the Washington Navy Yard; and the New York Historical Society. A fifth copy was advertised and sold on the Internet in 2002 to an undisclosed, presumably private collector.

33. Holland, "The Submarine Boat and Its Future," 894.

34. Storm, a talented inventor from New York, later a resident of Troy, patented devices for compressing air, "hydro-atmospheric power," steam engines, weapons, and on May 1, 1866, was issued Patent 54,448 for a "Submarine Explorer," which he noted was "taken from and what is known and patented as 'Ryerson's Submarine Explorer.'" Unlike Kroehl's craft, Storm's patent was for an improved diving bell. He used it in the summer of 1868 in the East River. His backers were William R. Taylor and J. A. Weisse. Dr. Weisse (1810–88) was a medical doctor and an emigrant from Alsace, who settled in New York and became both a well-known physician and a prominent philologist. He was also a member of the Masonic order. There was most likely, both through the Masonic order and the Ryerson patent, a link back to Julius Kroehl, then testing his own version of a "Sub Marine Explorer." Dr. Weisse apparently was not pleased with the Storm version of the Ryerson patent, patenting his own "Improved Diving Bell" (Patent 89,453) on April 27, 1869, basing it on the earlier Foreman/Sears bell. Taylor went his own way with the Storm bell, taking it to California to shovel up sand from the ocean floor off Gold Bluff, Calif., where the Klamath River was said to have deposited vast quantities of gold. A minor gold rush in the spring of 1851 brought miners and invited speculation, but it was soon proved that there was no gold in the sand, just "mere fancies." See Hittell, *History of California,* 3:151–52. Nonetheless, an article in the *San Francisco Daily Evening Bulletin* of July 29, 1872, reported that Taylor was in San Francisco, had chartered the schooner *Witch Queen,* and was going to take the 10½-foot-high, 9-foot-diameter Explorer to work the sands off Gold Bluff. "It is also the intention of this Company to work the bell submarines in the pearl fisheries on the coast of Mexico and in the Gulf of Dulce, on the

northern coast of Costa Rica." That Taylor and company would ship out the second and different "Submarine Explorer" at expense to chase the false dream of gold at Gold Bluff, a resource that 21 years earlier had been proven not to exist, and then chase after more pearls following the failure of the Pacific Pearl Company reinforces my point about the loose, often foolhardy nature of capitalist speculative ventures of the period.

35. "Sub-Marine Exploration: The Wreck of the Frigate *Hussar*," 105.

36. As cited in Hitchcock, "*Intelligent Whale*," 101–2.

37. The *Army and Navy Journal,* September 21, 1872. Also see the *New York Daily Tribune,* September 24, 1872.

38. As cited by Hitchcock, "*Intelligent Whale*," 104.

39. Ibid., 105.

40. Barber, Lecture on Submarine Boats, 17.

41. *New York Times,* October 9, 1897.

42. See, for example, Compton-Hall, *Submarine Pioneers,* 41.

43. Baird, "Submarine Torpedo Boats," 852. Baird and fellow engineering officer Alfred Colin had inspected captured Confederate submarines during the war. I am indebted to John McKee for pointing out that "Baird was also a good friend of naval engineer and Civil War veteran Rear Admiral Harrie Webster. Webster was married to Sophia's cousin Mary Hein, and had signed a notarized statement attesting to Sophia's widowhood during her pension application. Most likely, Baird got most of his information from Webster." In 1896 Baird, a lifelong member of the Masonic order, was grand master of the Washington, D.C., lodge. As a Mason, Baird had to have known Julius Kroehl. Alfred Colin was also a member of the Masonic order. Among his many associations was a tenure as special secretary to John Ericsson, the inventor of the ironclad USS *Monitor.*

44. Letter, Dudley W. Knox to Howard Kroehl, May 18, 1937, Z files, US Naval Historical Center, Washington Navy Yard.

45. E-mail from John McKee, December 28, 2007.

46. I am indebted to John McKee for drawing this latter point to my attention.

47. Julius Hermann Kroehl, Application for Passport, National Archives.

48. We came to this realization early on in assessing the submarine and the tower, and John McKee also noted it, commenting on it in his e-mail of December 28, 2007, in which he called Kroehl "an adaptive-innovator type—he could look at someone's efforts, then copy and improve on them—an ideal person for reverse-engineering efforts." This strength of Kroehl's was also a potential weakness in that his skill would not have made him popular—and his likeliest detractors would be Benjamin Maillefert, James Bogardus, and Van Buren Ryerson, despite Ryerson's licensing of the bell patent to the Pacific Pearl Company. A glimpse at a surviving letter from Ryerson in 1863 suggests he had a strained relationship with Kroehl, but unfortunately, the letter, as well as other Ryerson papers, is no longer available, at least at this time. I was contacted and offered the documents, including Ryerson's original patent, for sale. I sent a certified appraiser, registered with the National Archives of the United States and Canada, to assess the documents and offer a fair price so that the documents would be available for research and then be donated to the New York Historical Society. The price asked was above the appraised value, but

the sticking point was the realization that not every document had been shown to the appraiser, which left him (and me) very uncomfortable. Our offer was rejected, and subsequently the documents were offered for sale at the same price on eBay. The auction sale was not completed, although there was a rumor that a private dealer had purchased them outside of the eBay system. They have not since resurfaced. One of the greatest obstacles to research and preservation is the prevalent notion that the past is a commodity worth a great deal of money. It has, in my experience, led to many cases such as this—and as a result of someone's decision to try to maximize profit, and probably at no greater a price than we offered, the documents may be lost to history—and certainly were not available for this assessment.

49. Gayle and Gayle, *Cast-Iron Architecture in America,* 187.

50. Kahn, "Bogardus, Fire, and the Iron Tower," 197, 200–202. When researchers finally identified Julius Kroehl as the builder of the Mount Morris Park tower, they failed to fully credit him accurately; in the City Landmarks Registry and in all subsequent books and guides, the tower's builder is listed as "Julius B. Kroehl" instead of the proper "Julius H. Kroehl."

51. Holland, "The Submarine Boat and Its Future," 894.

52. There were 7,231 hits for "Julius H. Kroehl" on Google as of December 11, 2010.

53. Govier, *Three Views of Crystal Water,* 178–79.

54. Ibid., 182.

55. Miéville, *Kraken,* 288.

CHAPTER 8

1. See Church, "Republic of Panamá," 683. The tidal range in spring is from 10 feet below mean sea level to 10 feet above; neap tide ranges are within 7.9 feet. US Senate, *Message of the President of the United States . . . Report of Board of Consulting Engineers on Panama Canal,* 52.

2. These assumptions are based on the fact that the rocky cove provided no easy place for anchoring safely, and earlier accounts of *Explorer*'s layup after Kroehl's death indicated the submarine was beached, which makes sense. The position of the craft, and the prevailing patterns of the waves as they enter the cove, as well as the position of the craft, all suggest a position half up on the beach that in time saw *Explorer* shift and tilt in the sand, coming to rest on a substrata of cobble, driftwood, and bedrock in its current (as observed in 2001–2008) position.

3. Lidar survey of the hull in 2004 disclosed warping in the hull where the conning tower had shifted slightly due to a strong force pulling it seaward.

4. This is all based on archaeological examination of the hull between 2004 and 2008.

5. Parker, "Maritime Landscapes," 39.

6. Rainbird, *Archaeology of Islands,* 55–56.

7. Ibid., 67.

8. DeVine, "Mapping the CSS *Hunley.*" Also see Murphy, *H.L. Hunley Site Assessment.*

9. Delgado, "Archaeological Reconnaissance of the 1865 American-Built *Sub Marine Explorer.*"

10. E-mail message from John Blashford-Snell, March 4, 2005: "We are travelling to Panama in April with a 12 strong team. We plan on travelling to Isla San Telmo and would like to see if there is anything we could do raise funds to support your project to transfer the submersible to the Warren Lasch Conservation Center." After an exchange of e-mails and a telephone conversation, Colonel Snell reported back on May 3, 2005 in an e-mail: "We surveyed the 'Explorer' as promised. Roger Cooper, a British technologist and our chief diver[,] did the job. He has made some fairly detailed drawing for you and videoed the sub inside and out. As you know she has some fairly large holes in her hull. I know the Canadian Ambassador in Panama[,] David de Adam[,] and briefed him on your proposal. Alas he will return to Ottawa on 15 June but I'm sure he would put you in touch with his successor."

11. Roger D. Cooper sent me a manuscript report entitled "Scientific Exploration Society, Panama Expedition 2005, Expedition Survey Conducted between 19/20 April 2005, Submarine 'Explorer' built ca. 1864" in May 2005. The report is in my possession.

12. SES Press Release, "Gulf of San Miguel, Panama, 5–25 April 2005." The comment in the press release was "British technologist Roger Cooper of Market Harborough, who carried out the survey with three other divers, said 'Entering the submarine with its strange Victorian engineering reminded me of the Nautilus in the film *20,000 Leagues Under the Sea*. I would not have been surprised to see Captain Nemo at the controls in the Conning Tower.'"

13. "American Civil War Submarine Found," *The Times* (London), June 6, 2005.

14. In an initial e-mail on June 6, 2005, Colonel Snell wrote, "Some local papers in Britain have heard of our visit to 'The Explorer.' We have tried to make them understand that the credit for its 'discovery' belongs to you not to us. But journalists are not always accurate! I'm often asked what type of engine the Explorer had and how the lockout chamber worked. What sort of briefing apparatus did the crew have for use on the sea-bed? Can you enlighten me? Are you still planning to visit the sub later this year?" I responded with "Not a problem. I have seen the Times article. I know how reporters can mix things up. Thank you for your kind e-mail explaining the situation. I was wondering. P.S. Work started on the sub in 1864 but it was not completed until 1865, so the Times was wrong in saying 1864." On June 8 Colonel Snell answered, "Some of the British papers do mention your name and the museum. I will send copies. It is surprising that over a month after our return the press suddenly get interested. I think the new feature film 'Sahara,' about the search for a Civil War sub in the desert may have aroused interest. A Canadian radio station has contacted us and we suggested they speak to you. I hope all this interest may help you campaign to save the 'Explorer.'" On June 9 a separate e-mail arrived with this message: "For your information I have attached a copy of the original press release that we forwarded to the press agency. The Times journalist obviously played on the words. I am sorry for any trouble this might have caused you. We have done our best to correct any journalist who have made further enquiries circulating the attached."

15. Johnson, Wilson, Carr, Murphy, and Delgado, "Corrosion of Civil War Era *Sub Marine Explorer*."

16. McCarthy, "Report on the Wreck of the *Sub Marine Explorer*," 24.

CHAPTER 9

1. Baird, "Submarine Torpedo Boats," 852.

2. Holland, "The Submarine Boat and Its Future," on p. 902, notes that "thirty-three deaths were charged to her. As a matter of fact, she never lost a single life, though, Heaven knows, she was handled carelessly enough." The myth persists. Richard Compton-Hall, in *Submarine Pioneers,* 78, cites accounts of 39 "but more likely thirteen" men who drowned during tests of the craft.

3. See Hitchcock, "*Intelligent Whale:* A Historical and Archaeological Analysis of an American Civil War Submersible."

4. Compton-Hall, *Submarine* Pioneers, 81–106, passim.

5. See Westerdahl, "Maritime Cultural Landscape." Westerdahl defined his concept of the maritime cultural landscape as "human utilisation (economy) of maritime space, by boat, settlement, fishing, hunting, shipping and its attendant sub-cultures," 5. There have been some excellent studies following this line of research, for example, Ash, *Maritime Cultural Landscape of Port Willunga.*

6. Galtsoff, *Pearl-Oyster Resources of Panama,* 14, and Mackenzie, "History of the Pearl Oyster Fishery in the Archipielago de las Perlas," 58.

7. Nelson, *Five Years at Panama,* 74. Born in Montreal in 1846, Dr. Wolfred Nelson married an American, relocated to New York, but also traveled extensively in Mexico and Central America studying tropical diseases. He died in New York in 1913. *New York Times,* January 16, 1913.

8. "It is said, that Messrs. Rundell and Bridge, some time ago, paid down a sum of money for the right to monopolize the trade, and they sent out from England a diving-bell. . . . but the attempt was a vain one, in consequence of the rocky nature of the bottom of the bay, together with the very heavy ground-swell." Wortley, *Travels in the United States,* 333. Also see Mosk, "Capitalistic Development in the Lower California Pearl Fisheries," 462–63.

9. Robinson, *Panama: A Personal Record of Forty-six Years,* 198.

10. This view of the submarine's "deadly" nature may possibly come from an oral tradition that imperfectly recalls the craft's potentially deadly technology, as explained later in this chapter, or it may be a memory of the sub's impact in 1869 by locals who have condensed history and bypassed the century of the fishery that then followed *Explorer's* abandonment, or both. The pearl fishery in time recovered, and by 1900 was described as again active, with hired divers licensed by Panama City pearl merchants making free ascent dives twice a day and collecting between 40 or 50 oysters, and with the locals also diving "on their own hook." The fishery reportedly yielded $500,000 in pearls and $250,000 in shells each year. Curtis, *Between the Andes and the Ocean,* 36–37. However, overfishing led to a rapid decline after 1925, and as of 1998, the fishery was to all intents dead, in part also due to the decline in popularity and hence price for natural pearls. However, that year some 145 fishermen in the archipelago were also harvesting oysters one to three days a week. Mackenzie, "History of the Pearl Oyster Fishery in the Archipielago de las Perlas," 61–64.

11. Adas, *Dominance by Design,* 6.

12. McGuiness, *Path of Empire,* 7.

13. McGuiness notes the Panama Railroad was part of an effort by capitalists from the northeastern United States to "consolidate control over an economy that only a few years earlier had seemed to offer the possibility of fortunes for anyone with desire and a strong back" (ibid., 10). The same process happened in California's mines with a shift to quartz and hydraulic mining and the rise of companies and corporations that controlled California's gold region (ibid., 81–82). "In both Panama and the northern mines, companies financed by capital from the northeastern United States and the introduction of steam-powered technology played leading roles in the consolidation and conquest of once-booming economies" (ibid. 186).

14. Soulé, Gihon, and Nisbet, *Annals of San Francisco,* 53–54.

15. A focused history of slaves employed in the pearl fishery as well as in other diving pursuits, replacing native Indians, is Kevin Dawson's excellent essay "Enslaved Swimmers and Divers in the Atlantic World."

16. McGuiness summarizes attitudes, drawing on contemporary comments as well, in *Path of Empire,* 42–46.

17. As cited in Caughey, *Seeing the Elephant,* 40.

18. Letter, Sample Flinn to William Flinn, Panama, May 11, 1849.

19. Tyson, *Diary of a Physician,* 18, 22.

20. Ryan, *Personal Adventures,* 380.

21. Tomes, *Panama in 1855,* 226–28, passim.

22. Kessner, *Capital City,* xii–xiii.

23. Ibid., xiii.

24. Ibid., 42.

25. Ibid., 37.

26. Kessner, *Capital City,* 38, and Fite, *Social and Industrial Conditions,* 85.

27. Kessner, *Capital City,* 40.

28. Ibid., 49.

29. Ibid., 125.

30. Ibid., 124.

31. *Chicago Inter Ocean,* September 2, 1878.

32. *New York Times,* June 29, 1902. The *Times* reported that Poston died in Tucson; North in *Samuel Peter Heintzelman* states that Poston died in the Phoenix hotel.

33. North, *Samuel Peter Heintzelman,* 176.

34. The back of the share has a form to fill in, noting that for value received, Poston would "sell, assign and transfer" the stock. It was never executed. Pacific Pearl Company Stock Certificate, DB 52, F 1a, Item 11, Poston Papers, Sharlot Hall Museum.

35. Entry for Mark Brumagim, March 25, 1869, vol. 417, p. 198, Dun & Company Records, New York City.

36. Entry for Mark Brumagim, September 14, 1869, vol. 417, p. 198, Dun & Company Records, New York City Baker Library Historical Collections, Harvard Business School.

37. *New York Herald,* January 31, 1877.

38. Entry for Mark Brumagim, December 29, 1881, vol. 417, p. 200, Dun & Company Records, New York City.

39. Ibid., and entry for April 3, 1882.

40. "Verdenal's Chat—Old Californians in New York," *San Francisco Chronicle,* January 6, 1889.

41. Paulsen, "Legal Battle for the Candelaria Mine," 265. Brumagim died in New York City on December 23, 1914. *New York Times,* December 24, 1914.

42. *New York Times,* January 16, 1869.

43. The National Arms Company of Brooklyn manufactured weapons in Brooklyn beginning in 1864 and 1870, when it was acquired by Colt. Given William M. B. Hartley's Colt connection, one wonders if Tiffany was "parachuted" into National Arms in 1869 to facilitate the sale. National Arms was best known for its .32-caliber "Teat Fire" cartridge, which were developed specifically to circumvent the patented rimfire cartridges patented by Horace Smith and Daniel Wesson. By 1872, two years after the sale to Colt, the firm was defunct.

44. Entry for Wm. H. Tiffany, July 6, 1869, vol. 380, p. 200a/23, Dun & Company Records, New York City.

45. Entry for Wm. H. Tiffany, August 6, 1869, vol. 380, p. 200a/23, Dun & Company Records, New York City. Notes of testimony from a California court case in 1852 include a sworn statement from one B. F. Williams, former owner of the Parker House, a gambling establishment, in which he noted he had sold his property and assigned his lease to the Parker House as well as "everything I had for 15 or 17000 Thousand dollars to Wm. H. Tiffany." As part of the deal, Tiffany was to pay $2,000 of it directly to a creditor, William Chipman, but Tiffany never paid it to Chipman nor did Williams receive it. He also discussed a mortgage "on some billiard tables executed by Tiffany—Tiffany never paid me the sum for which the mortgage was given—the fire [of May 4, 1851] burned them. The amount secured was $2,000." William Chipman Papers, MS 373, Folder 1, California Historical Society.

46. Hartley, *Money and Usury,* 5. I am indebted again to John McKee for finding this book and for his review and comments on the subject.

47. See the Hartley obituary, *Central Law Journal,* February 12, 1875, 116.

48. Chadwick appears in the 1880 US Census with his wife, Julia, and daughter, Julia, as a "tile merchant." He died before 1900. US Census Bureau, Tenth Census of the United States, 1880, Microfilm Publication T9, Roll 891, Family History Film 1254891, p. 504C, Enumeration District 505, Image 0332, Records of the Bureau of the Census, Record Group 29, National Archives. Wrightson appeared in the 1880 US Census as a lawyer in Chicago. He died in Mexico City on April 7, 1895. I am indebted to John McKee, who notes that Wrightson married a distant cousin to Hartley's wife after 1870 and relocated to Chicago. He and his wife had two sons. Active in civic issues, Wrightson eventually became a judge. He was touted as a successor to John C. Frémont as governor of the Arizona Territory, but was not selected.

49. *New York Times,* August 29, 1869.

50. Straus and Aksenov, *Diving Science,* 8.

51. Ibid., 67.

52. Nelson, *Five Years at Panama,* 75–76.

53. Straus and Aksenov, *Diving Science,* 302–5.

54. Phillips, *The Bends,* 2.

55. Ibid., 48–57.

56. Ibid., 57, 49.

57. Ibid., 69.

58. Ibid., 73.

59. Ibid., 85–91, 93–94.

60. Ibid., 102–5, 110.

61. Ibid., 121–31, 2.

APPENDIX 1

1. Wood report and drawing, National Archives; "Apparatus for Submarine Exploration," Provisional Patent No. 2466, August 29, 1867, Woodcroft, *Alphabetical Index of Patentees.*

2. Boiler iron plate was rolled from iron bars. "Uniform thickness and good quality of iron are the main requisites," Osborn, *Metallurgy of Iron and Steel,* 795.

3. "Apparatus for Submarine Exploration," 1–2.

4. Hitchcock, "*Intelligent Whale,*" 137–38.

5. Ibid., 167.

6. Ibid., 170.

7. For example, see Peters, *Building the Nineteenth Century,* 38, in which he notes how early iron structures "imitated heavy timber connections."

8. "Apparatus for Submarine Exploration," 15.

9. Ibid.

10. *Pacific Pearl Company,* 1865.

11. US patent number 135,404, issued on February 4, 1873, incorporated the earlier work on the Cathcart propeller.

12. *Buffalo (New York) Commercial Advertiser,* August 16, 1871.

13. *New York World,* July 22, 1871.

14. Hitchcock, "*Intelligent Whale,*" 161.

15. "Apparatus for Submarine Exploration," 5.

16. Ibid., 4.

17. Ibid., 6.

18. Ibid., 2.

19. Maxwell, *Theory of Heat,* 198–99.

20. Davis, Gallman, and Gleiter, *In Pursuit of Leviathan,* 29, 56, and 344.

21. Wagner, *Handbook of Chemical Technology,* 634.

22. Wood report, 8–9.

23. "Apparatus for Submarine Exploration," 2.

APPENDIX 3

1. "N.G." stands for New Granada. At the time of Kroehl's death, Panama was part of "New Granada," now Colombia.

2. Patent dryer was used in paint. Dick's *Encyclopedia of Practical Receipts and Processes* (1872), 2739, describes how it was made: "Mix the following ingredients to a paste with linseed oil: 15 pounds dry sulphate of zinc, 4 pounds sugar of lead, and 7 pounds litharge. The mixture should be passed 3 or 4 times through a paint mill. When a tin of this is in use, the surface should be always smoothed down level, and kept covered with a thin layer of linseed oil."

3. This was most likely the style of brimless, round, black silk traditional Chinese hat manufactured today as a novelty item and popular in the nineteenth century among non-Chinese travelers.

4. Silver nitrate ($AgNO_3$). Kroehl used this expensive chemical to develop his photographs. An 1864 treatise on photography describes it: "NOTHING can be easier to prepare than the bath of nitrate of silver, and yet there is no preparation in the art of photography which produces so many difficulties and troubles to surmount as the sensitizing bath for the iodized or bromo-iodized collodion plates. In consequence of this it becomes a difficult task to prescribe rules by which such a bath can be preserved sensitive under the troubles with which it is so frequently beset. The origin of these troubles may be traced to the materials introduced by the immersion of the collodion plates; but these deteriorating materials are of such a heterogeneous nature, arising from the decomposition of the pyroxyline, of alcohol, of ether, of the iodides, the bromides, their bases, and of the elements combining with them, that it is as yet an unsolved problem, that of determining precisely the cause of any given abnormal action in the nitrate bath. It is true, as regards the introduction of injurious substances into the bath, all effects resulting from there can be avoided by using the solution of nitrate of silver only once. If this salt were not so expensive, this mode of avoiding trouble would be by far the wisest and the safest. In such a case the photographer would flow his plate with the silver solution in the same manner as with the developing or fixing solution, using just sufficient to cover the film and to sensitize it. All the residual part might be collected, decomposed, and fresh nitrate prepared. But because the silver salt is a dear material, we aim to economize by using the solution over and over again. For this purpose, glass, porcelain or photographic-ware baths are constructed for containing the fluid. They are made so as to accommodate the largest plate with the least quantity of the solution, a great mistake superinduced by false economy. In this country vertical baths seem to be the only ones employed; whereas in France and Germany, for economical and other special reasons already alluded to, horizontal dishes contain the solution, and the plates lie, as it were, collodion side downward in a thin layer of the same. Some of these baths are especially adapted for the tourist, admitting the fluid to be closed hermetically by means of India-rubber caps, screws and clamps. Nitrate of silver will permeate through the parietes of porcelain baths; the photographic-ware bath and the glass are not subject to this inconvenience." Towler, *Silver Sunbeam,* xv.

5. This is the receptacle Kroehl bathed his plates in using the silver nitrate.

6. Kroehl suffered from some form of hernia which had not been treated surgically, and wore these undergarment supports. An excellent contemporary description of the various types can be found in Warren, *Hernia,* 243–51.

7. Binoculars.

Bibliography

Abbot, Henry J. *The Beginnings of Submarine Warfare Under Captain Lieutenant David Bushnell.* Willet's Point, New York: Privately printed, 1881.

Abbott, Jacob. "The Novelty Iron Works." *Harper's New Monthly Magazine* 2, no. 12 (May 1851): 721–34.

Adas, Michael. *Dominance by Design: Technological Imperatives and America's Civilizing Mission.* Cambridge: Belknap Press of Harvard University Press, 2006.

Albion, Robert Greenhalgh. *Forests and Sea Power: The Timber Problem in the Royal Navy, 1652–1862.* Cambridge: Harvard University Press, 1926.

American Institute of the City of New York. *Annual Report of the American Institute of the City of New York.* Albany: C. Van Benthuysen, 1847.

Ash, Aidan. *The Maritime Cultural Landscape of Port Willunga, South Australia.* Flinders University Maritime Archaeology Monograph Series, Number 4. Adelaide: Flinders University, Department of Archaeology, 2007.

Bacharach, Arthur J. "The History of the Diving Bell." *Historical Diving Times,* no. 12 (Spring 1998): 18.

Bacon, George B. "One Night's Work, April 20, 1862: Breaking the Chain for Farragut's Fleet at the Forts Below New Orleans." *Magazine of American History* 16 (1886): 305–7.

Baird, G. W. "Submarine Torpedo Boats." *Journal of the American Society of Naval Engineers* 14, no. 2 (1902): 845–55.

Bancroft, Hubert Howe. *History of Central America.* Vol. 1. San Francisco: History Company, 1886.

Barber, Lt. F. M. "Lecture on Submarine Boats and Their Application to Torpedo Operations." Newport, R.I.: US Naval Torpedo Station, 1875.

Bauer, K. Jack. *Surfboats and Horse Marines: US Naval Operations in the Mexican War.* Annapolis, Md.: Naval Institute Press, 1969.

Belcher, Captain Sir Edward. *Narrative of a Voyage Round the World, Performed in Her Majesty's Ship Sulphur, during the Years 1836—1842, Including Details of the Naval Operations in China, from Dec. 1840, to Nov. 1841.* London: Henry Colburn, Publisher, 1843.

Bell, Andrew McIlwaine. *Mosquito Soldiers: Malaria, Yellow Fever, and the Course of the*

American Civil War. Baton Rouge: Louisiana State University Press, 2010.

Bethge, Hans-Georg. *Der Brandtaucher: Ein Tauchboot—von der Idee zur Wirklichkeit.* Berlin: Beilefeld, Delius, Klasing & Co., 1968

"The Blasting of Rocks Under Water without Drilling." *Hunt's Merchants' Magazine and Commercial Review* 27, no. 3 (September 1852): 320–29.

Blunt, Edmund M., and George W. Blunt, *The American Coast Pilot; Containing Directions for the Principal Harbors, Capes and Headlands on the Coasts of North and South America.* . . . 17th and 18th eds. New York: Edmund and George W. Blunt, 1854 and 1857.

Bohn, Casimir. *Bohn's Handbook of Washington.* Washington: Casimir Bohn and Taylor & Maury, 1852.

Borthwick, J. D. *Three Years in California.* Oakland: Biobooks, 1948.

Bourne, John. *A Treatise on the Steam-Engine.* London: Green, Longmans, Green, 1866.

Bourne, William. *Inunetions or Deuices Very Necessary for All Generalles and Captains, or Leaders of Men, as well as by Sea as by Land.* London: Thomas Woodcock, 1590.

A Brief Account of Submarine Machines, and Specially of Ryerson's Patent for Improvements in Submarine Explorers. Also Certificates of the Practicability and Use of the Machine. New York: Edward O. Jenkins, 1860.

Browne, J. Ross. *Resources of the Pacific Slope. Statistical and Descriptive Summary of the Mines and Minerals, Climate, Topography, Agriculture, Commerce, Manufactures, and Miscellaneous Productions, of the States and Territories West of the Rocky Mountains. With a Sketch of the Settlement and Exploration of Lower California.* New York: D. Appleton and Company, 1869.

Browning, Robert M. Jr. *From Cape Charles to Cape Fear: The North Atlantic Blockading Squadron During the Civil War.* Tuscaloosa: University of Alabama Press, 1993.

Buhl, Lance C. "Mariners and Machines: Resistance to Technological Change in the American Navy, 1865–1869." *Journal of American History* 61, no. 3 (December 1974): 703–27.

Burrows, Edwin G., and Mike Wallace. *Gotham: A History of New York City to 1898.* New York: Oxford University Press, 1998.

Carstensen, Georg, and Karl Gildemeister. *New York Crystal Palace: Illustrated Description of the Building.* New York: Riker, Thorne & Company, 1854.

Caughey, John Walton, ed. *Seeing the Elephant: Letters of R. R. Taylor, Forty-niner.* Pasadena, Calif.: Ward Ritchie Press, 1951.

Chase, I. McKim. *The Art of Pattern-Making: A Comprehensive Treatise. Numerous Examples of all Kinds of Pattern Work for Green-sand, Dry-sand, and Loam Moulding. Pattern Work for Marine Engines and Screw Propellers. Also Useful Information and Rules for the Practical Use of Pattern-makers and Others.* New York: John Wiley and Sons, 1903.

Chipman, William. Papers, 1850–1852. MS 373. California Historical Society, San Francisco.

Church, Col. G.E. "The Republic of Panamá." *The Geographical Journal, Including the Proceedings of the Royal Geographical Society* 22, no. 1 (July 1903): 676–85.

City of New York, Board of Aldermen. *Documents of the Board of Aldermen of the City of New York, from Nos. 23 to 35, June to December. Inclusive.* Vol. 26, pt. 2. New York: Charles W. Baker, Printer, 1859.

————. *Annual Report of the Comptroller of the City of New York, of the Receipts and Expenditures of the Corporation, for the Year 1852.* New York: McSpedon and Baker, 1853.

————. *Annual Report of the Comptroller of the City of New York, of the Receipts and Expenditures of the Corporation, for the Year 1858.* New York: McSpedon and Baker, 1859.

————. *Proceedings of the Board of Assistant Aldermen.* Vol. 61. New York: Board of Assistant Aldermen, 1856.

————. *Proceedings of the Boards of Aldermen and Assistant Aldermen, and Approved by the Mayor.* Vol. 24. New York: Board of Aldermen, 1856.

Clark, Christopher M. *Iron Kingdom: The Rise and Downfall of Prussia, 1600–1947.* Cambridge, Mass.: Harvard University Press, 2006.

Cloud, John. "Smart Germans in the Survey and Washington." NOAA Central Library, 2006. http://www.lib.noaa.gov/noaainfo/heritage/coastandgeodeticsurvey/smart_germans.pdf.

Cole, Ronald H. *Operation Just Cause: Panama.* Washington, D.C.: Joint History Office, Office of the Chairman of the Joint Chiefs of Staff, 1995.

Compton-Hall, Richard. *The Submarine Pioneers.* Phoenix Mill, U.K.: Sutton Publishing Ltd., 1999.

Corbin, Thomas W. *The Romance of Submarine Engineering.* Philadelphia: J. B. Lippincott Company, 1913.

Corporation of the City of New York. *Annual Report of the Comptroller, Exhibiting the Revenues and Expenditures of the City Government, Including the Operations of the Several Trust and Sinking Funds, for the Year 1860. Document 16, Board of Aldermen, August 5, 1861.* New York: Edmund Jones & Company, 1861.

Crackbon, Joseph. "Narrative of a Voyage from New York to California Via Chagres, Gorgona & Panama, Journey Across the Isthmus &c., Residence in Panama" [1849]. Manuscript. California State Library, Sacramento.

Cross, Ira B. *Financing an Empire: History of Banking in California.* Vol. 1. Chicago: S. J. Clarke Publishing Company, 1927.

Curtis, William Elroy. *Between the Andes and the Ocean: An Account of an Interesting Journey Down the West Coast of South America from the Isthmus of Panama to the Straits of Magellan.* Chicago: Herbert S. Stone and Company, 1900.

Davis, Lance E., Robert E. Gallman, and Karin Gleiter. *In Pursuit of Leviathan: Technology, Institutions, Productivity, and Profits in American Whaling, 1816–1906.* Chicago: University of Chicago Press, 1997.

Davis, Sir Robert H. *Deep Diving and Submarine Operations: A Manual for Deep Sea Divers and Compressed Air Workers.* 5th ed. London: Saint Catherine Press, 1951.

Dawson, Kevin. "Enslaved Swimmers and Divers in the Atlantic World." *Journal of American History.* 92, no. 4 (March 2006): 1327–55.

Delgado, James P. "Archaeological Reconnaissance of the 1865 American-Built *Sub Marine Explorer* at Isla San Telmo, Archipielago de las Perlas, Panama." *International Journal of Nautical Archaeology* 35, no. 2 (May 2006): 230–52.

"Description of a Diving Dress, invented and used by Charles Condert, of Brooklyn, New York." *Journal of the Franklin Institute* 20, no. 3 (September 1835): 147–49.

DeVine, Doug. "Mapping the *CSS Hunley*." *Professional Surveyor Magazine*. 22, no. 3 (2002): 6–16.

Dick, William B., ed., *Encyclopedia of Practical Receipts and Processes, Containing over 6400 Receipts; Embracing Thorough Information, in Plain Language, Applicable to Almost Every Possible Industrial and Domestic Requirement.* New York: Dick & Fitzgerald, 1872.

Dickinson, H.W. *Robert Fulton, Engineer and Artist: His Life and Works.* London: John Lane, Bodley Head, 1913.

Dickman, Howard L. "Captain James A. Whipple: Marine Salvor, Engineer, and Inventor." *American Neptune* 34, no. 2 (April 1974): 89–102.

"Diving Operations at Portsmouth," *Journal of the Franklin Institute* 25, no. 4 (April 1833): 265–66.

Donkin, R. A. *Beyond Price: Pearls and Pearl-Fishing, Origins to the Age of Discoveries.* Memoirs of the American Philosophical Society Held at Philadelphia for Promoting Useful Knowledge, vol. 224. Philadelphia: American Philosophical Society, 1998.

Drexler, Franklin B., ed. *Addresses of the Living Graduates of Yale College, June 1872.* New Haven, Conn.: Press of Tuttle, Morehouse & Taylor, 1872.

Driver, Felix, and Luciana Martins. "Shipwreck and Salvage in the Tropics: The Case of HMS *Thetis,* 1830–1854." *Journal of Historical Geography* 32 (2006): 539–62.

Dun, R. G., & Company Records (1840–1895), Mss. 791, Baker Business Historical Collections, Baker Library, Harvard University.

Duncan, Roland E. "*Chile* and *Peru:* The First Successful Steamers in the Pacific," *The American Neptune* 35, no. 4 (October 1975): 248–74.

Faust, Albert Bernhardt. *The German Element in the United States: With Special Reference to Its Political, Moral, Social and Educational Influence.* Boston: Houghton Mifflin Company, 1909.

Fendall, Clarence. Letters to F. H. Gerdes. Entry 103. Records of Assistant F. H. Gerdes. Records of the US Coast and Geodetic Survey, Record Group 23, National Archives, Washington, D.C.

Field, Cyril. *The Story of the Submarine from the Earliest Ages to the Present Day.* Philadelphia: J. B. Lippincott, 1908.

Figueroa, Alfredo Navarro, et al. *El Chorillo: Situación y Alternativas.* Panama City: IDEN, 1990.

Fischer, Thomas Alfred, and Ernst Ludwig Fischer. *The Scots in Eastern and Western Prussia.* Edinburgh: Otto Schultze & Co., 1903.

Fisher, Douglas A. *The Epic of Steel.* New York: Harper & Row, 1963.

Fite, Emerson David. *Social and Industrial Conditions in the North during the Civil War.* New York: Macmillan Company, 1910.

Flinn, Semple. Letters. Manuscript 723. California Historical Society, San Francisco.

Foote, H. S., ed. *Pen Pictures from the Garden of the World or Santa Clara County, California, Illustrated.* Chicago: Lewis Publishing Company, 1888.

Francis Metallic Life-Boat Company. *Francis' Metallic Life-Boat Company.* New York: William C. Bryant & Co., 1852.

Friedman, Norman. *US Submarines through 1945: An Illustrated Design History.* Annapolis, Md.: US Naval Institute, 1995.

Galtsoff, Paul. *The Pearl-Oyster Resources of Panama.* Washington, D.C.: US Fish and Wildlife Service, 1950.

Gardner, Charles K. *A Dictionary of All Officers, Who Have Been Commissioned, or Have Been Appointed and Served, in the Army of the United States . . . and of the Navy and Marine Corps. . . .* New York: G. P. Putnam and Company, 1853.

Gayle, Margot, and Carol Gayle. *Cast-Iron Architecture in America: The Significance of James Bogardus.* New York: W. W. Norton & Company, 1998.

"Gossip with Readers and Correspondents," *The Knickerbocker* 49, no. 2 (February 1857): 208–9.

Govier, Katherine. *Three Views of Crystal Water.* London: Fourth Estate, 2005.

Grimes, Hiram. Papers. MSS C-B 103. Bancroft Library, University of California, Berkeley.

Harrie, Patricia A. Gruse. *Great Lakes' First Submarine: L. D. Phillips' "Fool Killer."* Michigan City, Ind.: Michigan City Historical Society, 1982.

Hartley, W. M. B. *Harrison's Automatic Whistle for Locomotives, W. M. B. Hartley, Agent, 40 Broadway.* New York: Wynkoop, Hallenbeck & Thomas, 1857.

———. *Money and Usury.* New York: Privately printed, 1869.

———. Obituary in "Legal News and Notes," *Central Law Journal* (St. Louis) 2, no. 7 (February 14, 1875): 116.

Hazard, Rowland G., and Caroline (Newbold) Hazard. Papers. Files on Samuel Hallett and lawsuit against Hallett. Box 19, Folders 17–22, MSS 483 sag 5. Rhode Island Historical Society, Providence.

Hearn, Chester G. *Admiral David Glasgow Farragut: The Civil War Years.* Annapolis, Md.: Naval Institute Press, 1998.

———. *Circuits in the Sea: The Men, the Ships, and the Atlantic Cable.* Westport, Conn.: Praeger Publishers, 2004.

———. *The Capture of New Orleans, 1862.* Baton Rouge: Louisiana State University Press, 1995.

Hitchcock, Peter W. "*Intelligent Whale:* A Historical and Archaeological Analysis of an American Civil War Submersible." Master's thesis, Texas A&M University, 2002.

Holland, John P. "The Submarine Boat and Its Future." *North American Review* 171, no. 529 (December 1900): 894–903.

Hollister, John C. *Historical Record of the Class of 1840, Yale College.* New Haven: Tuttle, Morehouse & Taylor Press, 1897.

Holt, Michael F. *The Rise and Fall of the American Whig Party: Jacksonian Politics and the Onset of the Civil War.* Oxford, U.K.: Oxford University Press, 1999.

Homberger, Eric. *The Historical Atlas of New York City: A Visual Celebration of 400 Years of New York City's History.* New York: Henry Holt, 2005.

House of Representatives, *Journal of the House of Representatives of the United States: Being the Second Session of the Thirty-third Congress, Begun and Held at the City of Washington, December 4, 1854, in the Seventy-Ninth Year of the Independence of the United States.* Washington: A. O. P. Nicholson, 1854 [1855].

Houze, Herbert G., Carolyn C. Cooper, and Elizabeth Mankin Kornhauser. *Samuel Colt: Arms, Art, and Invention.* New Haven, Conn.: Yale University Press, 2006.

"Hurl Gate Rocks," *Hunt's Merchants' Magazine and Commercial Review* 21, no. 12 (December 1849): 664–65.

Irving, Washington. "Tales of a Traveller: Part Fourth." In *The Works of Washington Irving.* Vol. 2. New York: P. F. Collier, 1885.

Johnson, Donald L., Brent M. Wilson, James D. Carr, Larry E. Murphy, and James P. Delgado. "Corrosion of Civil War Era Sub Marine Explorer Intertidal Zone—Bay of Panama," Paper 08239, NACE International Conference, 2008. http://content.nace .org/Store/Downloads/7B450638EC-C651-DD11—889D-0017A446694E.pdf.

Kahn, David M. "Bogardus, Fire, and the Iron Tower." *Journal of the Society of Architectural Historians* 35, no. 3 (October 1976): 186–203.

Kemble, John Haskell. *The Panama Route, 1848–1869.* Berkeley: University of California Press, 1943.

Kessner, Thomas. *Capital City: New York City and the Men Behind America's Rise to Economic Dominance, 1869–1900.* New York: Simon & Schuster, 2003.

Kiaupa, Zigmantus, et al. *The History of the Baltic Countries.* Tallin: Avita, 2002.

Kirsch, George B., Othello Harris, and Claire E. Nolte, eds. *Encyclopedia of Ethnicity and Sports in the United States.* Westport, Conn.: Greenwood Press, 2000.

Kornblum, William. *At Sea in the City: New York from the Water's Edge.* New York: Algonquin Books, 2002.

Kroehl, Julius. Application for Passport, New York, August 31, 1854. Passport Applications (1795–1905), General Records of the Department of State, Record Group 59, National Archives, Washington, D.C.

———. Last Will and Testament, December 7, 1866, Surrogate's Court, New York County, New York, Index of Wills Probated in Kings County from January 1, 1850, to December 31, 1890, liber 35, p. 39.

Kroehl, Sophia R. "Widow's Naval Pension Application File" 1889, with supporting documents. Pension application files based upon service in the Civil War and Spanish-American War. Records of the Department of Veterans Affairs, Record Group 15, National Archives, College Park, Md.

Lain, J. *The Brooklyn City Directory.* Brooklyn: J. Lain & Company, 1864; 1865.

Langley, Henry G. *The San Francisco Directory for the Year Commencing September 1859.* San Francisco: Valentine & Co., Commercial Steam Press, 1859.

——. *The San Francisco Directory for the Year Commencing September 1860.* San Francisco: Valentine & Co., Commercial Steam Press, 1860.

——. *The San Francisco Directory for the Year Commencing September 1861.* San Francisco: Valentine & Co., Commercial Steam Press, 1861.

——. *The San Francisco Directory for the Year Commencing September 1862.* San Francisco: Valentine & Co., Commercial Steam Press, 1862.

LeCount and Strong's San Francisco Directory for 1854. San Francisco: LeCount and Strong, 1854.

Library of Universal Knowledge: A Reprint of the Last (1880) Edinburgh and London Edition of Chambers' Encyclopaedia, With Copious Additions by American Editors. Vol. 14. New York: American Book Exchange, 1881.

Linne, S., and M. Leijer. *Darien in the Past: The Archaeology of Eastern Panama and North-Western Columbia.* Goteberg: Elanders Bocktryeri Aktiebolog, 1929.

Lundeberg, Philip K. "Marine Salvage and Sea Mine Technology in the 1840s: The Taylor Connection." In *Ships, Seafaring and Society: Essays in Maritime History,* ed. Timothy J. Runyan, 106–16. Detroit: Wayne State University Press, 1987.

Lytle, William M., and Forrest R. Holdcamper. *Merchant Steam Vessels of the United States 1790–1868: "The Lytle-Holdcamper List."* Staten Island, N.Y.: Steamship Historical Society of America, 1975.

Mackenzie, Clyde L. Jr. "A History of the Pearl Oyster Fishery in the Archipielago de las Perlas, Panama." *Marine Fisheries Review* 51, no. 2 (1999): 58–65.

MacLeod, Donald. *Biography of Fernando Wood, Mayor of the City of New-York.* New York: G. F. Parsons, 1856.

Manning, William R., ed. *Diplomatic Correspondence of the United States, Inter-American Affairs, 1831–1860.* Vol. 5: *Chile and Columbia.* Washington, D.C.: Carnegie Endowment for International Peace, 1935.

Manstan, Roy R., and Frederic J. Frese. *Turtle: David Bushnell's Revolutionary Vessel.* Yardley, Penn.: Westholme Publishing, 2010.

"The Marine Armor," *The Knickerbocker* 12, no. 4 (October 1838): 373–74.

Marryat, Frank. *Mountains and Molehills; Or, Recollections of a Burnt Journal,* ed. Marguerite Eyer Wilbur. Stanford, Calif.: Stanford University Press, 1948.

Maxwell, James Clerk. *The Theory of Heat.* 2nd ed. London: Longmans, Green, and Company, 1872.

McCarthy, Michael. *Iron Steamship Archaeology: Sucess and failure on the S. S. Xantro.* New York: Kluwer Academic Publishers, 2000.

McCarthy, Michael. "Report on the Wreck of the *Sub Marine Explorer* (1865) at Isla San Telmo, Archipielago de las Perlas, Panama, and the 2006 Field Season," Report No. 221, Western Australian Maritime Museum, Perth, 2006. http://www.museum

.wa.gov.au/collections/maritime/march/documents/No.%20221%20SubMarine%20
Explorer.pdf.

———. "The Submarine as a Class of Archaeological Site." *Bulletin of the Australian Institute for Maritime Archaeology* 22 (1998): 61–70.

McGuiness, Aims. *Path of Empire: Panama and the California Gold Rush.* Ithaca, N.Y.: Cornell University Press, 2008.

Meyer, Carl. *Bound for Sacramento: Travel-Pictures of a Returned Wanderer.* Trans. Ruth Frey Axe. Claremont, Calif.: Saunders Studio, 1938.

Miéville, China. *Kraken.* New York: Del Rey, 2010.

Miller, Hunter, ed. *Treaties and Other International Acts of the United States of America.* Vol. 5: 1846–1852. Washington, D.C.: Government Printing Office, 1937.

Milligan, John D. *Gunboats Down the Mississippi.* Annapolis, Md.: United States Naval Institute, 1965.

Milner, Rev. Thomas. *The Baltic: Its Gates, Shores and Cities; With a Notice of the White Sea.* London: Longman, Brown, Green and Longmans, 1854.

"More about Newark," *Northern Monthly Magazine* 2, no. 1 (November 1867): 1–20.

Mosk, Sanford A. "Capitalistic Development in the Lower California Pearl Fisheries." *Pacific Historical Review* 10, no. 4 (December 1941): 461–68.

"Mother of Pearl and Its Uses," *The Technologist: A Monthly Record of Science Applied to Art and Manufacture* 1 (1861): 222.

Murphy, L.E., ed. *H. L. Hunley Site Assessment.* Santa Fe: National Park Service, Submerged Resources Center, 1998.

Nadel, Stanley. *Little Germany: Ethnicity, Religion, and Class in New York City, 1845–80.* Urbana: University of Illinois Press, 1990.

Nelson, William, ed. *The New Jersey Coast in Three Centuries: History of the New Jersey Coast with Genealogical and Historical-Biographical Appendix.* New York: Lewis Publishing Company, 1902.

Nelson, Wolfred. *Five Years at Panama: The Trans-Isthmian Canal.* New York: Belford Company, 1889.

Newhall, Beaumont. *The Daguerreotype in America.* New York: Dover Books, 1976.

New York City Court of Common Pleas. Record of Naturalization for Julius Kroehl, Bundle 91, Record 57.

The New York State Business Directory. Albany: C. Van Benthuysen, 1870.

The New-York Submarine Engineering Company. New York: George F. Nesbitt & Co., 1862.

North, Diane M. T. *Samuel Peter Heintzelman and the Sonora Exploring and Mining Company.* Tucson: University of Arizona Press, 1980.

Oddy, J. Jepson, and William Playfair. *European Commerce: Shewing New and Secure Channels of Trade with the Continent of Europe: Detailing the Produce, Manufactures, and Commerce, of Russia, Prussia, Sweden, Denmark and Germany; as Well as the Trade of the Rivers Elbe, Weser, and Ems; with a General View of the Trade, Navigation. . . .* London: W. J. and J. Richardson, 1805.

The Official History of Odd Fellowship: The Three-Link Fraternity, or the Antiquities, Creative Period, and Golden Age of Friendship, Love and Truth, Illustrated. Boston: Fraternity Publishing Company, 1898.

Osborn, Henry S. *The Metallurgy of Iron and Steel: Theoretical and Practical: In All Its Branches; With Special Reference to American Materials and Processes.* Philadelphia: Henry Carey Baird, 1869.

Overman, Frederick, and A. A. Fesquet. *The Moulder's and Founder's Pocket Guide: A Treatise on Moulding and Founding in Green-sand, Dry-sand, Loam, and Cement; The Moulding of Machine Frames, Mill-gear, Hollow-ware, Ornaments, Trinkets, Bells and Statues & Description of Moulds for Iron, Bronze, Brass and Other Metals; Plaster of Paris, Sulphur, Wax, Etc; The Construction of Melting Furnaces, the Melting and Founding of Metals; The Composition of Alloys and Their Nature, Etc., Etc.* Philadelphia: Henry Carey Baird, 1893.

The Pacific Pearl Company, Incorporated under the Laws of the State of New York. New York: E. S. Dodge & Co., Printers and Stationers, 84 John Street, 1865.

The Pacific Pearl Company: Incorporated under the Laws of the State of New York. New York: John B. Lyon, 1866.

The Pacific Pearl Company, New York. New York: W. Davison, Printer, 1863.

Parker, A. J. "Maritime Landscapes," *Landscapes* 1 (2001): 22–41.

Parks, E. Taylor. *Colombia and the United States, 1765–1934.* Durham, N.C.: Duke University Press, 1935.

Parsons, William Barclay. *Robert Fulton and the Submarine.* New York: Columbia University Press, 1922.

Paulsen, George E. "The Legal Battle for the Candelaria Mine in Durango, Mexico, 1890–1917." *Arizona and the West* 23 (August 1981): 243–66.

Perrin-Gouron, Gérard, "Le Docteur Prosper PAYERNE Sa Vie, son oeuvre." http://ubaye-haut-verdon.blogspot.com/. Accessed June 10, 2009.

Peters, Tom F. *Building the Nineteenth Century.* Cambridge, Mass.: MIT University Press, 1996.

Peverelly, Charles A. *The Book of American Pastimes: Containing a History of the Principal Base Ball, Cricket, Rowing, and Yachting Clubs of the United States.* New York: Published by the author, 1866.

Phillips, John L., M.D. *The Bends: Compressed Air in the History of Science, Diving, and Engineering.* New Haven, Conn.: Yale University Press, 1998.

Pierson, B. T. *Directory of the City of Newark for 1851–53,*17th ed. Newark, N.J.: Holbrook's Steam Press, 1851.

Port of New York. *The Centennial Hand-Book of the Naval Office of Customs at the Port of New York: Prepared and Published on Behalf of All Employed in the Office.* New York: John C. Rankin Jr., Printer, 1889.

Porter, Admiral David D. *The Naval History of the Civil War.* New York: Sherman Publishing Company, 1886.

Poston, Charles. Papers. ("Civil War and Later"), Record 2412, Certificate 5096, Can #234, Bundle #5. "List of Stocks left with George Wrightson, Attorney for Charles D. Poston," (undated), DB f.1a. Sharlot Hall Museum and Archives, Prescott, Ariz.

Probst, Nora. "The New York Turn Verein: Finding Aid of the Archival Documents (1850–2005)." New York Turn Verein Archives (1850–2005). American Turners New York, Bronx, New York.

Ragan, Mark K. *Submarine Warfare in the Civil War.* New York: Da Capo Press, 2002.

Rainbird, Paul. *The Archaeology of Islands.* Cambridge, U.K.: Cambridge University Press, 2007.

Rawson, Edward K., and Charles M. Stewart, eds. *Official Records of the Union and Confederate Navies in the War of the Rebellion,* ser. 1, vol. 8: *North Atlantic Blockading Squadron from September 5, 1862 to May 4, 1863.* Washington, D.C.: Government Printing Office, 1899.

————, eds. *Official Records of the Union and Confederate Navies in the War of the Rebellion,* ser. 1, vol. 9: *North Atlantic Blockading Squadron from May 5, 1863 to May 5, 1864.* Washington, D.C.: Government Printing Office, 1899.

Raymond, Rossiter W. *Mineral Resources of the States and Territories West of the Rocky Mountains.* Washington, D.C.: Government Printing Office, 1869.

"Report on Mr. L. Norcross's Diving Apparatus," *Journal of the Franklin Institute.* 29, no. 1 (January 1835): 25–26.

Richman, Irving Berdine. *The Spanish Conquerors: A Chronicle of the Dawn of Empire Overseas.* New Haven, Conn.: Yale University Press, 1919.

Ridgely-Nevitt, Cedric. *American Steamships on the Atlantic.* Newark: University of Delaware Press, 1981.

Ripley, George, and Charles A. Dana, eds. *The New American Cyclopaedia: A Popular Dictionary of General Knowledge.* New York: D. Appleton and Company, 1859.

Robinson, Tracy. *Panama: A Personal Record of Forty-six Years, 1861–1907.* New York: Star and Herald Company, 1907.

Roland, Alex. *Underwater Warfare in the Age of Sail.* Bloomington: Indiana University Press, 1978.

Ryan, William Redmond. *Personal Adventures in Upper and Lower California, in 1848–9; With the Author's Experience at the Mines.* London: William Shoberl, 1850.

Ryerson, Albert Winslow. *The Ryerson Family Genealogy.* Chicago: Privately printed for Edward L. Ryerson, 1916.

Scarlett, P. Campbell. *South America and the Pacific; Comprising a Journey across the Pampas and the Andes, from Buenos Ayres to Valparaiso, Lima and Panama, with Remarks upon the Isthmus.* Vol. 2. London: Henry Colburn, 1838.

Scott, Robert N., ed. *The War of the Rebellion: A Compilation of the Official Records of the Union and Confederate Armies,* Ser. 1, Vol. 24, Pt. 3: *Correspondence, Etc.* Washington, D.C.: Government Printing Office, 1889.

Sears, Henry B. "On Appliances for Facilitating Submarine Engineering and Explora-tion," *Journal of the Society of Arts* 5, no. 224 (March 6, 1857): 243–49.

Secretary of the Navy. Letters Received by the Secretary of the Navy From Commissioned Officers Below the Rank of Commander and From Warrant Officers ("Officers' Let-ters"), 1802–1884. Record Group 45, National Archives, College Park, Md.

———. Letters Sent by the Secretary of the Navy to Officers, 1798–1868. Record Group 45, National Archives, College Park, Md.

———. Miscellaneous Letters Received, January 3, 1801–December 31, 1884. Record Group 45, National Archives, College Park, Md.

———. Miscellaneous Letters Sent ("General Letter Books"), 1798–1886. Record Group 45, National Archives, College Park, Md.

———. "Report of the Secretary of the Navy." In *Message from the President of the United States to the Two Houses of Congress at the Commencement of the Second Session of the Thirty-Fifth Congress.* Vol. 3. Washington, D.C.: James E. Steedman, 1858.

Secretary of the Treasury. *Annual Report of the Secretary of the Treasury on the State of the Finances for the Year 1870.* Washington: Government Printing Office, 1870.

Shaw, William H. *History of Essex and Hudson Counties, New Jersey.* Vol. 1. Philadelphia: Everts & Peck, 1884.

Shea, William L., and Terrence J. Winschel. *Vicksburg Is the Key: The Struggle for the Mis-sissippi River.* Lincoln: University of Nebraska Press, 2003.

Silka, Henry. "Williamsburg, Brooklyn: The Home of the First Successful Commercial Submarine." *Long Island Historical Journal* 20, nos. 1–2 (Fall 2007/Spring 2008): 71–82.

Simon, John Y., ed. *The Papers of Ulysses S. Grant,* vol. 8: *April 1–July 6, 1863.* Carbondale: Southern Illinois University Press, 1979.

Slotten, Hugh Richard. *Patronage, Practice, and the Culture of American Science: Alexander Dallas Bache and the US Coast Survey.* Cambridge, U.K.: Cambridge University Press, 1994.

Smith, Gene Allen, and Larry Bartlett. "A Most Unprovoked, Unwarrantable, and Dastardly Attack: James Buchanan, Paraguay and the Water Witch Incident of 1855." *Northern Mariner* 19, no. 3 (July 2009): 269–90.

Smith, Walter George. *Life and Letters of Thomas Kilby Smith, Brevet General, United States Volunteers, 1820–1887.* New York: G. P. Putnam's Sons, Knickerbocker Press, 1898.

Soulé, Frank, John H. Gihon, M.D., and James Nisbet. *The Annals of San Francisco.* San Francisco: D. Appleton & Company, 1855.

Stadden, Coey Montague. "Hannis Taylor." In *Library of Southern Literature,* ed. Edwin Anderson Alderman, Joel Chandler Harris and Charles William Kent, 12:5179. New Orleans: Martin & Hoyt Company, 1910.

State of New York. *Documents of the Assembly of the State of New-York, Seventy-Fifth Ses-sion, 1852.* Vol. 7, No. 127 to 129. Albany: C. Van Benthuysen, 1852.

Stewart, Charles W., ed. *Official Records of the Union and Confederate Navies in the War of the Rebellion,* ser. 1, vol. 18: *West Gulf Blockading Squadron, from February 21 to July 14, 1862.* Washington, D.C.: Government Printing Office, 1904.

———, ed. *Official Records of the Union and Confederate Navies in the War of the Rebellion,* ser. 1, vol. 20: *West Gulf Blockading Squadron, from March 15 to December 31, 1863.* Washington, D.C.: Government Printing Office, 1905.

———, ed. *Official Records of the Union and Confederate Navies in the War of the Rebellion,* ser. 1, vol. 23: *Naval Forces on Western Waters, from April 12, 1862 to December 31, 1862.* Washington, D.C.: Government Printing Office, 1910.

———, ed. *Official Records of the Union and Confederate Navies in the War of the Rebellion,* ser. 1, vol. 24: *Naval Forces on Western Waters, from January 1, 1863 to May 17, 1863.* Washington, D.C.: Government Printing Office, 1911.

———, ed. *Official Records of the Union and Confederate Navies in the War of the Rebellion,* ser. 1, vol. 25: *Naval Forces on Western Waters, from May 18, 1863 to February 29, 1864.* Washington, D.C.: Government Printing Office, 1912.

Strauss, Michael B., M.D., and Ivan V. Aksenov, M.D., Ph.D. *Diving Science: Essential Physiology and Medicine for Divers.* Champaign, Ill.: Human Kinetics, 2004.

"Sub-Marine Exploration: The Wreck of the Frigate Hussar." *Scientific American* 19, no. 7 (August 12, 1868): 105.

"Submarine Blasting," *Hunt's Merchants' Magazine and Commercial Review* 30, no. 11 (February 1854): 191–96.

"Submarine Operations on the Rocks at the Gate, near New York." *Civil Engineer and Architect's Journal* 15 (1852): 119.

Swank, James M. *The History of Iron Manufacture in All Ages, and Particularly in the United States for Three Hundred Years, from 1585 to 1885.* Philadelphia: Published by the author, 1884.

Taylor, Bayard. *At Home and Abroad: A Sketch-Book of Life, Scenery and Men.* New York: G. P. Putnam's Sons, 1881.

———. *Eldorado; Or, Adventures in the Path of Empire. . . .* New York: Alfred A. Knopf, 1949.

Taylor, William H. *New and Alluring Sources of Enterprise in the Treasures of the Sea, and the Means of Gathering Them.* New York: J. Narine, 1838.

Ten Broeck, R. G. S. Diary, 1853. Manuscript HM 16999. Henry E. Huntington Library, Pasadena, Calif.

Theberge, Captain Albert E. *The Coast Survey, 1807–1867.* Vol. 1: *History of the Commissioned Corps of the National Oceanic and Atmospheric Administration.* http://www.lib.noaa.gov/noaainfo/heritage/coastsurveyvo11/CONTENTS.html.

Thompson, Jerry D. *Civil War to the Bloody End: The Life and Times of General Samuel P. Heintzelman.* College Station: Texas A&M University Press, 2006.

Thompson, Robert Means, and Richard Wainwright, eds. *Confidential Correspondence of Gustavus Vasa Fox, Assistant Secretary of the Navy, 1861–1865.* Vol. 2. New York: Printed for the Naval History Society by the De Vinne Press, 1919.

Timbs, John. *The Year-Book of Facts in Science and Art: Exhibiting the Most Important Discoveries and Improvements of the Past Year, in Mechanics, Natural Philosophy, Electricity, Chemistry, Zoology and Botany, Geology and Geography, Meteorology and Astronomy.* London: Charles Tilt, 1840.

Tomes, Robert. *Panama in 1855: An Account of the Panama Rail-Road, Cities of Panama and Aspinwall, with Sketches of Life and Character on the Isthmus.* New York: Harper & Brothers, 1855.

Towler, John. *The Silver Sunbeam.* New York: Joseph H. Ladd, 1864.

Trow, J. F., ed., *Trow's New York City Directory.* New York: J.F. Trow, 1850–1866.

Tuckerman, Bayard, ed. *The Diary of Philip Hone, 1828–1851.* Vol. 2. New York: Dodd, Mead & Company, 1889.

Tyson, James L. *Diary of a Physician in California: Being the Results of Actual Experience Including Notes of the Journey by Land and Water. . . .* Oakland, Calif.: Biobooks, 1955.

US Census Bureau. Seventh (1850), Eighth (1860), Ninth (1870), Tenth (1880), Eleventh (1890), Twelfth (1900), and Thirteenth (1910) Census of the United States, Records of the Bureau of the Census. Record Group 29, National Archives, College Park, Md.

US Coast and Geodetic Survey. Records. Record Group 23, National Archives, Washington, D.C.

US Coast Survey. *Report of the Superintendent of the Coast Survey, Showing the Progress of the Survey During the Year 1863.* Washington, D.C.: Government Printing Office, 1864.

US Customs Service. Records. Passenger Lists of Vessels Arriving at New York, New York, 1820–1897. Record Group 36. National Archives, Washington, D.C.

US Department of State. "Despatches, 1789–1906." Record Group 59, National Archives, College Park, Md.

———. General Records. Passport Applications, 1795–1905. Record Group 59, National Archives, Washington, D.C.

US District Courts. Records. "James Bogardus v. the Mayor and Aldermen of the City of New York." US Circuit Court for the Southern District of New York, Law Case Files, Docket No. L1–543, Judgment Records, Box 14, 1858, Folder 1. Record Group 21. National Archives.

US Patent Office. *Annual Report of the Commissioner of Patents for the Year 1855: Arts and Manufactures.* Vols. 1 and 2. Washington, D.C.: A. O. P. Nicholson, Printer, 1856.

———. *Annual Report of the Commissioner of Patents for the Year 1861: Arts and Manufactures.* Vol. 1. Washington, D.C.: Government Printing Office, 1863.

US Senate. *Message of the President of the United States, Transmitting the Report of the Board of Consulting Engineers and of the Isthmian Canal Commission on the Panama Canal, Together with a Letter Written by Chief Engineer Stevens.* S. Doc. No. 231, 59th Cong., 1st sess. Washington, D.C.: Government Printing Office, 1906.

Urquhart, Frank John. *A History of the City of Newark, New Jersey, Embracing Nearly Two and a Half Centuries, 1666–1913, Illustrated.* Vol. 2. New York: Lewis Historical Publishing Company, 1913.

Wagner, Frederick. *Submarine Fighter of the American Revolution: The Story of David Bushnell.* New York: Dodd & Mead, 1963.

Wagner, Rudolf. *A Handbook of Chemical Technology.* London: J. & A. Churchill, 1872.

Warren, Joseph H., M.D. *Hernia: Strangulated and Reducible.* Boston: Charles N. Thomas, 1881.

Weddle, Kevin J. *Lincoln's Tragic Admiral: The Life of Samuel Francis Du Pont.* Charlottesville: University of Virginia Press, 2005.

Wells, Albert C., Letter to "My Dear Sir," Panama, December 5, 1849. Manuscript. New York Historical Society, New York City.

Wells, David A., ed. *Annual of Scientific Discovery: Or, Year-Book of Facts in Science and Art for 1852. . . .* Boston: Gould and Lincoln, 1852.

Westerdahl, Christer. "The Maritime Cultural Landscape." *International Journal of Nautical Archaeology* 21, no. 1 (1992): 5–14.

Whipple, James A. *Circular of James A. Whipple, Submarine Engineer.* Boston: J. E. Farwell and Co., 1857.

Wills, Richard K. "The Louisiana State Museum Vessel: A Historical and Archaeological Analysis of an American Civil War-Era Submersible Boat." Master's thesis, Texas A&M University, 2000.

Wood, W. W. W. Letter and Report to the Honorable Gideon Welles, Secretary of the Navy, Washington, D.C., February 2, 1865. Records of the Office of the Secretary of the Navy. Record Group 45. National Archives, College Park, Md.

Woodcroft, Bennet. *Alphabetical Index of Patentees and Applicants for Patents of Invention, For the Year 1867.* London: George Edward Eyre and William Spottiswoode, Printers to the Queen's Most Excellent Majesty, 1868.

Wortley, Lady Emmeline Stuart. *Travels in the United States, Etc. During 1848 and 1850.* New York: Harper and Brothers, Publishers, 1851.

Yale University. *Obituary Record for the Undergraduates of Yale University, Deceased from June, 1880, to June, 1890.* New Haven, Conn.: Tuttle, Morehouse & Taylor, 1890.

Yates, Lawrence A. "Operation JUST CAUSE in Panama City, December 1989." In *Urban Operations: An Historical Casebook,* 325–72. Fort Leavenworth, Kans.: Combat Studies Institute, Command and General Staff College, October 2, 2002.

Index